THE DECLINE OF
ORGANIZED LABOR IN
THE UNITED STATES

THE DECLINE OF ORGANIZED LABOR IN THE UNITED STATES

Michael Goldfield

THE UNIVERSITY OF CHICAGO PRESS
Chicago and London

MICHAEL GOLDFIELD is assistant professor
of government at Cornell University.

The University of Chicago Press, Chicago 60637
The University of Chicago Press; Ltd., London

96 95 94 93 92 91 90 89 88 87   54321

Library of Congress Cataloging-in-Publication Data
Goldfield, Michael.
    The decline of organized labor in the United States.

    Bibliography: p.
    Includes index.
    1. Trade-unions—United States—History—20th century.
I. Title.
HD6508.G683   1987   331.88'0973   86-24890
ISBN 0-226-30102-8

Contents

List of Tables

List of Figures

Acknowledgments

Few intellectual projects take place in a vacuum, and this one is no exception. This volume originally grew out of a doctoral dissertation and thus has accumulated several waves of debts.

I would like first of all to thank the members of my dissertation committee at the University of Chicago for their patience and assistance: Lutz Erbring, Russell Hardin, Ira Katznelson, Adam Przeworski, and Philippe Schmitter. Valuable assistance was given to me by Mel Reder, Arnold Zellner, and others at the University of Chicago Business School's Workshop on Economics and Econometrics; by Richard Freeman, James Medoff, and Paula Voos. Critical advice and support was provided by a number of friends including Joanne Castle, Ed Cliffle, Ross Lambert, David Moberg, Marsha Rothenberg, and Mel Rothenberg. Mike Hamlin and Jim Jacobs provided early encouragement and much advice along the way.

In the transformation of the original manuscript, parts were read by Benjamin Ginsberg, Michael Hannan, Dale Hathaway, Steven Jackson, Theodore Lowi, George Ross, Martin Shefter, and Sidney Tarrow. I was fortunate enough to have comments on the full manuscript at various stages of its incarnation from Ronald Ehrenberg, Richard Freeman, Jonas Pontusson, Beth

Rubin, and John Sprague. And in an act of pure altruism, Peter Katzenstein gave me the benefit of a full set of comments on two separate versions.

Al Bauman of the Bureau of Labor Statistics and Bessie Jackson of the National Labor Relations Board provided help in the acquisition of data. Pieces or earlier versions of some of the material have appeared in articles in *Politics and Society, Research in Political Economy*, and the *Journal of Politics*; I appreciate the permission to draw from that material here. Jonathan Plotkin provided research assistance in the latter stages of this project and help with the tables and figures.

Finally, I wish to thank my parents, Roslyn and Joseph Goldfield, who have borne with me from the beginning, my children who have been my unwitting fellow travelers, and my wife, Evelyn, whose encouragement and support have been invaluable.

Introduction

In early 1946, trade unions appeared to be well-established in the United States and growing stronger. During World War II, union membership had increased from nine million to over fourteen million members. With wartime controls on unions removed, contract victories and extensive new organizing, particularly in the South, seemed inevitable. In 1945 alone, unions won 82.9 percent of the almost five thousand National Labor Relations Board (NLRB) bargaining elections, involving well over one million workers. Conservatives complained, not without some basis in fact, that the National Labor Relations Board, as well as other New Deal agencies, were riddled with Communists and other radicals; to most observers, the government did not appear to be unsympathetic to union demands. In late 1945 United Auto Workers first vice-president Richard Frankensteen came close to being elected the mayor of Detroit, despite vicious opposition from newspapers, auto companies, and other business interests. On the economic front, unions were pressing forward. Art Preis (1964, p. 262) describes the autumn of 1945 as "the greatest wage offensive in U.S. labor history":

In the twelve months following V-J Day more than 5,000,000 workers engaged in strikes. For the number of strikers, their weight in industry and the duration of the struggle, the 1945–46 strike wave in the U.S. surpassed anything of its kind in any capitalist country, including the British General Strike in 1926. (Preis, p. 276)

Union strength seemed so great, strike militancy so high, that many capitalists considered themselves lucky to gain some measure of class peace by granting substantial wage increases and new fringe benefits.

This period—before the passage of the antilabor Taft-Hartley Act in 1947, the purges in the Congress of Industrial Organizations (CIO), and the complete failure in organizing the South under Operation Dixie—stands in stark contrast to the situation at present. Today the tide is clearly flowing the other way. Among the most significant indicators is the drop in the percentage of U.S. workers in unions. This percentage (the union density) has fallen continuously since 1954, when over 34 percent of the labor force were union members; now the figure is well below 20 percent. Although trade unions in other economically developed countries have had their expansions and contractions, U.S. trade unions are the only ones to have suffered a continuous decline in union density over the last three decades. U.S. unions today are largely estranged from their natural allies among oppressed minorities, in the women's movement, and among more radical, left-wing elements in the population. Despite the growing weakness of the unions, public opinion polls indicate that the majority of U.S. citizens have little sympathy for labor unions' plight. Unions still are regarded as too powerful and untrustworthy.

In contrast to 1946, unions today are on the defensive and reeling from repeated defeats. Concessions to companies in recent contract bargaining; loss of any national political influence; employer-led union busting; failures in new organizing; and the disintegration of decades-long stable bargaining relations in many major industries, including construction, trucking, air, and coal mining, raise sharply the question of the continued existence of unions, at least in their present form, in the United States.

This situation demands explanation. Its beginning, its causes, its significance, as well as the prospects for its continuance or reversal, need to be identified and analyzed. In early 1985, I was talking to the Midwest director of a large government employees union. Why, I asked him, are unions in such trouble today? What are the reasons behind the dramatic losses in union membership, particularly in the private sector? He leaned a little closer, looked me straight in the eye, and said, "Mike, that is the $64,000 question." And, it is, of course, toward an answer to this question that the bulk of this book is directed.

The significance of what is happening to unions here is widely recognized. For many, a strong labor movement is the cornerstone of a liberal or social-democratic society. For others, unions serve merely to obstruct the unhindered functioning of an efficient capitalist market, depriving all of important freedoms. Union decline has also given new life to arguments for the waning significance of class in this country and in capitalist societies in general. Those of us who still cling to more traditional Marxist forms of class analysis, however, must examine carefully and provide plausible explanations for the trade union decline. If workers are indeed unwilling or incapable of forming elementary collective organizations for their own self-defense, then the prospects for independent working-class political organizations and the development of a distinct socialist class consciousness, not to mention the establishment of a socialist society, are dim at best. A workers' movement that cannot defend or reclaim its initial conquests will invariably fail in its new ones. Thus I view the attempt to understand the decline of labor unions in the United States as the beginning of an attempt to understand the conditions necessary for their future rebirth.

Most of this essay will examine the question of trade union weakness and decline from a less lofty perspective. Yet I mention certain of these broader questions because, in the end, it is upon these that I also hope to shed some light.

This book, the first of two projected volumes, examines the weakened state of U.S. labor unions. It places the recent decline in the context of a longer range deterioration going back over three decades and explores the reasons for that deterioration. I probe the significance of this decline for U.S. society in general and for the development of a broad revolutionary working-class movement. Finally, I evaluate the prospects for the rebirth, renewal, and resurgence of U.S. labor unions.

The second volume will examine the historical-political reasons behind the decline described and analyzed in the present volume.

Part 1

Organized Labor in the United States: Its General Weakness and Recent Decline

1

Introducing the Decline

In order to discover the reasons for U.S. trade union weakness and decline, one must first identify the phenomenon, describing its somewhat uneven contours.[1] In both the scholarly and popular literature, there is, however, a wide diversity of views. One approach, for example, argues that unions are weak and losing strength rapidly, that there has been a recent, precipitous fall in the fortunes of unions. Several years ago, this accelerating decline was located in the 1970s; today it is more fashionable to trace the roots to the Reagan administration. Still another approach views unions as strong and stable, seeing present trade union decline as little more than a cyclical drop in the long-range pattern of expected union growth. It is instructive to focus briefly on these two divergent views.

U.S. Unions Are Strong

Even today, there is not universal agreement that U.S. unions are weak and declining. The argument of former secretary of labor John Dunlop (1980) is representative of those who argue that

[1]. It is this unevenness that makes statements based merely on impressionistic evidence often so misleading.

3

U.S. labor unions are quite strong.[2] Dunlop notes that the membership of labor unions has grown substantially since 1948. Unions and employee organizations had increased their membership by 9 million members, from 15 million in 1948 to 24 million in 1980. Dunlop stresses that the present period stands in sharp contrast to that of the 1920s, when there was a "marked absolute decline" in membership, from 4.8 million in 1920 to 2.8 million in 1933. He argues against those who use the drop in union density (the percentage of the labor force in trade unions) as an indication of a weakening in union strength:

The share of the nonagricultural work force in labor organizations . . . is scarcely an all-purpose measure of union strength or influence—at the workplace, in a community, or in the larger society—on compensation, on the role of the strike, on legislative matters, on voting patterns, on the role of retired members who are not counted, or on public opinion or the community. *It is hard to believe that labor organization in the society today, in the year of the national accord, is one-fourth less in some gross sense, than it was in 1948, one year after the Taft-Hartley Act was enacted.* (Dunlop 1980, p. 399; emphasis mine)[3]

In opposition to the view of fellow Harvard economist Richard Freeman (1980), who argues that unions have declined in strength, Dunlop presents an impressive list of union achievements in order to indicate their power. He cites the important union influence on wages, benefits, personnel rules, and man-

2. While it is a common argument from business economists that organized labor has not declined significantly in strength and is, in fact, quite strong, it could still be found in the late 1970s among certain optimistic AFL-CIO (American Federation of Labor-Congress of Industrial Organizations) officials. See, for example, Kistler (1977). For an early pessimistic view that is not prolabor, see the article "American Union Busting" in the *Economist* of 17 November 1979.

3. Dunlop continued to hold to similar views in late 1982, as is clear from an interview printed in *Fortune*:

John Dunlop: Well, on your basic question about the union's declining share—I think you're taking a very short-run view . . . Henri Sée, the French historian, used to emphasize that a social movement operates like the wave of the sea eating away at the base of a cliff. For years nothing seems to happen. Then, one day, the side of the cliff falls in. That's the way our labor movement has grown. I remember the day people said you couldn't organize government workers. Then, bingo, in the Sixties and early Seventies the unions got half the state and local employees and two-thirds of the federal employees. Just like that! The labor movement has always grown in surges.

Fortune: But there hasn't been a surge in 30 years.

John Dunlop: That's not very significant. The white-collar people—more and more of them are in unions. The number of women is rising. The southern communities are changing. (Dunlop 1982)

agement practices in large nonunion establishments, claiming they are the result of collective bargaining and potential union organization. He mentions the triumph of union legislative goals, including equal opportunity legislation, pension plan regulation, OSHA (the Occupational Safety and Health Act), "the expanded scope of the obligation to bargain under the National Labor Relations Act," and statutes against age discrimination. He notes recent legislation on the handicapped. He points to improvements in social security and disability, and in minimum wages and hours. The list goes on. Dunlop is even audacious enough to speculate that there is a possibility that large companies may moderate their traditional hostility to unions; he finds evidence for this in the 1979 "neutrality letter" signed by General Motors with the UAW, which restricts the company from fighting union drives in its new plants, even with methods that are permitted by law.

The attempt to minimize the extent of current union setbacks is also reflected in the view of Dunlop and others (e.g., Flanagan 1984) that wage concessions made by unions in the 1980s are not signs of union weakness, but predictable recession-dictated patterns.[4]

U.S. UNION STRENGTH IS DWINDLING

The view that the strength of organized labor is seriously eroding has been put forward in the past, for example, by Bell (1953, 1954) and by Barkin (1961). More recently, however, an argument, frequently heard from AFL-CIO officials, has emerged that the policies and attitudes of the Reagan administration are responsible for a precipitous fall in labor's fortunes. As one federation publication argues,

It is not just a coincidence; the Reagan Administration has fostered carefully the notion that collective bargaining and trade unions are a worthless relic of previous years that interfere with his economic game plan. This has not gone unnoticed by union busters and employers. (AFL-CIO, *RUB*, June 1983, no. 38.)

Thus the reelection of Reagan in 1984 was a green light for further anti-unionism. According to AFL-CIO information direc-

4. The argument that U.S. unions are quite strong is also put forward forcefully by several left-wing writers who present their case in comparative perspective (Tronti 1972; Arrighi and Silver 1984).

tor Murray Seeger, "The union-busters are in hog heaven now" (Raskin 1985, p. 52).

This view too is, of course, not without its supporting evidence. Since the inauguration of Republican Ronald Reagan as the United States president in 1981, unions and their members have indeed taken a beating. For the first time since the early 1930s, the absolute number of union members has declined significantly. Unions have not only been beaten back in new organizing, but they have been driven out of previous strongholds in mining, trucking, and construction. Hard-nosed employer tactics and enormous union concessions have given unionized workers record-low wage increases leading to sharp actual declines in real wages.

It is hard to argue with AFL-CIO officials that they no longer have a friend in the White House. During its first year in office in 1981, the Reagan administration not only defeated a strike by PATCO (Professional Air Traffic Controller's Organization) but quickly proceeded to destroy the union. The appointment of anti-union members to the National Labor Relations Board sharply changed the complexion of that agency legally mandated to protect union organizing rights.

The aftermath of the 1984 presidential election further serves to underscore the administration's orientation. Much publicity was given to the attempt to obtain nonunion performers to provide free entertainment at Reagan's inauguration.[5] Also indicative were the publicly announced investigations of the presidents of the American Federation of Government Employees, the letter carriers, and the postal workers for supposed violations of the 1939 Hatch Act during the campaign. These presidents and their unions actively campaigned for challenger Walter Mondale against Ronald Reagan. The Hatch Act, of course, supposedly protects public employees from being forced to support the reelection of the administration that is their current employer.

Despite its prima facie plausibility, it is not obvious that the reasons for trade union decline in this country may all be found at Reagan's doorstep. There are those, for example, who trace the

5. The 4 January 1985 issue of *Backstage*, a show business trade publication, contains an advertisement for "clean-cut and all-American types" who are nonunion. For an extended comment, see Ledwith in the February 1985 issue of *Allegro*, the publication of the Associated Musicians of New York, Local 801 of the American Federation of Musicians.

problems that unions have faced under Reagan to factors that were quite strong during the 1970s. Political scientists Ferguson and Rogers (1979a, 1979b, 1981) argue that organized labor began losing strength especially rapidly during the 1970s. They describe union losses then as a "spectacular decline" (1981). They are less impressed than Dunlop by union political strength, talking instead about "the decay of organized labor as a force in American politics" (1979a, p. 20). They note the declines in union density, union legislative defeats, the intense management resistance to unions, and the fall in victory rates in NLRB union certification elections.

Ferguson and Rogers, writing about the defeat of the Labor Law Reform Act in June of 1978, refer to the decline of U.S. unions as follows:

Any number of statistics testify to the gravity of the situation. The percentage of the workforce organized into trade unions has dropped steadily since the mid-1950's, standing now at a postwar low of 20.1 percent. Organizing drives mounted by unions are increasingly ineffective. While as late as the mid-1950's unions won 60 percent of representation elections, by last year their percentage of victories *plunged* to 46 percent. (1979a, p. 11; emphasis mine)

If Ferguson and Rogers's description bears any relation to reality, then those who lay the cause of union woes at Reagan's doorstep must not be describing the whole story.

The extent to which each of these views has merit must be determined. Each of the various claims presupposes a general and precise analysis of organized labor's decline. Yet few of these commentators have clearly delineated the extent of this decline statistically, nor have they attempted to date the periods of decline with any degree of precision.[6] Key aspects of reality are missed by those who argue that union strength is still high as well as by those who attribute present union problems largely to the Reagan administration. Both assessments are also based on incorrect methodologies. There are actually two separate questions that are often mixed together. First is the question of whether U.S. trade unions are strong or weak. A discussion of

6. Their analyses lack even the degree of accuracy argued by Dunlop (1948) and I. Bernstein (1954a), who, of course, had much cruder instruments. This is particularly true with respect to NLRB union certification elections. Typical is the statement by the economist Joseph Krislov (1979). In comparing the period 1954–55 with the period 1976–77, he merely says, "In recent years, unions have been less successful in certification elections."

this issue can only be fully informative in the context of a comparison with unions in other countries. Hardly anyone who emphasizes current union strength does so in a comparative context. Second is the question of trade union decline, a slightly different issue than the relative strength of U.S. unions. Those who place the onus for trade union decline exclusively on recent factors (particularly those who argue for an accelerating decline) do so in an ahistorical framework. The nature of trade union decline, however, can only be ascertained in a many-decades-long historical context.

In part 1, I delineate the degree of weakness of U.S. unions via international comparisons and trace the historical extent of their decline. This chapter will attempt to sketch certain quantitative indicators of trade union strength, most notably union membership figures and new organizing through the National Labor Relations Board. Chapter 2 covers union political influence, including its status in public opinion polls. Chapter 3 discusses U.S. labor-management relations, focusing on strike militancy, contract strength, concessions, the decline of real wages, the disintegration of previously stable bargaining relationships, union leadership, and union busting. Chapter 3 concludes with an assessment of the special responsibilities of the Reagan administration. Within each section, the questions of weakness and decline are in general noted separately.

MEMBERSHIP

Dunlop is, of course, right that the period of the 1970s has been very different from that of the 1920s. Then, as a result of the post–World War I open-shop crusade, trade union membership declined from over 5 million members in 1920 to 3.5 million in 1923, dropping to less than 3 million in 1933.[7] Unlike the early 1920s, the absolute number of members in national trade unions in the United States in 1980 had not declined in any several-year

7. For union membership figures for these years, see Troy (1965, p. 1) and Wolman (1936, pp. 138, 139). The Wolman and Troy data series were maintained periodically by the National Bureau of Economic Research (NBER). Bureau of Labor Statistics (BLS) figures for the period prior to 1930 are available in the *Handbook of Labor Statistics* (1950), but their accuracy is highly debatable. For an early discussion of the relative merits of the NBER and BLS figures, see Wolman (1936). For a more recent discussion of the strengths and weaknesses of each statistical approach, see Bain and Price (1980). Since these and other series all have important differences, union membership data for this country should in general only be considered as indicative.

period since the early 1930s.[8] Even the drop in union membership in the first half of the 1980s (much of it due to the serious
recession and the sharp declines in employment in the heavily
unionized steel, auto, and rubber industries) is on a scale far
smaller than that of the 1920s. In order to resolve certain of the
interpretive questions about U.S. union membership, it is useful
to look at actual union membership figures.[9] Partly because of
problems of data consistency, it is helpful to look at the pre-1980
period before looking at the post-1980 years (see tables 1 and 2
and figures 1, 2, and 3).

The period up until 1980 may be evaluated using the long-
standing Bureau of Labor Statistics (BLS) series. The pre-1980
period is characterized by the steady decrease in the percentage
of the work force organized into trade unions since the mid-
1950s. As indicated in table 1, union density for the country as a
whole has decreased from 34.7 percent of the nonagricultural
workforce in 1954 to 23.6 percent in 1978.[10] Figures 2 and 3
clearly indicate that there does not appear to be an accelerating
decline. They also raise the question of whether there has been

8. New figures by Troy and Sheflin (1985) attempt to place a peak in 1975,
although even these figures indicate little substantial falls in absolute membership until 1980. Their figures, however, are disputed in another new data set
developed by Kokkelenberg and Sockell (1985).

9. There are a variety of problems with various union membership statistical
series for this country. I will be mentioning the most significant ones in the text
and notes of this section. For example, until 1968, BLS figures for unions did not
include data for employee associations. During the 1960s, however, a number of
employee associations (most notably the National Education Association and the
American Nurses Association) began to act like unions, especially in their role as
negotiators of contracts. Many researchers and Department of Labor publications
began to consider it appropriate to include employee organization membership
figures in that of union membership series. Some commentators prefer to refer to
the unions and these employee associations as "bargaining associations." What is
important to recognize, however, is that the combined series, which was the one
kept current by the BLS until 1980, only begins in 1968 and is not strictly
compatible with the older series, which ended in 1978.

10. Calculations of union density, especially, should only be viewed as
suggestive. First, union density is a category difficult to calculate accurately; for
a while, even the BLS stopped computing it. The BLS estimates that over 5
percent of union members may now be retirees, a substantial rise in the last
decade. Since retirees are not counted in the labor force, the ratio of union
density no longer makes strict sense. Second, the union membership figures
themselves, in my opinion, became increasingly suspect during the 1970s. The
large percentage rises during this period in per capita taxes, payable to the
AFL-CIO have probably vastly increased underreporting and eliminated most of
the previous overreporting by certain unions. Many unions, for this reason,
probably began dropping laid-off members from their counts much sooner. These
changes are very difficult to estimate.

TABLE 1		National Union Membership as a Proportion of Labor Force and Nonagricultural Employment, Selected Years, 1930–1978			
	Number of Members	Number in Labor Force	Percentage Union	Number Nonagricultural Workers (in thousands)	Percentage Union
Year	(in thousands)				
1930	3,401	50,080	6.8%	29,424	11.6%
1931	3,310	50,680	6.5	26,649	12.4
1932	3,050	51,250	6.0	23,628	12.9
1933	2,689	51,840	5.2	23,711	11.3
1934	3,088	52,490	5.9	25,953	11.9
1935	3,584	53,140	6.7	27,053	13.2
1936	3,989	53,740	7.4	29,082	13.7
1937	7,001	54,320	12.9	31,026	22.6
1938	8,034	54,950	14.6	29,209	27.5
1939	8,763	55,600	15.8	30,618	28.6
1940	8,717	56,180	15.5	32,376	26.9
1941	10,201	57,530	17.7	36,554	27.9
1942	10,380	60,380	17.2	40,125	25.9
1943	13,213	64,560	20.5	42,452	31.1
1944	14,146	66,040	21.4	41,883	33.8
1945	14,322	65,300	21.9	40,394	35.5
1946	14,395	60,970	23.6	41,674	34.5
1947	14,787	61,758	23.9	43,881	33.7
1948	14,319	62,080	23.1	44,891	31.9
1950	14,267	63,858	22.3	45,222	31.5
1952	15,892	65,730	24.2	48,825	32.5
1954	17,022	66,993	25.4	49,022	34.7
1956	17,490	69,409	25.2	52,408	33.4
1958	17,029	70,275	24.2	51,363	33.2
1960	17,049	72,142	23.6	54,234	31.4
1962	16,586	73,442	22.6	55,596	29.8
1964	16,841	75,830	22.2	58,331	28.9
1966	17,940	78,893	22.7	63,955	28.1
1968	18,916	82,272	23.0	67,951	27.8
1970	19,381	85,903	22.6	70,920	27.3
1972	19,435	88,991	21.8	73,714	26.4
1973	19,851	91,040	21.8	76,896	25.8
1974	20,199	93,240	21.8	78,413	25.8
1975	19,611	94,793	20.7	76,945	25.5
1976	19,634	96,917	20.3	79,382	24.7
1977	19,695	99,534	19.8	79,382	24.8
1978	20,246	102,537	19.7	85,763	23.6

Source: BLS series (U.S. Dept. Labor, BLS 1980b, table 165, p. 412).
Note: Series ends in 1978.

TABLE 2   National Union and Employee Association Membership as a
Proportion of Labor Force and Nonagricultural Employment,
1968–1982

Year	Number of Members	Number in Labor Force	Percentage Union	Number Nonagricultural Workers (in thousands)	Percentage Union
	(in thousands)				
1968	20,721	82,272	25.2%	67,897	30.5%
1969	20,776	84,240	24.7	70,384	29.5
1970	21,248	85,903	24.7	70,880	30.0
1971	21,327	86,929	24.5	71,214	29.9
1972	21,657	88,991	24.3	73,675	29.4
1973	22,276	91,040	24.5	76,790	29.0
1974	22,809	93,240	24.5	78,265	29.1
1975	22,361	94,793	23.6	77,364	28.9
1976	22,662	96,917	23.4	80,048	22.3
1977	22,456	99,534	22.6	82,423	27.2
1978	22,757	102,537	22.2	86,697	26.2
1979	22,579	104,996	21.5	89,886	25.1
1980	22,366	106,821	20.9	90,657	24.7
1982	19,763	110,204	17.9	96,125	20.6

Source: 1968–79 data are from U.S. Dept. of Labor, BLS 1980a (table 6, p. 59);
1980 data from Labor-Management Relations Division, BLS; 1982 union membership data from BNA 1984; 1982 employment figures from U.S. Dept. of Labor,
BLS 1985a.

Note: BLS union membership series ends in 1980.

any weakness or a decline at all during the period up to 1980.
Dunlop contends that unions make major organizing breakthroughs or spurts at infrequent times. In the "normal state of
affairs," as in the present period, "the labor movement has had a
hard time standing still" (Dunlop 1980, p. 398). Yet Dunlop's
argument with respect to overall membership figures is belied
by international comparisons. U.S. trade unions are the only ones
in the economically developed capitalist countries to have suffered a continuous decline during this period.[11] Further, the

11. When I speak of the economically developed countries, I refer to those in
Western Europe and to Japan, the United States, Canada, Australia, and New
Zealand. For short-hand purposes, occasionally I say "developed capitalist" or
merely "developed" countries, implying no judgment on the political or social
system. The term "advanced industrial societies," I find ambiguous and misleading.
It begs the question concerning the ways in which this highly diffuse category of
countries are advanced besides economically and technically. It also tends to
blur the important distinctions between capitalist and noncapitalist countries.

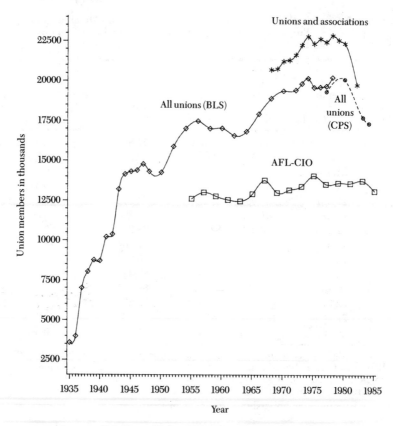

Source: U.S. Dept. of Labor, BLS 1979e, 1980a, 1980b, 1981e, 1985a; BNA
1984; AFL-CIO 1985.

FIGURE 1.   Membership of U. S. national unions by year

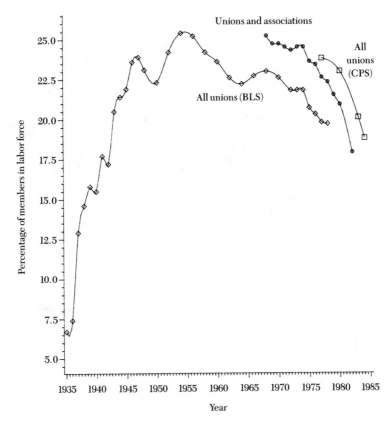

Source: U.S. Dept. of Labor, BLS 1979e, 1980a, 1980b, 1981e, 1985a.

FIGURE 2.   Union membership as a percentage of total labor force

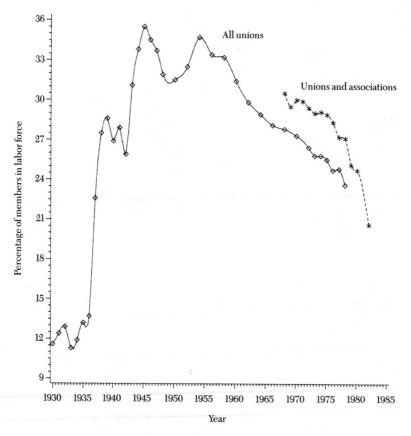

Source: U.S. Dept. of Labor, BLS 1980a, 1980b. 1985a.

FIGURE 3.   Union membership as a percentage of employees in non-agricultural establishments by year

United States has one of the lowest union densities of any of these countries.[12] This may be seen from the comparative figures of union membership presented in table 3 below.[13]

Even the relatively stable size (or slight growth) of U.S. union membership from the early 1960s until 1980 is deceptive. In part because the United States is a large country, its contours of unionization are highly uneven. It is essential to dissect and disaggregate membership figures. The aggregate figures actually hide an absolute decline in union members in the private sector during the 1960s and 1970s. What these statistics conceal are the large-scale gains in membership made by unions in the governmental sector during this period. Union membership in the public sector increased from a bare 13 percent in 1956 to over 50 percent in 1980 (Freeman 1984).[14] For example, the American Federation of State, County, and Municipal Employees (AFSCME) went from 220 thousand members in 1962 to 444 thousand in 1970 to over a million in 1978. The American Federation of Government Employees (AFGE) went from 106

12. It might, of course, be argued that France, for example, has a lower percentage of union members in its work force than is true in this country. Such an assertion, however, would not be based on a consistent definition of what it means to be a union member. In France a union "member" is an activist. Fifty such members might conceivably constitute themselves as an organizing committee in a plant of many thousands and receive a majority vote as the plant bargaining representatives. In the United States, on the other hand, a fifty-member committee that won majority support in a large plant would automatically gain thousands of members. Taking these differences into account between the United States and France, one would not want to say that the United States had a larger percentage of union "members." Information about French trade union behavior may be gleaned from Reynaud (1967, 1975); Hoyles (1969); Dubois, Durand, and Erbes-Seguin (1978); Gaillie (1980); Ross (1982); Lange, Ross, and Vannicelli (1982); Ross and Martin (1980); Kesselman (1982); and Jenson and Ross (1984).

13. The best set of comparative figures, but not quite as recent as those presented in table 3, are those compiled by Bain and Price (1980). The uniqueness of U.S. unions' continuous decline in union density from the 1950s is apparent from looking at either set of figures. Britain, for example, showed a stagnation in membership from 1950 to the late 1960s similar to that of the United States, then began a steady increase to almost 50 percent by 1974. Japan has had ups and downs in the 1950s and 1960s, suffering a not insubstantial decline in union density since the middle 1960s.

14. Estimates for federal government union membership often vary widely. Paid-up dues-paying members sometimes are said to constitute only 40 percent of federal employees (see, e.g., Troy and Sheflin 1985). Federal employees who are represented by unions, however, are clearly a majority. Some public sector union officials claim that the elimination of ineligible managerial, supervisory, and technical employees from the calculus would raise this latter figure to 75 percent. Similar caveats could be made for many of the figures for state and local government employee union membership.

TABLE 3   Comparison of Union Membership in Thirteen Countries as a
Percentage of Nonagricultural Employees, 1955–1985

Year	United States	Australia	Belgium[1]	Canada	Denmark	France[1]
1955	34%[2]	64%	NA	32%	70%	23%
1960	32[2]	61	62	31	70	24
1965	29[2]	59	62	28	68	23
1970	31	52	66	32	66	22
1975	29	58	75	35	74	23
1976	29	57	NA	36	76	NA
1977	NA	NA	NA	NA	NA	NA
1978	27	57	NA	37	81	NA
1979	25	58	NA	NA	85	NA
1980	25	58	75–80	36	89	28
1981	NA	57	75–80	36	93	28
1982	NA	58	NA	38	96	NA
1983	20	58	NA	38	99	NA
1984	19	57	NA	38	98	NA
1985	18	NA	NA	37	NA	NA

	Germany	Italy[1]	Japan	Netherlands	Sweden	Switzerland	UK
1955	46%	NA	38%	43%	70%	34%	46%
1960	41	55–60	34	43	68	35	45
1965	38	55–60	36	41	71	32	45
1970	37	50–55	35	39	79	31	52
1975	41	50–55	35	43	84	36	54
1976	41	NA	34	43	87	38	56
1977	NA	NA	33	44	89	37	58
1978	42	NA	33	43	92	36	59
1979	42	NA	32	43	89	36	58
1980	42	55–60	31	42	90	35	57
1981	42	55–60	31	40	91	35	56
1982	43	NA	31	40	93	35	55
1983	43	NA	30	39	94	35	55
1984	43	NA	29	37	95	35	53
1985	42	NA	NA	NA	NA	NA	NA

[1]For Belgium, France, and Italy, union membership is a percentage of all wage and salary employees.

[2]Excludes members of employee associations.

Source: Unpublished data from U.S. Dept. of Labor, BLS, Division of Foreign Labor Statistics.

thousand members in 1962 to 325 thousand in 1970. Postal workers became almost 90 percent organized during the past two decades. Teachers have also unionized heavily. The American Federation of Teachers (AFT) went from 71 thousand members in 1962 to 205 thousand in 1970 to 500 thousand in 1978. The National Education Association grew from 1 million in 1970 to 1.7 million in 1978. The Classified School Employees Association went from 97 thousand in 1972 to 150 thousand in 1978 (U.S. Dept. of Labor, BLS 1980a, pp. 91–92).[15] This enormous growth in public sector unionism had largely tapered off by the late 1970s.

Subtracting the several million union members gained in the public sector from the totals, one may see that a substantial absolute decline occurred in union membership in the private sector during the two decades from 1960 to 1980.[16] In addition, there is strong evidence that those areas previously regarded as traditional union strongholds are not exempt from drops in union density. A look at table 4 shows a decline in labor-management agreement coverage in metropolitan areas from 1960 to 1981, from 73 percent to 56 percent for the country as a whole. In manufacturing during this period, the decline has been from 79 percent to 65 percent (see table 5). Whereas the Midwest (i.e., the North Central region) offers a picture of somewhat more stability, the Northeast shows a significant organizational decline (77 percent to 62 percent for industry as a whole, 81 percent to 65 percent in manufacturing).[17]

Table 6 indicates that the industrial states that have been the most unionized have fallen in union density. Among these states are West Virginia, Wisconsin, Pennsylvania, Michigan, Illinois, Indiana, Minnesota, New Jersey, and California. Only New York State, which has led the nation in hospital, public employee, and

15. It should be mentioned that a minority of school employees are not public employees. A small amount of the increases for the AFSCME and the AFT are due to mergers with other unions. These mergers, however, in no way diminish the large-scale patterns of growth in actual new members in these two unions. For additional information on public employee union membership, see Lewin, Feuille, and Kochan 1977; Burton 1979; Kochan 1980; and Freeman 1984.

16. These estimates are confirmed by both the estimates of public sector unionism by Burton (1979) and the estimates of private sector unionism by Freeman and Medoff (1979a).

17. The declines in labor-management coverage by industry are again confirmed in the estimates of coverage by industry from the Freeman and Medoff study (1979a).

TABLE 4   Labor-Management Coverage, Metropolitan Areas, 1960–1984

Year	All	Northeast	South	North Central	West
1960–61	73%	77%	48%	80%	80%
1963–64	70	74	47	78	73
1964–65	69	74	47	79	71
1965–66	69	73	46	79	72
1967–68	68	73	46	78	71
1969–70	67	72	45	77	68
1971–72	65	71	45	75	64
1972–74	63	69	43	75	63
1974–76	61	66	39	75	59
1977	59	66	38	75	58
1981	56	62	34	73	53
1982	54	61	34	71	53
1983	53	59	33	70	52
1984	51	57	32	69	48

Source: Dept. of Labor, BLS 1979d (table 157, p. 546); 1977 and 1981–84 data are unpublished (from BLS Labor-Management Division).

TABLE 5   Labor-Management Coverage, Manufacturing Plants, 1960–1984

Year	All	Northeast	South	North Central	West
1960–61	79%	81%	60%	86%	83%
1963–64	77	79	59	85	76
1964–65	77	79	60	86	74
1965–66	76	78	57	87	73
1967–68	76	77	57	85	73
1969–70	76	78	59	86	72
1971–72	76	78	59	86	70
1972–74	75	77	58	86	68
1974–76	71	72	51	86	64
1977	69	72	49	85	62
1981	65	65	45	84	55
1982	63	64	45	81	55
1983	62	62	44	82	53
1984	60	60	42	80	50

Source: U.S. Dept. of Labor, BLS 1979d (table 157, p. 546); 1977 and 1981–84 data are unpublished (from BLS Labor-Management Division).

TABLE 6   Union and Employee Association Density by State, 1970–1978

State	1970	1972	1974	1976	1978
California	35.7%	34.5%	33.3%	32.2%	28.8%
Illinois	37.3	37.8	37.1	34.3	33.4
Indiana	37.5	36.0	36.2	33.4	31.9
Michigan	43.5	42.6	42.4	36.6	38.5
Minnesota	31.9	31.6	38.3	28.7	27.6
New Jersey	31.2	32.7	32.3	29.9	27.3
New York	40.2	41.2	45.4	44.8	41.0
Pennsylvania	40.0	41.3	40.9	39.7	37.3
West Virginia	46.8	45.4	41.9	42.6	40.4
Wisconsin	33.3	31.7	32.1	32.3	30.5

Source: U.S. Dept. of Labor, BLS 1980b (table 166, p. 414).

sales-force organizing seems to have resisted this trend in the 1970s (U.S. Dept. of Labor, BLS 1980b, p. 414).

The bottom line is that union membership strength is eroding, not merely because of difficulties in organizing new constituencies or in less organized parts of the country. Union organization is weakening even in those areas of traditional strength. Thus our examination of the unevenness of the rise in union membership in the two decades from 1960 to 1980 and a comparison of U.S. figures with those of other developed countries indicates that Dunlop's remarks on union strength in this respect are overstated. On the other hand, the decline of the 1970s is similar to that of the 1960s and late 1950s. Even the current disintegration of traditional union strongholds (e.g., trucking, mining, and construction) has not yet reached the general level of the 1920s, although it certainly may if present trends continue unabated (see table 7).[18]

18. Troy and Sheflin are clearly in error when they state, "The nine year, 16% decline in total membership from the cyclical and historical peak in 1975, represents the most sustained, significant decline suffered by U.S. unions in the twentieth century" (1985, p. 1.1). From 1920 to 1933, union membership declined 42 percent; even excluding the depression years, membership dropped 34 percent from 1920 to 1929, a decade of supposed prosperity. These percentages are based upon figures in the Wolman series (1936, p. 16) whose methodology Troy and Sheflin explicitly emulate. See Griffin, Wallace, and Rubin (1986) for an account of union setbacks before the Great Depression. Freeman and Medoff (1984b, p. 221) similarly fail to consider the post–World War I period when they assert that the 1956–80 decline is "unprecedented in American history." At the other extreme is the analysis by Kokkelenberg and Sockell (1985), which attempts to exclude those barred from unionization (e.g., supervi-

TABLE 7   AFL-CIO Paid Membership, 1955–1985

Year	Number of Members (in thousands)
1955	12,622
1957	13,020
1959	12,779
1961	12,553
1963	12,469
1965	12,919
1967	13,781
1969	13,005
1971	13,177
1973	13,407
1975	14,070
1977	13,542
1979	13,621
1981	13,602[1]
1983	13,758[1]
1985	13,109

Source: Report of the Executive Council to the AFL-CIO Sixteenth Convention, Anaheim, Cal., 28 Oct. 1985.

[1]Just before the 1981 convention, the one-million-member UAW rejoined the AFL-CIO. Its full membership is not counted until the 1983 convention.

The period from 1980 to 1985, the beginning of the Reagan years, is less easy to evaluate for a number of reasons. Not the least of these is the problem of finding a suitable time series for union membership data.[19] Still, by even the most conservative interpretation of this data, union losses were quite substantial. In addition, the trends of major losses in traditionally unionized sectors were especially sharp during the post-1980 period. This

sors) or unlikely to join (e.g., managers); they argue that there has been very little decline from 1973 to 1981.

19. The long-standing BLS series, based on extensive surveys of individual unions, was discontinued in 1980. The series was picked up by the Bureau of National Affairs, who published the BLS surveys for 1980, then did their own in 1982. As the new BNA data for 1982 indicate, unions have suffered large-scale losses. Yet these figures tend to exaggerate the degree of those losses. It is probably wrong to compare the new BNA figures with the older BLS figures. It was clear even before its figures were announced that the BNA series would understate union membership because of the BNA's obvious inability to gain the degree of cooperation in surveying unions that the BLS has had historically. A further indication of the degree of understatement may be seen by looking at the AFL-CIO series in table 7 and the Current Population Survey figures in table 8. The more recently released series by Troy and Sheflin (1985) and by Kokkelenberg and Sockell (1985) have already been mentioned.

can be seen in general from the figures in table 5 concerning labor-management coverage. More detailed breakdowns (see table 8), reported from the Current Population Survey (CPS),

TABLE 8   Union Membership Based on CPS Surveys, 1977–1984

Year	Number Eligible (in thousands)	Number Organized (in thousands)	Percentage Organized	Number Covered (in thousands)	Percentage Covered
1977	81,334	19,335	23.8%	21,535	26.5%
1980	87,480	20,095	23.0	22,493	25.7
1983	88,290	17,717	20.1	20,532	23.3
1984	92,194	17,340	18.8	19,932	21.6

Source: 1980 and 1983–84 data from U.S. Dept. of Labor, BLS 1985a (p. 208); 1977 data from U.S. Dept. of Labor, BLS 1979e, 1981e.

confirm this trend (U.S. Dept. of Labor, BLS 1985a, pp. 208–9). The industry where unions have suffered the largest proportional loss is mining, where membership dropped from 285,000 to 162,000 from 1980 to 1984, the proportion of union members in the industry falling from 32 percent to 17.9 percent (Adams 1985; U.S. Dept. of Labor, BLS 1985a, 1981e).

These losses, however, while they should not be minimized, must be put into context. They have taken place during the most severe economic downturn since the Great Depression. There are almost always losses of union membership in recessions. Significant losses can be seen even in the 1974–75 period as well as during earlier recessions. Members are laid off, the ease of replacement of workers and the difficulty of getting a new job make organizing risks more severe, while the wage gains by new unions are likely to be low. In the most recent recession, highly unionized manufacturing was hit especially hard, and its recovery, if it can be said to have had one, has been very slow. As the data in tables 1 and 2 indicate, unions have, however, historically rebounded somewhat during economic recovery periods.

The trends in the early 1980s show a steady continuation of the previous losses in membership by private sector unions, no longer masked by the earlier public sector gains. None of this is meant to belittle the seriousness of these losses in membership, only to place them in their proper perspective.

Many of the signs are indeed ominous for U.S. trade unions. Union membership in heavy industry is unlikely to recover to anywhere near its prerecession levels. The deregulated industries will not be easy to reorganize. The slow quantitative losses—a steady trend from the mid-1950s to the mid-1980s—have qualitatively changed the strength of unions. Totally contrary to Dunlop's complacent assessment, 1946 and 1986 are worlds apart. Quantity (slow and cumulative) has indeed changed into quality. Trends in union membership growth find U.S. unions both comparatively weak and steadily declining over a period of more than three decades.

NLRB CERTIFICATION ELECTION RESULTS

It is also instructive to look at the fall of union success rates in NLRB certification elections, the main arena for private sector union organizing for the last fifty years. Union victory rates in NLRB certification elections may be examined with a linear model.[20]

Let us start with a simple linear model that regresses the percentage of union victories over each successive year. This model takes the preliminary form

$$Y_t = \beta_0 + \beta_1 X_t + U_t,$$

where Y is the dependent variable, percentage of union victories or percentage of workers voting for unions; X is the independent variable, year; β_0 is the intercept; β_1 is the parameter for X; and U is the stochastic or random variable. Y and X are real observations.

The model was then adjusted to separate the start-up period 1935–37, the first several years of NLRB functioning before the Wagner Act was upheld by the Supreme Court, from the rest of the years. This was done by creating a dummy variable for this period.[21]

20. A brief word on linear models is perhaps necessary for those unfamiliar with least-square estimators. The aim of a linear model is to find the linear equation (often represented graphically by a straight line) that best captures the relationships between the variables under investigation. Least-square estimators attempt to minimize the divergences of each data point from this straight line. How well the model "fits" the data is found by examining the divergences or residuals of each point from the predicted value in the equation. A good fit means the model *may* be reasonable. A poor fit means that the model is bad, the process may not even be linear, or that there exists no predictable relationships between the variables under examination.

21. Dummy variables are used to place qualitative explanatory variables in quantitative statistical models. Essentially, they are variables that have binary or dichotomous values, that is, they may be either present or not. Examples might be sex (female or not-female), season (winter or not-winter), or as in our case, the start-up period or not. (see Hanushek and Jackson 1977, p. 58).

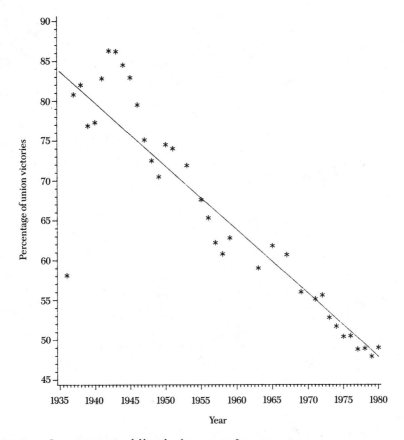

Line represents model based on least squares fit.
Symbol * represents the actual values.

FIGURE 4.   Percentage of union victories in NLRB elections by year: Actual values with least squares fit

Our new model thus is

$$Y_t = \beta_0 + \beta_1 X_t + \beta_2 S_t + U_t,$$

where S is the start-up period, β_2 is the new coefficient parameter, and U is the stochastic term, as before.

When this model was estimated, several interesting results occurred (see figures 4 and 5).[22] First, the decline since the 1950s

22. Note the error in Goldfield 1982 in the data on the war period. This error has been corrected in the present series, eliminating the use of a dummy variable for the period when the War Labor Board was responsible for many certification elections.

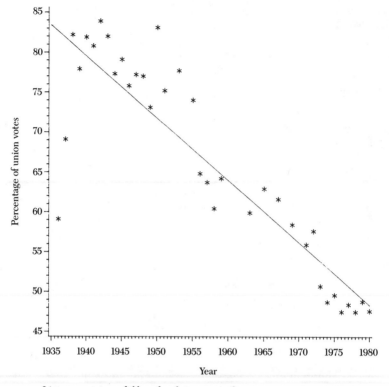

Line represents model based on least squares fit.
Symbol * represents the actual values.

FIGURE 5.   Percentage of union votes in NLRB elections by year: Actual
                 values with least squares fit

seems quite linear, constant in slope. Second, the period from
1972 to 1980 appears near the center of the new linear model,
indicating that the decline during this period may have been no
more drastic than that of other periods. The thesis that unions
have been doing well is thus not confirmed by our model. The
view that unions have suffered a greater degree of decline in the
1970s than previously, however, is also suspect on the basis of
NLRB certification results, as well as unionization figures.[23]

23. At first sight, it seems that the best means for determining exactly whether
an accelerated decline has taken place or not is to calculate the slopes of various
OLS segments in the model. This calculation and comparison can, of course, be
easily done by taking the first derivative of the model. The slope (i.e., the first
derivative) of the period, say, 1972–78 may then be compared with the slope for

Declines in NLRB victory rates from 1980–84 also seem to follow this general trend, with a slight increase in the postrecessionary years of 1983 and 1984. Certainly, the lowered victory rates during this latter period are not a qualitatively new type of phenomenon that began with the Reagan administration.

CONCLUSION

Thus it is reasonable to conclude from an examination of both union membership figures and NLRB union organizing rates that union strength has steadily eroded over the last three decades. An examination of union membership figures over time has shown U.S. trade unions to be weak compared to unions in other economically developed capitalist countries.

1936–71 or 1955–70. Although it is instructive to make the comparisons of a variety of slopes, this procedure does not conclusively solve our problem. The small number of data points in each segment makes the slope vary greatly depending on which points are included. Thus, 1968–78 gives a very different slope from that of 1972–78, and 1956–69 gives us a markedly different slope from 1951–74. Much now becomes arbitrary, since there is no overpowering reason for including one or two years on one side of the supposed decline or the other.

2

National Political Influence

The weakness of trade unions in the United States and their long-term decline are again confirmed by examining their influence in national politics. Compared to their counterparts in Japan, Australia, New Zealand, Canada, and Western Europe, the political influence of U.S. unions is not great. This can be demonstrated by a number of stark comparisons; one important indication of this weakness is the historic state of social welfare and economic policy in this country.[1] Union political influence,

1. For comparative material, I have relied heavily on Wilensky (1975); Stephens (1979); Rein and Rainwater (1981); Flora and Heidenheimer (1981); Shalev (1983); Wilensky, Luebbert, Hahn, and Jamieson (1983); Esping-Anderson and Korpi (1983); Cameron (1984); and Pontusson (1984). With the exception of Pontusson's study, much of this work, while descriptively rich and often insightful, is limited by its narrow committment to either liberal or social democratic normative and descriptive assumptions. In reviewing much of this literature, Shalev comments that most omit discussions of the importance of radical left parties and movements pushing reformists in power to enact pro–working class policies; Shalev also notes the "obliviousness" of this literature to the "structural veto of capital" in the limits of welfare state policy. Fortunately, most of these general limitations do not bear heavily on the comparative discussions here. For general assessments of U.S. social policies, I have relied on Piven and Cloward (1971), Kudrle and Marmor (1981), Skocpol and Ikenberry (1982), Swank (1984), Hicks and Swank (1984), Browning (1985), and Weir (1986).

comparatively weak, also appears to have declined steadily since the 1930s.[2] While there are no simple measures for this latter assessment, it is perhaps best reflected in the deterioration of union and worker political rights. It can be argued further that the diminished union ratings in public opinion polls are also not unrelated to this weak and declining political influence.

SOCIAL WELFARE LEGISLATION

Unions are not the only political forces in developed capitalist countries that strive for the institution of large social welfare programs. They are, however, by far the most powerful and influential. It is also recognized by many writers that a strong, organized labor movement is often a key determinant in the passage of social legislation; conversely, the lack of strong social welfare programs in an economically developed capitalist country is often due to the weakness of organized labor.[3]

While there have been many qualifications to this thesis in recent years (particularly to the argument that there is a strict correlation between social-democratic strength in government and the scope of the welfare state), few would argue that the weakness of social welfare programs in the United States is unrelated to the weakness of unions here. Esping-Anderson and Korpi (1983) assert that the tendency of labor movements to "seek to institutionalize social rights that are independent of market exchange" is universal in capitalist democracies. Kudrle and Marmor see U.S. trade unions as strong supporters of "universalistic social programs" (1981, p. 115). Thus the state of social welfare in the United States may reasonably be taken as related to the state of trade unions here.

2. I, of course, do not argue that unions have no political influence. The passage of the Occupational Safety and Health legislation (setting up OSHA) may be attributed to general union influence, just as the increased federal mine safety standards and black lung settlements were, almost certainly, a direct result of militant protests by miners. It is also apparent that in some states, for example, Michigan and New York, organized labor has had and continues to have large influence within the Democratic Party. See J. David Greenstone's classic, although now somewhat dated, study of the influence of organized labor in the Democratic Party (Greenstone 1977).

3. This theme was developed in two key studies in the 1970s. Berkeley sociologist and industrial relations researcher Harold Wilensky argues: "A large, strongly organized working class with high rates of participation in working class organizations . . . fosters pro–welfare state ideologies and big spending" (1975, p. 65). Likewise, Stephens claims "that the growth of the welfare state is a product of the growing strength of labour in civil society" (1979, p. 89).

Welfare state measures are considered here to include the national health service (in the United States, medicare, medicaid, and veterans' medical care), social security, public assistance, rent and utility subsidies, unemployment compensation, and various forms of workmen's compensation and disability benefits.[4] More generally, one might accept the functional definition noted by Shalev that welfare state policies are those that universally guarantee a "minimum standard of living designed to cushion the impact on citizens and their families of some of the major insecurities, deprivations, and inequalities of the market economy" (1983, p. 9).

A comparative examination of social welfare programs might begin by noting that the United States continues to resist having any national health plan, long after every other economically developed country has accepted the idea (Wilensky 1975, p. 27; Kudrle and Marmor 1981, p. 83). The comparatively modest proposals by Senator Edward Kennedy in the 1970s, heavily supported by the AFL-CIO and other unions, have met with little success in Congress, even at the height of Democratic congressional strength. At the other end of the spectrum, a national health system arrived in Germany in the late nineteenth century under Bismarck. Organized labor in the United States has certainly been weak in this regard.

By almost every reasonable criterion, the United States lags in social welfare programs. Unemployment compensation in this country is less automatic, covers a smaller percentage of a worker's pay, and lasts a shorter time than in virtually any European country (Sorrentino 1976; Magaziner and Reich 1982, p. 15; OECD 1984).

Comparative welfare state studies have mushroomed since the middle 1970s. Collectively they view an assortment of indicators purporting to measure the strength of social welfare policies and, hence, the degree of development of the welfare state. Two early efforts by Wilensky (1975) and Stephens (1979) look at aggregate welfare spending data for a variety of countries. Wilensky examines the percentage of GNP (Gross National Product) spent on social welfare programs as a rough indicator of

4. I exclude education, for reasons argued by Wilensky, with whom I concur. Wilensky concludes that education is not social welfare but, in general, a "transfer payment from the parents of the less affluent to the children of the more affluent" (1975, p. 5). He argues that this is even the case in California, which supposedly has the most democratic higher education system in the world.

the "welfare effort." He finds that, of the twenty-two "rich countries" in his study, the United States ranks twenty-first on social security spending (1975, pp. 30–31). He attributes much of the "special reluctance" of the United States to what one might characterize as a series of antilabor "cultural values."[5]

Stephens, while critical of Wilensky's methodology and indices, arrives at similar results. He produces evidence that shows that the United States ranks lowest in welfare spending in comparison to seventeen other economically developed capitalist countries that he examines.[6] It also ranks high in terms of economic inequality based on the distribution of wealth (Stephens 1979, p. 118). He argues convincingly in two chapters, both entitled "Labour Organization and the Welfare State," that the strongest explanatory variables for welfare spending and income distribution are degree of labor organization and extent of what he calls "socialist rule," which is a rather loose category including governmental control by various labor parties.[7]

By a similar index, Kudrle and Marmor (1981) find the United States, along with Canada, a welfare laggard in comparison with eleven other countries. They also find the United States to be behind other developed capitalist countries by a variety of additional indicators. The United States, for example, ranks last among seven large capitalist countries in the dates in which a series of selected programs—all of direct interest to workers— were first introduced; these programs include pensions, unemployment insurance, and accident insurance (Canada, however, introduced unemployment insurance in 1940, while the United States introduced it in 1935).

Shalev argues that there are criteria other than the amount of social welfare that also reflect the class biases of programs (1983, pp. 16–17, 18–19). These include the scope of the coverage, the way it is administered, and the criteria by which eligibility is determined. Esping-Anderson and Korpi (1983, p. 5) likewise discuss attempts by working-class movements to "marginalize" traditionally punitive, means-tested poor relief. They discuss the struggles by labor organizations over the conditions for entitle-

---

5. Wilensky describes these "cultural values" as "economic individualism, our unusual emphasis on private property, the free market, and minimum government" (1975, p. 32).

6. These countries are the United States, Canada, Australia, New Zealand and thirteen Western European countries.

7. For a critique of Stephen's general view, see Pontusson (1984).

ment, such as waiting days, contribution requirements, employment experience, and benefit duration. By these criteria, the
United States also ranks low. Piven and Cloward (1971) give
eloquent testimony to the demeaning features of the various
forms of relief in this country. Extensive waiting periods, means-
and employment-related criteria, and the capricious denial of
many benefits (including relief and unemployment compensation) make social welfare a form of subjection and insecurity,
rather than a reliable form of maintenance of standard of living.
Procedurally as well as substantively, the United States is far
behind other economically developed capitalist countries.

Thus, in contrast to the impressionistic arguments of Dunlop
and others, by a variety of quantitative and other carefully
delineated criteria, U.S. labor unions may be regarded as quite
weak in their influence on social legislation.[8] Further, it cannot
reasonably be argued that labor unions in this country are
unsuccessful in promoting social legislation merely because they
are less interested. Their efforts belie this. First, as noted by
Dunlop, they have been successful in enacting many small
pieces of social legislation, including minimum wages and
OSHA and CETA (Comprehensive Educational Training Act)
appropriations.[9] In those states where unions have had more
political influence than they have nationally, they have fought,
successfully in many cases, for more comprehensive social
legislation. These actions certainly suggest "interest."

One of the biggest indicators of the lack of political influence
of organized labor on the national level has been its failure to
affect government responsiveness to high and rising rates of
unemployment (Weir 1986). Levels of unemployment that are in
this country generally considered low (e.g., 4 and 5 percent)
were until the late 1970s often deemed unacceptable in many

8. On income distribution, see the careful study by Peter Wiles (1974). See
also Magaziner and Reich (1982, p. 16).

9. See Kau and Rubin (1981) for an attempt to develop a quantitative
assessment of labor's political impact. Their paper shows that unions act
rationally in making campaign contributions, in order to optimize the number of
congressmen who will support economic legislation in which unions are interested. Kau and Rubin find that unions exercise political power both through the
power of union members as voters and through campaign contributions made by
unions to representatives. They erroneously conclude, based on the fact that
unions have some influence and act rationally to use it, that unions have
substantial amounts of political power. A comparison with other developed
countries would have yielded a different conclusion about the extent of union
national political influence.

other developed countries (Freeman 1977, p. 181). In few other developed countries would unemployment be considered a valid consequence of controlling inflation. In a number of countries in Western Europe, a major stated purpose of government spending has been the maintenance of full employment. Whatever the validity and effectiveness of such schemes, this goal—strongly endorsed by major U.S. unions—has never been a politically dominant one here.[10]

One telling commentary on both the legislative weakness of organized labor and its interest in social legislation is that its ability to gain the passage of even minor reforms often depends on extreme forms of disruption sometimes coupled with alliances with other social forces. One would, of course, expect that major reforms (like the eight-hour day or national health care) would entail major upheavals. The Railway Labor Act of 1926, a relatively minor piece of labor legislation, was the result of several years of turmoil involving strong dissident groups among railway workers. The Mine Safety Act of 1972 was passed after widespread wildcat strikes in the coal fields; black lung benefit legislation was enabled after insurgent miners, organized independently of their unions, demonstrated by the tens of thousands in West Virginia. The major pieces of social legislation (still far less than in most other economically developed capitalist countries) were only passed as the result of the upheavals in the 1930s and 1960s. In the 1930s, labor unions were allied in supporting legislation with the massive, but short-lived, unemployed movement and the black movement (Goldfield 1985a). In the 1960s, major disruptions by blacks (from sit-ins and demonstrations to ghetto rebellions) led to the successful passage of social legislation, some of which unions had been pressing unsuccessfully for many years (Piven and Cloward 1971, 1977).

Despite the difficulties unions have had, they have been far more successful in obtaining social welfare and economic legis-

10. Note the effect of the 1946 Full Employment Act (for an interesting discussion see Domhoff 1979, pp. 109–17), and the failures to gain consideration in the 1970s of the Humphrey-Hawkins "full" employment bill and the more recent Conyers bill, which supposedly aims at creating full employment by shortening the workweek. Margaret Weir lays great emphasis on the importance of programs developed by experts and the structure of government in the blocking or advancing of key incomes policies. She asserts that opportunities for achieving such goals were more real than most commentators suggest. Still, she argues that "more than many advanced industrial nations . . . the U.S. lacks a ready-made proponent for active involvement in employment because of its weak labor movement" (1986, p. 29).

lation than in gaining their own legal rights and narrow economic goals.[11] Moreover, their influence in this regard would seem to be declining.

UNION LEGAL RIGHTS

As far as their own rights go, U.S. unions appear to be in a worse situation than their counterparts in other economically developed capitalist countries.[12] In no other developed capitalist countries are unions as legally constrained as in the United States (although in France they have few legal rights). The degree of injunctive powers possessed by the courts and the ability of employers to sue unions are unmatched elsewhere. The web of Taft-Hartley restrictions (while being mimicked in several other places) is nowhere as extensive as in the United States.

It is here that the question of unions' decline in political influence may be most fruitfully examined. Their political influence seems to have fallen steadily in recent decades. While it is important not to exaggerate the political influence of organized labor within the New Deal Democratic Party, it is clear that it was substantial.[13] By 1947, labor's influence, still strong by many accounts, was already weakening. A full mobilization by organized labor in that year failed to prevent the passage of Taft-Hartley over President Truman's veto. The inability of organized labor even to slow the passage of the Landrum-Griffin bill of 1959 demonstrated even greater ineffectiveness. This was, of course, during the Republican Eisenhower administration. In

11. See Freeman and Medoff (1984b, pp. 191–206) for a similar conclusion.
12. Workers themselves have fewer rights as employees than in most other developed capitalist countries, France perhaps being a partial exception. To take one example, the United States is one of the few such lands where workers may be arbitrarily fired without immediate legal recourse or injunctive relief (Estreicher 1984).
13. Gross (1981), for example, argues that the anti-NLRB hearings of the Smith Committee in 1939 and 1940 could not have taken place without the explicit support of the AFL, in part a product of its conflict with the CIO. These hearings, according to Gross, paved the way for the Taft-Hartley bill of 1947, regarded by labor unions as the "Slave Labor Act." For an argument that labor had little influence even during the New Deal, see Harris (1982a, 1982b). Ferguson and Rogers (1981), on the other hand, find the Truman veto of Taft-Hartley an indication of greater union influence in national politics than exists today. Montgomery (1979) views the 1934–38 period as the height of labor's political influence. Rubin, Griffin, and Wallace (1983), employing a broad view of union power, see the whole 1933–46 period as a highpoint. I consider labor militancy and pressure to be the primary cause for the passage of New Deal (1933–38) labor legislation (Goldfield 1985a).

succeeding years, organized labor failed, with a heavily Democratic Congress and Democratic presidents, to get even the most noxious sections of Taft-Hartley repealed (like 14b on "right-to-work" laws). Common situs picketing (allowing one construction craft to strike a whole construction site) passed both houses, but was vetoed by President Gerald Ford, who had originally supported it. By the mid-1970s the NLRB itself was being gutted by legal maneuvering and other forms of employer resistance.[14] A full-scale mobilization by organized labor failed miserably in its attempt to pass the tepid Labor Law Reform Act in 1978, which would have provided only partial remedies to the growing ineffectiveness of the NLRB.[15]

One of the few national legislative successes concerning the rights of private sector unions during the post–World War II period involved the extension of NLRB coverage to hospital workers.

BAD PRESS AND PUBLIC OPINION

The weakness of unions is also reflected in their long-term decline in public opinion. It is reasonable to ask what difference public opinion makes at all. For example, the 1943 strike by the United Mine Workers (UMW) during World War II, in defiance of President Roosevelt, did not receive favorable ratings in the polls. Publicly opposed even by major CIO leaders, it nevertheless galvanized support from large numbers of militant unionized workers in other industries. The miners, however, did not need public opinion on their side. Their industry was fully organized, and it was strategically located. Their historically militant work force was united. They could not be replaced by scabs—and they knew it. In many other situations, particularly those in which unions are newly organizing, public opinion can be important. Recently, a Long Island Teamsters local was successful in organizing a small fabricating plant owned by a large conglomerate. The union not only organized the work force, but publicized the way the plant was polluting the surrounding community. They exposed the ownership and orga-

14. See chapter 9 for a fuller discussion of employer resistance.

15. See Knight (1979) for a description of the issues involved in the Labor Law Reform Act of 1978. Ferguson and Rogers (1979a) give an analysis for the causes of the defeat of the bill. For a less sanguine view of the NLRB than Knight's, and for estimates of the extent of time delays in various NLRB steps, see Hook (1982). For remarks on the concessions in negotiations with Democratic Party congressional leaders that weakened the bill, see Raskin (1978).

nized a community dump-in at the conglomerate's headquarters. Maintaining their unity and aided by favorable publicity and community support, the workers got their union and a first contract.

The 1936–37 Flint sit-down strike that led to the unionization of General Motors depended in part for its success, according to many commentators, on the strong public support for the rights of labor. Clearly, this support was anchored on the militancy and power exhibited by workers in Flint and other parts of the country. Strong pro-union public opinion was most likely a result both of the growing strength of the labor movement and the sympathy large numbers of people had for the conditions under which U.S. workers were forced to earn their living. Liberal politicians, including Michigan governor Frank Murphy and President Franklin D. Roosevelt, proved responsive to this strong public support for the Flint strikers.

As James Medoff argues in his near exhaustive study of U.S. public opinion polls about unions (1984), the public image of trade unions does affect, at least to some degree, their success as organizations. First, there is a strong correlation between how people vote in representation elections and their image of unions; second, votes of local, state, and federal politicians are in part responsive to public opinion; third, the ability of companies to commit unfair labor practices without public outcries is based partly on the low degree of sympathy for unions.

There does appear to be a long-term decline in the image of labor unions (as measured in national surveys) since the middle 1950s, a trend that seems to be somewhat more accentuated since the middle 1960s. This can be seen in table 9 below.

Large-scale publicity seems to have occasionally had a big impact on public opinion on unions. This has particularly been the case when highly negative, well-publicized congressional hearings have been held.

From 1935 to 1937, according to polls, unions were highly rated by the public at large. Gross notes the degree of success the Smith Committee had during 1939–40 in discrediting both the NLRB and the union movement. According to Gallup polls, 16 percent more of the general population thought employers were unfairly treated by the NLRB, favoring pro-employer revision of the National Labor Relations Act, after the hearings had gotten under way (Gross 1981, p. 187).

A casual survey of the press gives the impression that labor

TABLE 9   Public Approval of Labor Unions, 1936–1985

Year	Approve	Disapprove	No Opinion
1985[1]	58%	27%	
1981	55	35	10%
1979	55	33	12
1978	59	31	10
1972	59	26	15
1967	66	23	11
1965 June	70	19	11
February	71	19	10
1963	67	23	10
1962	64	24	12
1961 May	63	22	15
February	70	18	12
1959	68	19	13
1957 September	64	18	18
February	76	14	10
1953	75	18	7
1949	62	22	16
1947	64	25	11
1941[2]	61 (67)	30 (33)	9 (10)
1940	64	22	14
1939	68	24	8
1937	72 (76)	20 (24)	8
1936	72	20	8

Note: This is a corrected and updated version of a similar table appearing in Medoff 1984.

[1]1985 figures are reported in *New York Times*, 19 May 1985.

[2]Other data appear in Gallup Report No. 191 (August 1981), where the question asked was, "In general, do you approve or disapprove of labor unions?" In additional yearly Gallup reports, the question for 1936–1941 was, "Are you in favor of labor unions?" (where different, the values for these reports are given in parentheses).

has generally been on the defensive in the post–World War II period.[16] In the late 1940s and early 1950s, the labor movement was not only attacked for having radicals and Communists in key leadership positions, but even for harboring them in its ranks. By the late 1950s, the charges of gangsterism and corruption were given full play, eventually providing the rationale for the Landrum-Griffin Act of 1959. As can be seen from table 9, favorable opinions toward unions, as measured by the Gallup

16. This phenomenon was also noticed by Bell (1953).

polls, dropped from 75 percent before the McClelland hearings to 68 percent afterward, remaining at that level through the 1960s then falling to an average of only 60 percent in the 1970s. This drop took place across many occupational groups (including professional and business, white-collar, blue-collar, and farmers). During the 1970s, it took place most sharply among those under thirty years of age. Much has been made in the 1970s and early 1980s of the declines in productivity of U.S. industrial workers (particularly in comparison to workers in Japan and West Germany). Some of this reporting either implicitly or explicitly blames a lack of "hard work" or loss of the "work ethic" by U.S. workers.[17]

In contrast to these negative attitudes toward unions, it is interesting to note the high favor in which unions and their leaders have stood among their membership. The polls also indicate a large number of contradictory findings among both the population at large and among union members themselves. First, people are often quite knowledgable and have surprisingly positive views on certain aspects of unions. Unions are considered necessary for complaints and grievances to be heard (in a 1984 Harris poll, 92 percent of union, 82 percent of nonunion respondents agreed), to protect workers' rights (1978 PIOR, 59 percent of all respondents agreed), to improve wages, working conditions, and job security (1982 ABC/*Washington Post*, 78 percent of respondents concurred). Workers should have the right to join unions (1984 Harris, 94 percent of union, 81 percent of all respondents answered affirmatively). Unions are viewed as a "good force" in promoting social needs (1984 Harris, 88 percent of all respondents agreed) and as a good check on "the power of big business" (1984 Harris, 61 percent of respondents concurred).

Yet by 68 percent to 17 percent, those polled consider "unions that do not fairly represent their members" to be a bigger problem than "companies that deny workers a chance to join a union" (1978 PIOR). Unions also have too much influence in "American life and politics" (1981 CBS/*NYT*, 60 percent). One explanation for these negative findings may be that public opinion ranks labor leaders low in confidence (1982 Harris) and in ethical standards (1983 Gallup). In the latter category, only 12

17. Victor Perlo (1982) documents certain of these charges against U.S. workers. He also goes on to present an interesting argument that the claim of declining productivity not only is used for antilabor purposes, but is in fact false.

percent of the respondents gave high marks to union leaders, below realtors and insurance salesmen (13 percent), building contractors (18 percent), lawyers (24 percent), television reporters (33 percent), college teachers (47 percent), doctors (52 percent), druggists (61 percent), and clergymen (64 percent). Only car salesmen (6 percent) and advertising practitioners (9 percent) ranked lower.[18]

Thus we find that both union members and the population at large have rudimentary knowledge of unions and think positively of them as institutions but are quite skeptical of their leadership. This is quite a subtle, not to say astute, evaluation.

Public opinion polls in other developed capitalist countries are not easily compared to those taken in this country. International results are contradictory. Although fewer people in other economically developed capitalist countries seem to judge trade union leaders as corrupt, inefficient, or unethical than in this country, the general degrees of positive evaluations for trade unions are similar. Because of the differing nature of the polls, it is difficult to make more than tentative judgments on this score.[19]

CONCLUSION

The social legislation of the 1930s successfully brought the United States out of the nineteenth century. The many small pieces of legislation cited by Dunlop and others, however, while certainly important, only indicate that the United States in comparison to other developed countries is still a reluctant participant in the twentieth century. Even before the initial dismantling of social welfare programs by the Reagan administration, this country was marked by the slippage in certain New Deal social programs, the increasing erosion of the progressive nature of the income tax, and the lack of headway on the issues of national health care and unemployment. That much of the legislation cited by Dunlop and others was, however, passed in the late 1960s and early 1970s also indicates that the decline in influence of U.S. unions, certainly before Reagan, has been neither precipitous nor terminal.

18. Although I have checked the original sources for the preceding polls, it was the comprehensive study by Medoff (1984) that led me to the majority of this material.

19. See, for example, Gallup (1976, 1981a, 1981b) and Hastings and Hastings (1984).

The analysis of unions' direct and indirect legislative influence, as well as the less favorable ratings in public opinion polls, make it only fair to conclude that labor's political influence is quite weak in this country, and if anything declining.[20]

20. It is interesting to note that this was also Samuel Gompers's assessment, according to William Z. Foster. Foster writes: "Another aspect of American Labor's political weakness is the reactionary course of labor legislation in the United States." He then quotes Gompers's "Charges against the National Association of Manufacturers, etc.," written in 1909, after a visit to Europe:

We are, in the United States, not less than two decades behind many European countries in the protection of life, health, and limb of the workers. . . . We are behind England 10 years. We are behind Germany 20 years.

Foster continues:

In the 13 years that have elapsed since this comparison was made the situation has become much more unfavorable for the United States, because during that period, and especially since the war, nearly all the European countries have made great strides forward in labor legislation while this country has gone steadily backward. (Foster 1922, p. 4)

3

The Collective Bargaining System

It might be argued that U.S. labor unions, though they are weak and ineffective in national politics, make up for this defect by exerting considerable economic power at the plant and firm level.[1]

To see whether this argument has substance, we shall now look at seven aspects of labor-management relations: worker militancy, contract strength, concession bargaining, job and income security, the recent disintegration of many previously stable collective bargaining relations, union leadership, and union busting.

WORKER MILITANCY

Those who argue that unions exercise considerable economic (even monopoly) power at the plant and firm level often point to the high strike rates of workers in the United States. Various

1. This is the current orthodox argument quite common in the industrial relations literature. For a clear formulation, see Kochan (1980). Several others cited in this essay who note the proposition approvingly are Voos (1982) and Roomkin and Juris (1978). For a sustained critique, see Hyman (1982). Michael Wallerstein (1985) argues that national union movements make rational choices over whether to get many benefits for their members through nationally legislated social welfare programs or through the incorporation of these benefits in their contracts.

studies and statistical compilations indicate that U.S. strike rates, particularly in the post–World War II period, are among the highest in the developed capitalist countries. The United States is not merely characterized by a high level of strike activity, but by a comparatively high level of violence in labor-management conflict throughout its history.

Until 1980, there was little evidence that strike activity had dwindled in this country. Rather, as can be seen in figure 6, the number of strikes by year seems to follow a cyclical pattern. In 1980, the Department of Labor stopped reporting detailed strike statistics. Unpublished figures for 1981, however, indicate that while the number of strikes began declining, those that did take place were much lengthier. For later dates, one must rely on the less informative BLS series that records strikes of over one thousand workers of at least one day, thus failing to capture most wildcat stoppages. This series tends to reflect official strikes in large firms, which clearly diminished from 1980 to 1982. This decline in strike activity, rather than being traceable to policies of the Reagan administration, is more likely attributable to the economic recession, high unemployment, and the especially weakened state of manufacturing. This speculation is confirmed by the sharp increase in some measures of strike activity for 1983 (with the beginning of an upturn in the economy).

Though U.S. workers and their unions do not generally seem to have been the passive recipients of whatever the employers have to offer, it is not clear that they have been able to mobilize for more than sectoral struggles. Among the failures of such narrowness has been the inability or unwillingness of the official labor organizations to mobilize more than token support for beleaguered strikers, among whom are numbered coal miners in 1978, PATCO in 1981, Greyhound strikers in 1983, the Phelps-Dodge copper workers in 1983–84, and Hormel workers in 1986. Still, it might be argued that unionized workers have not done so poorly in the post–World War II period. One might conclude that union tenacity in collective bargaining (reflected in lengthy and frequent strikes) rather than national political influence was the means for gaining social benefits for union members.

CONTRACT STRENGTH AND JOB AND INCOME SECURITY

It might thus be argued that many unions have not needed strong national social legislation since they achieve their aims more fully in their contracts. Pensions, supplementary unemployment

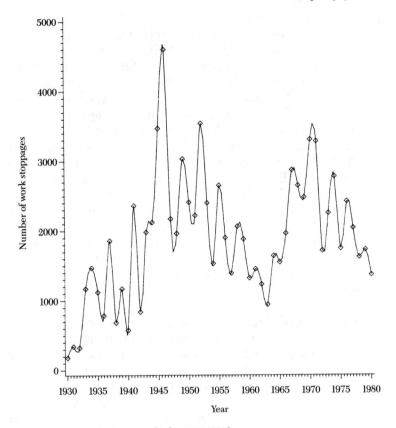

Source: U.S. Dept. of Labor, BLS 1982f.

FIGURE 6.   Number of work stoppages in the U. S. by year

benefits, and extensive medical coverage are indeed features of certain union contracts, for example, those of the United Auto Workers (UAW) and Steelworkers (USA). There is, of course, an important element of truth to the claim that key social welfare measures are enbodied in some union contracts. These provisions, however, are not necessarily an adequate counterbalance to weak union influence in national politics. First, a majority of the work force is unorganized. Since there exists a high disparity of wages and benefits between organized and unorganized workers, most nonunion workers tend not to enjoy union-negotiated social benefits.[2] Pensions and full medical coverage are

2. The existence and causes of union/nonunion wage (and benefit) differen-

among the more common benefits not enjoyed by nonunion workers. Second, even most union members do not receive many of the supposed benefits of strong collective bargaining. Most union members, for example, do not have full medical coverage. Few union pension plans pay more than meager supplements to social security. In addition, while the percentage of pension plans that fail is still small, some companies (eyeing the cash assets) have recently forced their employees to give up their pensions through "negotiations," as happened at Braniff Airlines. Third, a big problem with even the best of contracts is that the benefits usually only last for as long as a worker is employed at the particular firm. This problem is especially stark today. Even many steelworkers and UAW members (in auto, farm, and construction equipment) have lost benefits due to the extensive layoffs in their industries. Thus a comprehensive national social welfare program not based upon employment at a particular firm would benefit not only unemployed, nonunion, and laid-off workers, but even those in industries with supposedly strong contracts.

The argument that unions (and workers in general) receive the potential benefits of national social welfare programs through their union contracts rather than through national legislation is hardly convincing.[3] While there does seem to exist some collective bargaining strength among strong unions in this country compared, for example, to unions in weak bargaining countries like France and Italy, this would not appear to be an adequate substitute for national social welfare legislation. Moreover, there

---

tials are discussed in a growing literature. Their existence is well documented. Figures for 1984 show that the average weekly earnings for all unionized workers was $404, while that of nonunionized workers was $303. The disparity is even greater for nonwhite workers: $352 to $236 for black workers, $346 to $238 for Hispanic workers (U.S. Dept of Labor, BLS 1985a, p. 210). Much of the debate concerns whether high-wage industries are more open to unionism or whether unionization is in whole or part a cause of the differentials. See Kahn (1979) and Lewis (1983) for a discussion of the issues and extensive references. The best overall summaries are by Freeman and Medoff (1981, 1983). For our purposes here, it is enough to note that nonunion employees tend *not* to enjoy the level of wages or benefits that their union counterparts do. This differential is more extreme for many benefits (Freeman and Medoff 1984b).

3. Magaziner and Reich (1982) discuss the question of the inferior social benefits in chapter 1 of their work. Among other things, they note the far more liberalized vacations in other developed countries. Rein and Rainwater (1981) attempt to account for privately funded benefits in assessing social welfare; they still find that the United States ranks near the bottom.

are many developed capitalist countries (e.g., Sweden, Germany, Britain, and Australia) where bargaining covers a larger percentage of the work force and where the bargaining leverage is not inferior to that in this country.[4]

Union collective bargaining strength is not as weak in this country as are its political influence and membership strength. We should be clear that the militancy of many workers and the high strike rates have indeed helped workers win better conditions and in some cases better contracts. Their ability to win wage benefits is not inferior to that of workers in several European countries. Yet this collective bargaining strength is not able to compensate them (particularly in terms of job security) for the meager social legislation existing in the United States. Even further, there has been a decline in bargaining strength, quite evident over the last decade. U.S. unions have been unable to protect their members from forced and totally uncompensated losses of real wages due to inflation as has been done partially by Swedish and German unions, among others. They have bargained away, in many cases, the right to strike during the life of their contracts, and in the extreme case of steel (with the Experimental Negotiating Agreement), the right to strike over contracts. Until recently, unions have been all too ready to grant uncompensated major concessions to their employers—in contrast to the stance of many of their counterparts in other countries. All these things may be taken as indications of declining bargaining strength.

CONCESSION BARGAINING

One sign that the collective bargaining strength of major unions is weakening may be found in the widespread nature of concession bargaining, particularly as it developed in the early 1980s. Concession bargaining involves wage freezes, wage decreases, foregoing raises due under existing contracts, and giving up previously won fringe benefits; it often involves reopening of contracts in order to give these concessions to the companies. Concession bargaining has sometimes meant the giving up of long-cherished work rules and the acceptance of highly divisive two-tier wage systems, that is, lower wage scales for the same

4. For comparative material on bargaining in other developed countries, see Clegg (1976), OECD (1979), Martin and Kassalow (1980), Barkin (1975), von Behme (1980), Crouch and Pizzorno (1978), and Juris, Thompson, and Daniels (1985), among others.

jobs for newly hired, temporary, or even low-seniority workers. There are some who argue that these concessions are largely a result of cyclical economic activity, brought on by the severity of the recession (Dunlop 1982; Mitchell 1982; Flanaghan 1984); contract bargaining will presumably return to "normal," that is, concessions will be reversed, when the economy picks up. Others, however, see the 1980s concession bargaining as something new that portends extensive changes in U.S. collective bargaining behavior (Freedman 1982, 1985; Cappelli 1982, 1983).

To answer the questions about the nature of concessions, it is instructive to look at the special characteristics of the early 1980s bargaining agreements. Such concessions may be said to have begun with the government mandated wage cuts for Chrysler workers in 1979, but they did not really become a major trend until 1981. Many factors have contributed to the rise in the number and percentage of contracts involving major concessions. First, the general economic crisis (or recession) beginning in 1979 undoubtedly was a key component; unemployment rose officially to almost 11 percent in 1982, the highest level since the 1930s. Second, the recession created special havoc for workers in a series of distressed industries. These included newspapers, printing, and meatpacking, whose economic problems had been manifest for decades, and construction, where high unemployment and diminished building had been endemic since the middle 1970s. Third, those industries that were subject to increasing foreign competition were hit especially hard; these included auto, steel, tires and rubber, and ship building. Further, farm and construction equipment suffered greatly as a result of the crises in the sectors they supplied. Finally, deregulation intensified the recessionary difficulties for unions in trucking and air.

There have been concessionary negotiations in the past, including those during the 1930s depression, the post–Korean War givebacks in the garment and textile industries, the attempts to get Studebaker and Kaiser-Willys workers to accept wage cuts, supposedly to aid their dying companies. According to Robert J. Flanaghan however, the "scale of present concession bargaining is unprecedented" (1984, p. 184). As Flanaghan notes and BLS figures corroborate, wage decreases were virtually unheard of in major collective bargaining agreements up to 1981. By 1983, one-third of all workers covered by new contracts were taking wage reductions; in steel, air, and meatpacking these ranged from 10 percent to 20 percent during the first year. By way of contrast, first-year increases were almost 10 percent for contracts negotiated from 1974 to 1979, topping 10 percent in 1980 and 1981. These averages dropped to slightly over 3 percent in contracts signed in 1982 and 1983. In the first quarter of 1983, as a result of the steel settlement, median wages in major industrial settlements dropped 1.6 percent (3.7 percent in those with COLA clauses). As an indication of the extent of the concessions, it is worth noting that average union wage increases in manufacturing were over 1 percent less in 1983 (3.6 percent) than were wage increases among nonunion workers (4.7 percent) who were unable to apply any bargaining leverage.[5]

The scale of recent wage givebacks has not been seen since the 1930s. Then, however, the degree of unionization was negligible in mass production industries. Another unique feature of the recent period includes the large number of contract reopeners, for the purpose of making concessions, proposed by companies and accepted without serious resistance by the unions.

In the early 1980s, many economists claimed that these concessions were largely a result of conjunctural factors (Dunlop 1982; Mitchell 1982; Flanaghan 1984). They argued that the ending of the recession and the return of profitability to many distressed industries would see a regaining of union losses. But 1984, supposedly a year of recovery and declining official unemployment, brought with it continued concessions and even lower first-year wage increases in new contracts. Against the optimistic predictions for cyclical recovery, few gains in concession-prone industries seem to have been registered.[6] Even 1985 saw the acceptance of a sharp two-tiered wage system in the Master Freight Agreement by the Teamsters and successful demands by United Airlines, the biggest and a highly profitable airline, that its pilots accept a two-tiered scale that would eventually lead to a 50 percent lowered wage for pilots. Thus the continuing decline of union strength has made union "recovery" from the deep economic recession especially difficult.

Flanaghan and others cite the decreased number of strikes between 1980 and 1983 involving more than 1,000 workers to show the lack of union militancy. What they neglect to mention, however, are the sharp increases in 1983 in the number of workers

5. See various issues of *Current Wage Developments* for the years 1977–85.
6. See the informative analysis by Kim Moody (1985).

involved in strikes (909,000 in 1983 compared to 795,000 in 1980, 729,000 in 1981, and 656,000 in 1982), the number of working days lost (17.5 million in 1983 compared to 9.1 and 16.9 million in 1982 and 1981 respectively), and even the days lost per 1,000 workers (195 in 1983, 102 in 1982, and 172 in 1981). All this suggests that strikes have become much longer and possibly more bitter while unions have become less effective.

Contrary to the views of those who see the concessions merely as a response to various temporary conjunctural factors, they are more likely also a reflection of long-term union weakness and declining strength.

DISINTEGRATION OF STABLE BARGAINING RELATIONS

Further evidence of recent weakening in union collective bargaining strength in the United States is found in the disintegration of former stable bargaining relations in many industries and the break-up of industrywide bargaining relations in others (Freedman 1982).

Although full-scale industry bargaining was established in coal mining during the 1930s, the pacesetter for stable, industrywide bargaining has been the automobile industry. Here the relation was fully institutionalized beginning with the United Auto Workers–General Motors 1950 five-year contract, at the time popularly called the "Treaty of Detroit." Other industries, including steel, rubber, and farm and construction equipment, emulated the automobile industry. The last major sector to develop such bargaining was trucking. In 1964 the Master Freight Agreement was signed between the Teamsters (IBT) and almost ten thousand trucking companies employing over three hundred thousand workers. Grocery workers (now covered by the newly amalgamated United Food and Commercial Workers), brewery workers, and others followed the IBT patterns.

This system had established industrywide patterns of wages, benefits, and working conditions "insensitive to competitive conditions in separate industries and product lines" (Freedman 1982). These relationships, seemingly stable as late as 1980 except in several minor areas, have all but crumbled. In construction, mining, and trucking, previously highly unionized industries, huge losses in union membership and the rise of nonunion operations have effectively destroyed industrywide bargaining.

Even in those industries where membership remains high, unions have shown an increased willingness to make concessions tied to the profitability of companies. Such concessions in the auto, steel, airline, and meatpacking industries have effectively ended the patterns. In some instances, highly aggressive companies have used a variety of tactics to break out of previously negotiated industry standards. In 1983, Continental Airlines reorganized itself under Chapter 11 of the 1978 bankruptcy provisions, cut wages and benefits in half, fired a majority of its employees, and declared itself nonunion. In the wake of the defeat of the 1983–84 Phelps-Dodge copper strike, various copper companies, many of whom had lost money owing to the low price of copper on the world market, demanded a reopening of the 1983 three-year agreement. Companies sought from $2.50 to $6.00 per hour in immediate concessions.

Some claim that the reestablishment of industrywide standards would be equivalent to putting Humpty-Dumpty back together again. Of course, there is still the possibility that such standards might prevail without unions reasserting their power. This would undoubtedly have to be on terms that unionized workers would hardly approve. There is a trend for the more profitable companies in a distressed industry to want the same concessions, if not more, than those given to their weaker competitors. Greyhound, with large profits the previous year, still fought successfully for major wage and benefit cuts during the 1983–84 strike. GM wants what the Chrysler workers gave up, while American Motors wants even more. United Airlines, not facing the financial difficulties of Eastern, wants their "pattern." Other companies implicitly demand parity with their Third World competitors.

Such competition between workers in different companies and in different countries ultimately destroys workers' minimum goal for a living wage. There is always a lower wage somewhere that can be claimed by an employer to be the standard. John L. Lewis, in an exchange with Charles L. Schwab, then chairman of Bethlehem Steel, states this succinctly. During the 1920s, the United Mine Workers (UMW) had refused a wage cut in response to growing losses by coal companies. Schwab argued that the union scale should be reduced from $7.50 to $5.00 per day, since that is what many nonunion mines were paying.

Mr. Lewis: Do you know we have evidence before this committee to show that wages have been reduced in some instances as low as $2.50 and $3 in certain mines in West Virginia? Where is the bottom?

Mr. Schwab: You will not prevent the bottom being reached by keeping wages so high that the man cannot work.

Mr. Lewis: Do you approve of a wage policy that will permit the most unfortunate, the most isolated, the most dependent foreign miner in West Virginia to become the yardstick that would measure the wages of organized labor in America? (I. Bernstein 1966, p. 129)

Just as the destruction of the union standard in mining during the 1920s was a significant indicator of growing union weakness in the UMW, so the destruction of industrywide union standards in numerous industries today is one more sign of declining union strength.

While there have been unsuccessful attempts to decentralize collective bargaining in other economically developed capitalist countries (e.g., Sweden, France, and West Germany), forced concessions and the destruction of industrywide patterns have been primarily a U.S. phenomenon. The partial exception is Britain, where miners withstood for a year a vicious onslaught by the Thatcher government in 1984–85. Otherwise, no changes in collective bargaining comparable to those in the United States have even been attempted in these other countries.

WEAKNESSES OF TRADE UNION LEADERSHIP IN THE UNITED STATES

The role of the AFL leadership is to chlorophorm the working class while the capitalist class goes through its pockets. (Debs 1905)

The weakness of U.S. trade union leadership has been a complaint of radicals (and even many who were not so radical) for almost a century. Many of the criticisms from radicals in the 1920s or those who were to form the CIO leadership in the mid-1930s have a familiar ring today.[7]

7. For example, William Z. Foster, in his classic pamphlet *The Bankruptcy of the American Labor Movement* (1922), writes:

With almost unfailing regularity those nations with developed industrial systems also have well developed labor movements, and those that are backward industrially are also backward in working class organization. The one glaring exception is the United States.

Among the causes, according to Foster, are the union leaders:

The prevailing type of American labor leadership is a sore affliction upon the working class. Our higher officialdom swarms with standpatters and reactionaries such as would not be tolerated in any other country. Mr. Gompers himself personifies the breed. He is the arch-reactionary, the idol of all the holdbacks in the labor movement . . . . In many respects he is even more reactionary than the very capitalists themselves. (Ibid., pp. 13–14)

Workers in even the strongest industrial unions with strong contracts are plagued with problems of business unionism unheard of in most European countries.[8] The UMW, for example, continues to lose leverage in dealing with the coal companies by refusing to organize the growing number of strip miners. Other unions, like those in construction, which often are unwilling to

---

8. The term "business unionism" most assuredly originates in the United States, the country to which it finds most ready application. Whether Hyman (1973) is right in attributing the term to Hoxie is uncertain, for it was in common use before the publication of Hoxie's book on trade unions in 1915 (reprinted 1966). The usage, however, has varied. Hoxie uses the term to refer to what many call pure and simple trade unionism as opposed to either class or revolutionary unionism:

> Business unionism . . . is essentially trade-consciousness, rather than class-consciousness. That is to say, it expresses the viewpoint and interests of the workers in a craft or industry rather than those of the working class as a whole. It aims chiefly at more, here and now, for the organized workers of the craft or industry, in terms mainly of higher wages, shorter hours, and better working conditions, regardless for the most part of the welfare of the workers outside the particular organic group, and regardless in general of political and social considerations, except in so far as these bear directly upon its own economic ends. It is conservative in the sense that it professes belief in natural rights, and accepts as inevitable, if not as just, the existing capitalistic organization, the wage system, as well as existing property rights and the binding force of contract. It regards unionism mainly as a bargaining institution. (1966, p. 45)

This view of business unionism is shared by Debs (1921), who calls it the "old unionism," contrasting it with the revolutionary industrial unionism of the IWW. Daniel De Leon (1921) put forth a similar view in 1919.

With the establishment of industrial unionism, a derivative usage developed, which distinguished business unionism from pure and simple unionism. This refers to business unionism as the literal running of a union as a business. Lens (1949, 1959) adopts this usage. There are two manners of running a union as a business. One is the concern for the union primarily as a solvent financial organization, seeing it as a dues collection organization whose major function is to preserve its income, not deplete its resources unnecessarily. Such a stance may mean the avoidance of strikes, careful investment of funds, even alliances with employers to preserve its solvency. If the preservation of the business union requires the bureaucratic domination of the membership, the submergence of the rights of the rank-and-file whose desires and goals might present organizational risks, then so be it.

The second perspective involves, not merely the treatment of the union as a business by the leaders, but its operation as a business for their own personal aggrandizement, involving high salaries, expense accounts, and occasional swindles and money on the side. Here one sees the willingness to sacrifice even the business interests of the union for the personal finances of its leaders. Gangster-dominated unions are, of course, a subset of this type of business union.

None of these forms is pure. Even a gangster-dominated union must occasionally defend the interests of its members. When I refer to business unionism in this essay, I use the term as Lens does, in the sense of running a union as a business.

organize residential construction workers, have until recently seemed content to rule over a shrinking base. Most industrial unions fail to take a strong stand against the subcontracting of their work or for transfer rights for their members when plants close. Thus even a number of strong unions in this country fail to make efforts to stem loss of membership and bargaining leverage. In other developed countries, such failures are less frequent and acceptable.

To these weaknesses, we must add certain characteristics that are somewhat unique to U.S. labor unions. They are the only ones whose top leadership are virtually all procapitalist.[9] Furthermore, while the extent of corruption and gangsterism in certain unions in this country is greatly exaggerated by the mass media and by politicians, it does indeed exist. This phenomenon is almost unknown in other developed capitalist countries.[10]

Union leadership in this country is considerably weaker than in other developed countries. These weaknesses seem to have grown in the last few decades; yet this is difficult to prove in a rigorous manner. Thus, again, while the weaknesses are sharp, the decline, to the degree it has occurred, is less than momentous.

9. There are, of course, some notable exceptions like the IAM's Winpisinger and various of the UAW tops who are members of the Democratic Socialists of America (DSA). But these are the exceptions that prove the rule.

As noted in the *Economist*, certainly not a prolabor publication, in an article dated 17 November 1979, "The American labour movement can be forgiven for thinking that life is unfair. Compared with its brethren on the other side of the Atlantic, it is the most pro-private enterprise of the lot" ("American Union Busting," p. 1). Prosten also has some sarcastic remarks on the subject: "American business appears clearly unhappy about the continued existence of a labor movement that generally endorses capitalism—a courtesy unlikely to be extended to these or other companies operating in other Western countries" (1978, p. 243).

Montgomery (1979) sees a growing tendency among union tops to adopt moderate social-democratic stances, a tendency he attributes to the increasing failure of traditional reformist approaches to collective bargaining in this country.

10. While many people believe that there are gangster-dominated unions in Italy, experts on Italian labor assure me that this is not the case. In this country, there has, of course, been long-standing public exposure of the corruption and gangsterism that is widespread in the Teamsters union. Information on another union, the Hotel and Restaurant Employees Union, may be gleaned from testimony before the Committee on Government Affairs of the U.S. Senate (1982). Recent investigations of UAW Region 4 (Illinois, Iowa, and part of Wisconsin) suggest corruption among several previous regional directors. Freeman and Medoff (1984b) also mention the ILU (East Coast longshoremen) and the building trades. Such corruption is not new, but neither is it necessarily permanent. The Fur and Leather Workers Union, for example, was completely gangster-dominated until the late 1920s when members elected Communists to the leadership and drove the gangsters out (See Foner 1950).

UNION BUSTING

All evidence points to the fact that union busting by major U.S. businesses has risen greatly during the 1970s. This phenomenon represents a weakness of organized labor vis-à-vis the capitalists in this country, without parallel in other developed countries. The initial resistance of General Motors to UAW organizing in its new plants in the South (while the UAW represented virtually all other GM production workers in the United States) would be unheard of in Western Europe. The opposition of employers to unions in this country is not disputed by any serious commentators; it is acknowledged, even by Dunlop (1980), who naturally desires it to change.

Anti-union activities by employers have risen dramatically over the last several decades. The inability of unions to stem the use of these tactics by political or other means is another reflection of their gradual decline in strength. Certain components of this heightened employer resistance are worth mentioning here. Many of the particulars will be discussed in more detail later.

Contrary to popular belief, many employers have never given up such tactics as blacklists, the hiring of armed thugs, and the use of other forms of violence. It is debatable, however, whether these weapons have been employed significantly more often during the past period of growing anti-union activity, although some argue that they have.[11] Other tactics, however, have sharply risen during past decades. Certain of them register in NLRB statistics. Among them are

1. The almost twofold increase during the 1970s of unfair labor charges against employers by the NLRB.

2. The growing number of election delays by employers in the holding of certification elections (Prosten 1978; Hook 1982). Virtually all commentators agree that such delays make it more difficult for a union to become successfully certified as a bargaining agent.

3. The rising number of decertification elections (see table 10). Though the volume of decertifications, as the AFL-CIO

---

11. McConville (1975, 1980) presents this argument forcefully. Commonplace are stories like the one from Battle Creek, Michigan, where the management consulting firm of Nuckols, Inc., showed up "in a caravan with the scabs and carstens and got out of their cars and unstrapped their 45s" (AFL-CIO, *RUB*, no. 38, p. 6).

TABLE 10   Decertification Election Results, 1968–1984

Year	Number Elections	Number Won	Percentage Won	Number of Workers Eligible	Number of Workers Retained	Number of Workers Lost
1968	239	83	34.7	15,554	10,750	4,804
1969	293	99	33.8	21,771	12,422	9,349
1970	301	91	30.2	20,344	11,786	8,558
1971	401	122	30.4	20,726	9,953	10,773
1972	451	134	29.7	20,790	10,762	10,028
1973	453	138	30.5	20,007	9,913	10,094
1974	490	152	31.0	24,697	13,227	11,470
1975	516	137	26.6	23,817	9,968	13,849
1976	611	166	27.2	28,426	13,123	15,303
1977a	174	29	16.7	9,321	3,832	5,489
1977	849	204	24.0	41,850	19,452	22,398
1978	807	213	26.4	39,555	19,691	19,884
1979	777	194	25.0	39,538	17,450	22,088
1980	902	246	27.3	42,781	21,532	21,249
1981	856	215	25.1	45,406	17,899	27,257
1982[1]	869	208	24.1	39,138	17,110	22,028
1983[1]	922	235	25.4	33,341	14,714	23,656
1984[1]	874	207	23.7	37,801	13,759	24,042

[1]Years after 1981 are calculated from NLRB raw data tapes. Figures may differ from final NLRB results by as much as several tenths of a percent due to different methods of cleaning and analyzing the data.

Source: Material for 1968–81 is from NLRB annual reports by fiscal year. Years until 1977 are from 30 June of previous year to 30 June of current year. 1977a is the transitional quarter. Years 1977 on are from 30 Sept. of previous year until 30 Sept. of current year.

clearly points out,[12] does not affect a significant percentage of the members of organized labor, it is not a positive sign for unions. Both the increasing degree of success by employers in these elections and the growing frequency with which they occur render them one more powerful weapon in the employer arsenal.

Thus the sanguine view of Dunlop that employer hostility to unions may be moderating would seem largely misplaced. We may conclude that the growing anti-union tactics of employers display a certain weakness of U.S. unions and a serious threat to their long-term strength (and are potentially even the cause of a future drastic decline).

12. See the October 1982 issue of the AFL-CIO *Statistical and Tactical Information Report.*

CONCLUSION

Although trade unions in this country have won important legislative gains, increased their absolute membership steadily during the decades prior to the late 1970s, begun large-scale organizing of public employees, have a high rate of strike militancy, and in certain cases have won strong collective bargaining contracts, they must be regarded as weak in comparison to their counterparts in other developed capitalist countries. Their weakness is especially evident in their low rates of penetration, their small legislative influence, their inability to extend their organizing (particularly in the private sector), their unwillingness or inability to break out of concession bargaining, the breakup of formerly stable collective bargaining patterns, and their weaknesses in resisting the increased anti-union drives by their employees. Thus those who portray U.S. unions as strong, rather than weak, especially in comparison to unions in other capitalist countries, are certainly mistaken.

Even on their own terms, U.S. unions have declined in economic strength and political influence over the last several decades (by their own terms, I mean their lack of radicalism and supposed commitment to "bread-and-butter" unionism). This decline is especially evident in the falling union density, their loss in absolute numbers in the private sector, and their decreasing percentage of victories in NLRB union certification elections. These declines, however, seem to have been relatively steady from the mid-1950s to the present. The same steady decline also appears to have taken place in legislative influence, public opinion polls, and the unions' inability to beat back the current wave of union busting.

The special responsibility of the Reagan administration labor policies for the plight of unions is not very convincing. It is certainly true that these policies are more overtly anti-union than those of any administration since Herbert Hoover's (1928–32). Their effects, however, are completely entangled with the sharp economic recession and the resulting high unemployment that would certainly have found unions on the defensive, even were Jimmy Carter or a more liberal "prolabor" Democrat in office. Further, few of the problems of unions under Reagan began in the 1980s. Virtually all can be understood, explained, and extrapolated from trends that have been developing for decades.

We do not seem to be witnessing a decline that has started or accelerated dramatically in the 1980s or even in the 1970s. The importance of this conclusion for our investigation is the follow-ing: If an accentuated decline is quite recent, then one will want to look at factors that are quite specific to the last decade or so. On the other hand, if the decline has been long term, we will want to look not merely at recent factors, but at ones that started many decades ago or have continued to operate since that time.

Part 2
The Significance and Meaning of Union Decline

4

The Significance of the Trade Union Decline

INTRODUCTION

Part 1 has sketched in some detail the relative weakness and several-decades-long decline of trade unions in the United States. The full significance, however, of diminished unions power in the society is not necessarily obvious. Skeptics might surely ask, "So what?" All sorts of organizations come and go as part of normal societal development. The nineteenth-century Know Nothing and Populist parties came and went as did the early twentieth-century Bull Moose Party. Wagon-wheel makers and coopers are no more. The percentage of workers employed in agriculture has been diminishing for decades. The Boy Scouts grew rapidly, flourished, and may be declining. Perhaps the waning importance of trade unions in late twentieth-century America is no more momentous.

There are other skeptics who take an even more negative view. For these people, U.S. trade unions have always been, are now, or have recently become narrow special interest groups. For them, trade unions are merely corrupt organizations led by dictatorial, high-salaried leaders, sheltering overpaid, lazy, featherbedding workers whose low productivity and defense of outdated work-rules hold back innovative technology, raising prices of both manufactured goods (e.g., cars, tires, steel, and appliances) and construction (homes, highways, and government buildings). If this be so, who needs them? Why not good riddance to bad rubbish? This chapter will attempt to address these and other questions concerning the significance of recent trade union decline.

It is perhaps initially worth taking a brief look at certain perspectives that do not regard trade union weakness and decline as a loss to working people or society in general. There is, of course, a right-wing critique of trade unions. For many free market economists and other conservatives, unions are monopolies that hold back the efficient functioning of the free market, lowering profits, decreasing the total social goods for everyone (not to mention the profits of the very rich). Such a view is expressed in the 1908 Supreme Court decision in the *Danbury Hatters* case, where the hat workers union was found guilty of restraining trade in their attempt to organize via boycott Loewe's hatmaking firm based in Danbury, Connecticut. Conservatives have more recently asserted successfully in both the NLRB and the Supreme Court that many standard trade union activities are an unwarranted infringement on the rights of individual workers.[1] For those with such perspectives, the decline of union strength in American society may be a social blessing.[2]

For many liberals, the claim of the trade union to wide societal support beyond its own ranks is based on its broad democratic, progressive character. Thus its supposed autocratic structure and narrowed social vision (exemplified perhaps by its unwillingness to defend illegal Mexican workers and its lack of aggressiveness on minority and women's issues) weakens its legitimate claims to broad support and assistance. Radicals, as well as liberals, have cringed at the conservative nature of AFL-CIO foreign policy, often critical of Ronald Reagan from the right.

1. The economic arguments may be seen in various comments by Friedman (1962). A good summary of the restraint-of-trade decisions of the Supreme Court may be found in Gregory and Katz (1979). A milder view, claiming that trade unions hinder the efficient functioning of business and the mutual collaboration of workers and managers, is put forth by various industrial sociologists, for example, Mayo (1960); this standpoint is also discussed by Kochan (1980, pp. 10–11). The political arguments are a central thread running through dozens of major decisions by the Dotson-led NLRB from 1983 on. Among the useful summaries are those published in hearings before the House Subcommittee on Labor-Management Relations (U.S. Congress 1985), including Gould's (pp. 82–90), Kane's (pp. 108–9), Klare's (pp. 773–82), and Levy's (pp. 598–630).

2. See Kaus (1983) for a neoliberal version of this argument.

Union internationalism often is displayed only in support of right-wing "patriots."

Further along the political spectrum, there has been a traditional "left" critique of trade unions, put forth by various anarchists, whose influence in the labor movement internationally was especially strong until the early twentieth century. These views emphasize the degree of entwinement (or collaboration) of unions with the bosses (or capitalist managers) and the state. Most unions, by their acceptance of contracts, by their tacit or explicit recognition of managerial rights, accept the legitimacy of capitalism. They participate in and help legitimize the domination of capitalism over workers' lives. The role of unions is thus to stifle the revolutionary, anticapitalist aspirations, desires, and experiences of workers. In short, trade unions under capitalism have always been or have now become obstacles to working-class struggle. These ideas were expressed by the early syndicalists, some of whom had substantial influence in their respective labor movements—the Industrial Workers of the World in the United States, the syndicalists who dominated the French labor movement until World War I, the Spanish Anarchists whose influence lasted until the late 1930s. Anarchist and syndicalist ideas about unions gained brief popularity in the late 1960s and early 1970s. Lotta Continua in Italy achieved relatively large size and support; in the United States this trend was represented by several small groups including Facing Reality and Sojourner Truth, and partially by the much larger League of Revolutionary Black Workers in Detroit. From this standpoint, of course, few tears would be shed over the failing fortunes of U.S. unions.

Another perspective, while less harsh in its evaluation of unions, sees the decline in membership, combativeness, strength, and influence as part of the natural evolution of industrial or postindustrial society. This view, as argued by Bell (1960), Lipset (1960), Ross and Hartman (1960), and Kerr, Dunlop, Harbison, and Myers (1960), asserts that class cleavages, organizations, and conflict are the product of early capitalism. Initial industrialization creates deprivation and inhumane conditions for the workers who fuel its growth. As industrialization progresses, however, conditions become more tolerable and consumer goods of all types (whether food, housing, clothes, transportation, or leisure articles) become widely available; working hours shorten and living standards (as measured by life expectancy, health, and education) rise. As workers become more integrated into a homogenized middle class, their militancy and their organizations of struggle decline. All this is part of the natural development of capitalism, an inversion of Marx's scenario of growing class polarization.

From all these quarters, the current decline of U.S. unions may not be viewed as a problem at all but rather as a sign of social progress and social development. But each of the above characterizations is in part false. To applaud the decline would indeed be shortsighted. All these views err in their one-sidedness. The significance of U.S. trade union decline and its traditional weakness cannot be evaluated without first comprehending the role and the contradictory nature of trade unions in capitalist societies. In order to deal with these underpinnings, this chapter takes something of a diversion. Its purpose is to place the question of trade union decline in a deeper theoretical context.[3]

The Nature of Trade Unions under Capitalism

Capitalism is characterized by, among other things, the existence of two classes of people. There are on the one hand capitalists, who own the means of production and other enterprises (mines, manufacturing, banks, services, etc.) referred to by Marx as private property. There are on the other hand workers, who own no means of employment, though they may own varying degrees of personal property. Although there may be other classes and strata (among whom are counted small businessmen, independent professionals including doctors and lawyers, gentleman farmers, idle rich, college students, and beggars), it is the activities of capitalists and workers that determine and reflect the basic dynamics of capitalist society per se.

Business (the institutional reflection of the capitalists) buys raw materials, additional instruments of production, and labor power (by the hour, week, or month).[4] Products are produced

3. My understanding of U.S. unions and trade unions in general draws on a number of sources, including my own years of trade union activity. In addition, I draw heavily on the writings of Marx, Engels, Lenin, and Trotsky, as well as the works of many non-Marxist theorists including the Webbs, Commons, Perlman, Hoxie, and Dunlop. Of special importance have been the writings of Antonio Gramsci and Richard Hyman. The latter is one of the most astute theorists writing about unions today.

4. Marx insisted that the distinction between labor and labor power was the key to understanding capitalism; I have followed his terminological usage here.

and sold by capitalists for a profit. Capitalism is characterized not merely by the distribution of means of production between the few that own them and those that do not. It is also characterized by the pervasiveness of its commodity markets in raw material, means of production, final products, and ultimately in labor power itself. Workers confront capitalists in the labor market formally as equals (they are sellers, as both neoclassical economics and its philosophical reflection in modern contract theory spell out) and as subordinates in the production process.

In the early stages of capitalist development, the capitalists have a distinct and overwhelming advantage over the workers in the labor market as well as in the sphere of production. The workers, existing in large numbers, must compete as individuals with one another to earn their livelihood. They must sell their labor power for whatever terms the capitalist, their employer, offers. If they do not like the terms, another hungry worker is there to take their place. This competition among individual workers allowed the early capitalists to increase the hours of work to the laborer's physical limits, often to fourteen or more hours a day, raising the intensity of labor to the breaking point, lowering the pay (or price of labor power) to the bare minimum necessary for survival. Men, women, and children were forced by necessity to earn their daily bread under terrible conditions. In England, Marx describes the creation of a short-lived, starving, physically deformed (by hard work and limited job motions) race of workers.[5] A similar process is presently visible in parts of South Africa, where the primitive exploitative conditions of early capitalism are combined with cruel forms of national oppression and political domination, exemplified by the slave-like conditions, perhaps unique in the world today, forced upon the migrant African mineworkers (Magubane 1979).

Labor refers to the actual exertion of the laborer doing work. What the capitalist buys is not a certain amount of exertion by the worker, but the use of his or her energies for a certain amount of time. If the capitalist is able to work the laborers hard and productively, he may make a profit. Even if the work is unproductive, however, and there is no profit, the capitalist still must pay for the *labor power* (or potential labor) that he bought. Marx's use of this distinction first appears in the *Grundrisse* ([1857] 1973) and is used throughout *Capital* ([1867] 1977). Engels explains the importance of this distinction and its role in Marx's economic analysis (Marx and Engels [1897] 1968, pp. 65–70).

5. For the conditions of workers under early capitalism, see, for example, Marx's lengthy discussion in volume one of *Capital* (1977), Engels ([1845] 1968), Dobb (1963), and Hobsbawm (1967, pp. 75–140).

Trade union organization was originally a response to these conditions of early capitalism. Such organizations emerge virtually everywhere that capitalism develops; one might say they are a natural development. Even where they are banned and violently repressed, as in South Africa, they often succeed not only in organizing, but in forcing their recognition (MacShane, Plant, and Ward, 1984).

Trade unions are organized to limit the self-destructive competition among individual workers and thereby to gain for them elementary dignity and living conditions, in the form of higher wages, less intense work, and eventually, the establishment of a shorter workweek. As trade unions became stronger in the more developed capitalist countries, they gained influence in the political arena, broadening the electoral franchise, outlawing child labor, and establishing national limits on the legal length of the workday, first at ten, then eventually at eight hours. Thus trade unions are formed under capitalism to gather the collective strength of the workers, whose only power in bargaining with their employers and influencing the state is in their unified numbers.

INHERENT NECESSITY OF CONFLICT BETWEEN WORKERS AND EMPLOYERS

A number of questions and arguments arise about the role that these elementary workers' organizations play. One such dispute involves the degree to which conflict between labor and management under capitalism is inherent in the nature of their relationship.

CURRENT ORTHODOXY

Current orthodoxy in industrial relations studies in this country and in Britain sees no inherent conflict of interest between workers and capitalists. J. R. Hicks (1963), for example, views wages as largely determined by the market. Lowering wages below market value would create adverse effects in terms of lowered efficiency and disgruntled, uncooperative employees whether workers were organized in a union or not. Although Hicks does not express the strong anti-union sentiments of the right, he does argue that strikes are in general unnecessary, usually the result of faulty judgment or lack of skill on the part of the bargainers (1963, p. 146).

Modern pluralists, whose views dominate industrial relations research in Britain as well as in the United States, accept the necessity of strikes and conflict, although they see no inherent opposition in fundamental interests. Strikes are a normal part of the bargaining process, often involving tests of strength. Mature bargainers, however, although they cannot totally eliminate conflict, can certainly minimize it.[6]

These views, while containing valid perceptions and elements of truth, are, in my opinion, wrong in their fundamental assumptions. A more balanced, realistic, and accurate view is contained in the Marxist approach to labor conflict.

THE MARXIST VIEW OF LABOR CONFLICT

Institutionalists and other orthodox pluralist writers make an unquestioned normative assumption. They assert that stable and orderly relations between workers and capitalists are both normal and desirable. They assume that there exists or can exist a stable set of labor-management relations where the basic needs of both capitalists and workers may be met. They fail to comprehend that the structure of ownership and control of industry and the nature of the labor market creates an inherent source of irreconcilable conflict between workers and their employers.

On the most elementary level, the strivings of workers, their grievances, aspirations, their desire for a better life (of which wages and working conditions are a part), which they *naturally* seek, confront the capitalist as a cost (diminishing his profits) that he quite *naturally* resists. The pressure of competition under capitalism forces capitalists, even were they to feel personally benevolent and magnanimous toward their employees, to economize their labor costs. All other things being equal, they desire lower rather than higher wages, more production out of fewer workers. These competitive pressures confront them, as current international market pressures on U.S. business serve to underscore, as imperatives behind which lurks the threat of bankruptcy and extinction. These pressures provide the impetus both for the technological advances of capitalism, particularly in its

6. For a useful critique of industrial relations pluralism in Britain with extensive references, see Goldthorpe, Lockwood, Bechhofer, and Platt (1974). See also Hyman (1982). Ingham (1974) perhaps occupies a middle ground in this debate, seeing conflict as inherent but diminished (as it becomes managed) when it is institutionalized in highly developed forms of collective bargaining.

early stages, and for the continuous instability and insecurity of a large part of the working population.

As J. R. Hicks (1963) and, more recently, Sabel (1982) note, there are limits to the degree to which an individual capitalist or even capitalists as a whole can resist the demands of workers before their employees become completely uncooperative, unproductive, or even physically and culturally unable to perform their work. Still, the range of this floor is wide. As Marx notes explicitly in *Capital,* this bottom limit, the subsistence level, is socially determined, a product of continuous struggle between the classes of workers and capitalists. Thus conflict exists, sometimes acute, more often subdued, informal, implicit.

This conflict takes place not merely between unions and management as sellers and buyers in the labor market over the terms for their sale of labor power (i.e., over wages and terms of employment). It also takes place continually between workers and their supervisors over a variety of workplace conditions, rules, and patterns of behavior. Although there are often lengthy periods of seeming acceptance of management rights, prerogatives, and directives, these are at best partial and temporary. This acceptance, however, contrary to those more anarchist views that posit continual struggle and conflict, is real and based upon key aspects of production relations under capitalism. Management's role in production itself is contradictory. Management, especially in a large enterprise, plays an indispensable organizing role in production, a role that workers as producers recognize and, in general, accept. On the other hand, management plays the role of guardian of the capitalist's profits, getting more work out of fewer workers for less money. And it is here, in the arena of what Richard Hyman (1975) refers to as the frontier of control, that a frequent struggle takes place between workers and management. Marxists, unlike anarchists, thus want to understand the basis of consent as well as the basis for conflict in any particular situation. Unlike the pluralists, however, Marxists tend to target workers' self-activity, self-organization, class struggle, and the existence of the organizational forms in which these struggles are embodied.

This contradictory, inherently conflictual relationship between workers and capitalists provides, as I shall argue shortly, a basis for understanding the significance of U.S. trade union decline. The above analysis should also serve to underscore the degree to which the decline itself can only be understood in the context of battles between workers and capitalists. These battles, which help determine the fate of unions, include not merely the day-to-day skirmishes mentioned above, but also the major class offensives and retreats on the part of workers and their organizations and on the part of capitalists and their organizations. I shall return to these points later.

CONTRADICTORY NATURE OF TRADE UNIONS

It is within the vortex of continual conflict and compromise in the sphere of production and the competition for the sale of labor power on the market that an understanding of modern trade unions must be rooted. It is important to note that the terms of this conflict and compromise differ at various "stages" of trade union development. In understanding the present stage, it is useful to understand the earlier ones.

EARLY TRADE UNIONS

As labor historians and economists have noted, early trade unions became organized and gained members with economic prosperity. With the coming of the downside of the business cycle, trade unions were crushed by the employers or lost significant numbers of their membership. This phenomenon is noted for Europe by Hobsbawm (1967) and for the United States by Commons and his colleagues (1918, 1958). The Commons school argue forcefully that union growth and decline is directly related to the business cycle. They provide graphs of wholesale prices, which they argue are the key indicators of the business cycle, from 1820 to 1908, whose peaks correspond with upsurges of union organization:

Each upward turn of the curve of prices points to a period of business prosperity, each pinnacle is a commercial crisis, and each downward bend is an index of industrial depression. During a time when the level of prices is rising, employers generally are making profits, are multiplying sales, are enlarging their capital, are running full time and overtime, are calling for more labor, and are able to pay higher wages. On the other hand, the cost of living and the hours of labor are increased, and workmen, first as individuals, then as organizations, are impelled to demand both higher wages and reduced hours. Consequently, after prices are well on the way upward the "labor movement" emerges in the form of unions and strikes, and these are at first successful. Then the employers begin their counter organization, and the courts are appealed to. The unions are sooner or later defeated, and when the period of depression ensues, with its widespread unemployment, the labor movement either subsides or changes its form to political or socialist agitation, to ventures in cooperation or communism, or to other panaceas. This cycle has been . . . consistently repeated, although with varying shades and details." (Commons et al. 1958, pp. 19–20; see also Commons et al. 1918, pp. 3–21).

TRADE UNION ILLEGALITY

One important underlying reason for the wide fluctuations in early trade union membership and for their lack of stability was that they were often illegal, generally not fully recognized by the employers. The early stages of capitalism have all been characterized by what I call trade union illegality.

Trade union illegality is a de facto state based on the unwillingness of companies and the government to accept fully the rights of workers to be represented collectively by an organization of their own, whatever the extent of de jure trade union rights. Under conditions of trade union illegality, not only do the laws make it difficult for unions to function, but even illegal actions against them by the companies are often overlooked by the government. These illegal activities by the capitalists are accepted because unions are de facto illegal. Periods of trade union illegality have existed in the early phases of capitalist development in all major capitalist countries and continue to exist today in many places. In some countries, at certain times, the demanding of trade union rights by workers (the right to organize, the right to bargain collectively, the right to be dealt with in a legal, nonarbitrary manner by the employer, the right to strike) have been insurrectionary demands. This was certainly the case in Nazi Germany, under fascism in Portugal and Spain, in Bolivia during the 1950s, and in Chile, Brazil, and Paraguay during the mid-1980s, to name but a few examples.

Trade union illegality existed in the United States during the nineteenth and well into the twentieth centuries. Through much of the nineteenth century, membership in trade unions and participation in strikes were often grounds for being charged with criminal conspiracy. Trade unions had only semilegal existence. Thus Chicago labor leaders were convicted and hanged after the Haymarket affair of 1886. Eugene Debs's American Railway Union was bloodily suppressed in 1894. Labor leaders were tried for conspiracy and sedition during World War I. And striking steelworkers at Republic Steel became victims of the Chicago police in the Memorial Day Massacre of 1937, almost two years after the passage of the National Labor Relations Act.

U.S. trade union illegality has been characterized by the extensive use of company-employed private police forces, from the infamous "Pinkertons" to the coal company police that so successfully kept unions out of the coal fields in the 1920s, to Henry Ford's private army of spies and thugs who served to intimidate workers at the huge River Rouge Ford complex until the UAW victory in 1941.[7]

Under conditions of trade union illegality, struggles are often quite intense. Organizational survival, even the livelihoods of many leaders and activists are at stake. Possibilities for class collaboration and trade union narrowness (i.e., narrow interest group activity) are more limited. Workers and their unions are more willing to ally themselves with and take support from radical groups.

Despite the revolutionary overtones that the simple demand for trade union recognition takes on at certain times and places, even during the early periods of trade union development, one may trace a certain narrowness. Marx took due note of this characteristic of trade unions even during the period when he was most optimistic about their anticapitalist potential.

INITIAL VIEW OF MARX

Marx, like the modern institutionalists and other contemporary pluralists, noted the narrow basis on which most nineteenth-century unions were formed. The foremost reason was often for the protection of the wages that were depressed by the competition among workers. The limited aims of workers for the best wages and conditions in their work unit, factory, craft, or area were often pursued in conflict with similar goals of workers in other areas or occupations. Trade unions, as Marx saw them, often became too "exclusively bent upon the local and immediate struggles with capital" ([1866] 1974, p. 91). One can, of course, still see this narrowness today, as unions refuse to support each other's struggles, give mere lip service to the fights

---

7. For general information about organized repression by corporations, see Boyer and Morais (1970) and Goldstein (1978). For descriptions of Ford's eight-thousand-member "Service Department," see Preis (1964) and Meier and Rudwick (1979).

for survival of PATCO or the British miners, and even at times cross each other's picket lines.

Yet trade unions also have, according to Marx, an implicitly broader class basis. They serve not merely as organizations in the "guerrilla fights between capital and labour," but as organizing centers in the struggle for "complete emancipation" (1974, pp. 91–92). There are several reasons for this. Not the least of these is the confidence and increased fighting capacity that trade union struggles give workers as a class. Indeed their challenge to the rights and free reign of capital is recognized by business even under the most collaborative arrangements (as previously existed in the United States). Ultimately, however, the narrow struggles of most workers could not be successful without mutual support and a broad class program uniting other sectors of the population.

Although Marx viewed this trade union activity as central to the revolutionary mission of the working class, he did not regard it as sufficient. Even in many of his earlier writings he argued for the necessity of a workers' party that would represent the broader, more emancipatory, class interests of the workers ([1848] 1972b).

PERIODIZATION OF TRADE UNION DEVELOPMENT

There are many theories about trade union development. Some very narrowly focus on the United States and posit stages of development from broad class unions (like the Knights of Labor and the Industrial Workers of the World) to craft unions to industrial unions. Others suggest the development of trade union organization from early more militant forms to more mature, peaceful forms (Golden and Ruttenberg 1942; Lester 1958) or even to their decline and demise (Bell 1960; Lipset 1960; Kerr et al. 1960). Other theories look at the cycles of trade union growth, tying it to periods of social upheavals (I. Bernstein 1954a, 1954b; Dunlop 1948) or to the economic business cycle (Commons et al. (1958; Ashenfelter and Pencavel 1969; Bain and Elsheikh 1976). These theories, whether they posit cyclical, linear, or trajectory patterns of development, are united in their failure to identify the most important watershed in trade union functioning—the attainment of trade union legality. Of central importance is the degree to which this watershed determines and shapes the various forms of struggle and a recognition of the extent to which this boundary is historically temporary, something that will ultimately be fought and struggled over again and again (see Rubin, Wallace, and Griffith 1983 for a thoughtful discussion of some of these issues).

TRADE UNION LEGALITY

The acceptance of trade union legality marks a major change in the day-to-day relations between workers and capitalists. The establishment of the NLRB in 1935 was a legal turning point in the history of labor-capital relations in this country. It reflected the emerging recognition by the government and major capitalists in the United States that trade unions were legitimate institutions. The establishment of the NLRB was the product of large-scale social unrest in general and of intense struggles by the working class in this country (Goldfield 1985a). This de jure recognition of trade union rights was not yet—but only the beginning of—the de facto recognition of trade union legality in major industrial areas of the U.S.A.

I use the term "trade union legality" to describe the general acceptance by both employers and employees (through their unions) of a certain degree of orderliness in their relations, involving both rights and obligations. The capitalist recognizes the union, bargains with it, and accepts grievance claims. The union guarantees that its members respect their contractual obligations, including the foregoing of the right to strike over every grievance.

Trade union legality is related to, although not coincident with, the labor laws that govern labor-capitalist relations. This distinction is important. There may be laws that ensure trade union rights in a country yet parts of the country or certain industrial sectors where the employers do not recognize trade union legality. The inverse has also occasionally happened, although it is somewhat less common.[8]

The CIO period (roughly 1937–41), the period of organizing basic industry, marked the general acceptance of trade union legality by U.S. capitalists. In order for capitalists to accept trade union legality, trade unions must be organized on a national scale with demonstrated power to disrupt major sectors of the economy. The acceptance of trade union legality, however, is a

8. I rely heavily on Antonio Gramsci's insights in his 1919–20 articles from the Italian weekly journal *Ordine Nuovo*, especially "Unions and Councils II," 12 June 1920, where he discusses the industrial "legal order" (see Gramsci 1968).

compromise between workers (through their unions) and the capitalists. The capitalists provide organizational stability for the union and consequently some consistency in wages and benefits (the price of labor power) and working conditions. The unions restrain the disruptive tendencies of the work force and help the capitalists discipline the work force in varying ways. The contradictory nature of trade unions arises from their dual role as joint upholders of the class compromise of trade union legality—the industrial legal order, as Gramsci calls it—and as the representative of the trade union demands of their members.

This structure of ambivalence pervades the union hierarchy from top to bottom, albeit in different ways. Even without no-strike clauses and involvement in the punitive discipline of workers (which weighs the compromise even more heavily on the side of the capitalists), the union must attend to the "interests" of the company. The national leadership must know the "reservation price" of the company, both for normal bargaining situations and for strike confrontations (e.g., at contract times), being sure not to raise the stakes so high as to precipitate a "fight to the death." Accommodating leaderships aim much lower, often not to offend at all. Industrial legality requires the maintenance of the "good will"of the employer and the state by the unions.

At the local level, even the most militant shop steward is affected by this compromise. Aggressive stewards with organized constituents can often gain more for their members than passive leaders. Yet even the militant steward knows or comes to know that there is a line somewhere, no matter how vague its exact location, beyond which the company will give in on nothing and will quickly respond with repression (often in alliance with local and even national union officials). In most such situations, few constituents will feel that their representatives are doing their job. This line, of course, may drastically change its location depending on the militancy of the national union, the degree of broader support, and the general level of working-class turbulence—but it is always there.

The winning of trade union legality is a highly positive, yet contradictory, victory for workers. It undoubtedly gains them more strength on the labor market, where their greater numbers allow them to obtain better terms in the sale of their labor power. At the point of production, the mere existence of the union often strengthens the hands of informal work groups and local mili-

compromise between workers (through their unions) and the capitalists. The capitalists provide organizational stability for the union and consequently some consistency in wages and benefits (the price of labor power) and working conditions. The unions restrain the disruptive tendencies of the work force and help the capitalists discipline the work force in varying ways. The contradictory nature of trade unions arises from their dual role as joint upholders of the class compromise of trade union legality—the industrial legal order, as Gramsci calls it—and as the representative of the trade union demands of their members.

This structure of ambivalence pervades the union hierarchy from top to bottom, albeit in different ways. Even without no-strike clauses and involvement in the punitive discipline of workers (which weighs the compromise even more heavily on the side of the capitalists), the union must attend to the "interests" of the company. The national leadership must know the "reservation price" of the company, both for normal bargaining situations and for strike confrontations (e.g., at contract times), being sure not to raise the stakes so high as to precipitate a "fight to the death." Accommodating leaderships aim much lower, often not to offend at all. Industrial legality requires the maintenance of the "good will" of the employer and the state by the unions.

At the local level, even the most militant shop steward is affected by this compromise. Aggressive stewards with organized constituents can often gain more for their members than passive leaders. Yet even the militant steward knows or comes to know that there is a line somewhere, no matter how vague its exact location, beyond which the company will give in on nothing and will quickly respond with repression (often in alliance with local and even national union officials). In most such situations, few constituents will feel that their representatives are doing their job. This line, of course, may drastically change its location depending on the militancy of the national union, the degree of broader support, and the general level of working-class turbulence—but it is always there.

The winning of trade union legality is a highly positive, yet contradictory, victory for workers. It undoubtedly gains them more strength on the labor market, where their greater numbers allow them to obtain better terms in the sale of their labor power. At the point of production, the mere existence of the union often strengthens the hands of informal work groups and local mili-

thing that will ultimately be fought and struggled over again and again (see Rubin, Wallace, and Griffith 1983 for a thoughtful discussion of some of these issues).

TRADE UNION LEGALITY

The acceptance of trade union legality marks a major change in the day-to-day relations between workers and capitalists. The establishment of the NLRB in 1935 was a legal turning point in the history of labor-capital relations in this country. It reflected the emerging recognition by the government and major capitalists in the United States that trade unions were legitimate institutions. The establishment of the NLRB was the product of large-scale social unrest in general and of intense struggles by the working class in this country (Goldfield 1985a). This de jure recognition of trade union rights was not yet—but only the beginning of—the de facto recognition of trade union legality in major industrial areas of the U.S.A.

I use the term "trade union legality" to describe the general acceptance by both employers and employees (through their unions) of a certain degree of orderliness in their relations, involving both rights and obligations. The capitalist recognizes the union, bargains with it, and accepts grievance claims. The union guarantees that its members respect their contractual obligations, including the foregoing of the right to strike over every grievance.

Trade union legality is related to, although not coincident with, the labor laws that govern labor-capitalist relations. This distinction is important. There may be laws that ensure trade union rights in a country yet parts of the country or certain industrial sectors where the employers do not recognize trade union legality. The inverse has also occasionally happened, although it is somewhat less common.[8]

The CIO period (roughly 1937–41), the period of organizing basic industry, marked the general acceptance of trade union legality by U.S. capitalists. In order for capitalists to accept trade union legality, trade unions must be organized on a national scale with demonstrated power to disrupt major sectors of the economy. The acceptance of trade union legality, however, is a

---

8. I rely heavily on Antonio Gramsci's insights in his 1919–20 articles from the Italian weekly journal *Ordine Nuovo*, especially "Unions and Councils II," 12 June 1920, where he discusses the industrial "legal order" (see Gramsci 1968).

tants, as officials occasionally wink at their behavior, but more often, even as these union leaders faithfully fulfill their roles in containing, frustrating, and disciplining working-class struggle.

CONSERVATIVE TRENDS

On the other hand, trade union legality accelerates a number of conservative trends already inherent in its narrow explicit purposes. In the United States, where social (read socialist) vision and purpose are lacking, the collaborative relations over which union leaders preside set the stage for cynicism and corruption. What is most surprising is not that there is corruption, but how little there is.[9]

These tendencies have been analyzed by a number of theorists. C. Wright Mills (1948) prophetically, even if highly exaggeratedly, described the growing bureaucratization of the post–World War II union leadership and their close entwinement with the capitalist managers. What the pluralists describe as "maturity," Mills describes as an antidemocratic "conspiracy."

Cooperative relations between business and labor are rooted in the desire for peace and stability on the part of businessmen, labor leaders, and political officials. . . . This conspiracy does not include the extremists in any of the camps. . . .
Stabilization requires further bureaucratization of business enterprise and labor union. Given present industrial arrangements, it also involves amalgamating the union bureaucracy with the corporation's. . . .
If the union is efficient, the worker's gripes will . . . if necessary, go on up the union and company hierarchies. . . . This is the power of the arrangement and its mechanics from the worker's point of view. . . .
But for something gained, something must be given. (1948, pp. 223–24)

What is given up, according to Mills, is the democratic responsibility of the union leaders, including the stewards, to the rank and file who elected them. Rather, they have become "whips" to maintain labor discipline.

These antidemocratic, highly conservative trends have been of special interest to many Marxists. Lenin, for example, identified factors that tended to make labor unions in economically developed capitalist countries more conservative. He attributed much of the conservatism of various labor movements to the

9. See Freeman and Medoff (1984b, pp. 213–17); see also AFL-CIO comparative bonding figures reported in issue number 1 (November 1980) of its *Statistical Information Report*.

disproportionate influence of a stratum of workers and officials whom he dubbed, following Marx and Engels, the labor aristocracy. This stratum, according to Lenin, had two components. First, there was a small layer of privileged, usually skilled, workers who received cultural and economic privileges from the superprofits that their countries gained from less developed countries abroad. Second, there was a stratum of labor leaders, administrators, journalists, and others with strong ties to the nonworking-class world of politicians, publishers, cultural figures, and so on. The relationships and privileges that this grouping within the labor movement enjoyed were in substance a bribe for its general support of capitalism and capitalist interests abroad.

According to Lenin, the labor aristocracy was both a base for conservative forces within the labor movement and the breeding ground for the procapitalist leadership of the labor movement as a whole. The labor aristocracy had real strength within the labor movement both because of its (largely informal) ties to the capitalists and the state and because it was much more highly organized than other groupings within the unions (inverting the traditional anticommunist analysis, one might call the labor aristocracy the real antidemocratic subversives).

All who have looked for privileged strata and "opportunist," procapitalist labor leaders within the U.S. labor movement have not been disappointed in their search. And it has not escaped the notice of many who see merit in Lenin's analysis that the richest, most developed capitalist country in the world should have the largest, best organized labor aristocracy.

Leon Trotsky presents an analysis that is an extension of Lenin's. Like Lenin, Trotsky saw various structural obstacles to the development of revolutionary class consciousness among workers and of independent class organization. Thus he argues against the French syndicalists:

Were the proletarians as a whole capable of grasping its historical task immediately, it would need neither party nor trade union. Revolution would be born simultaneously with the proletariat. But in actuality the *process* by which the proletariat gains an insight into its historic mission is very long and painful. (Trotsky [1923–37] 1969, p. 8)

Trotsky argues that trade unions are

expressive of the top layers of the proletariat. . . . In periods of acute class struggle, the leading bodies of the trade unions aim to become masters of the mass movements in order to render it harmless. This is already occurring during the period of simple strikes, especially in the case of the mass sit-down strikes which shake the principle of bourgeois property. (1969, p. 60)

Thus trade unions have natural tendencies toward conservatism. These tendencies, according to Trotsky, are accelerated with the growth of monopoly. Trade unions tend to become more and more subordinate to the bourgeois state.

Monopoly capitalism does not rest on competition and free enterprise initiative but on centralized command. The capitalist cliques at the head of the mighty trusts, syndicates, banking consortiums, etc., view economic life from the same heights as does state power, and they require at every step the collaboration of the latter. In their turn, the trade unions in the most important branches of industry find themselves deprived of the possibility of profiting by competition among the different enterprises. They have to confront a centralized capitalist adversary, intimately bound up with state power. Hence flows the need of the trade unions—insofar as they remain on reformist positions, i.e., on positions of adapting themselves to private property—to adapt themselves to the capitalist state and to contend for its cooperation. In the eyes of the bureaucracy of the trade union movement, the chief task lies in "freeing" the state from the embrace of capitalism, in weakening its dependence on the trusts, in pulling it over to their side. This position is in complete harmony with the social position of the labor aristocracy and the labor bureaucracy, who fight for a crumb in the share of superprofits of imperialist capitalism. The labor bureaucrats do their level best in words and deeds to demonstrate to the "democratic" state how reliable and indispensable they are in peacetime and especially in time of war. (Trotsky 1969, p. 69)

These tendencies are in evidence to greater or lesser degrees in all economically developed capitalist countries. Thus according to this argument, there are, in all these countries, numerous structural factors that lead to conservatism among trade union organizations. These include, according to Trotsky, the existence of the labor aristocracy (as described and analyzed by Lenin), the organization of the more privileged, hence more conservative layers of the working class disproportionately into trade unions, and the greater entwinement of the unions with the state.

RADICAL TRENDS

But there exists another pole in the contradictory nature of trade unions under capitalism. They are more than organizational bureaucracies that accept economic and organizational benefits in return for enforcing workplace discipline and ensuring more or less political quiescence. They are also democratically responsive (if not always controlled) organizations of struggle that must, if only in part, respond to the grievances, aspirations, and pent-up frustrations of their constituents.[10]

Unions must thus occasionally engage in struggle, use tactics, and make demands that lie outside the previously agreed upon parameters of compromise. In times of crisis, these limits are sometimes grossly exceeded. The reason unions are often forced to play such a role, even occasionally against the desires of the leaders, is that union members never quite see the compromise embodying industrial legality in the same terms as do the leaders and the employers. The union is their organization; its purpose is to represent their claims, to fight for them, not to hinder them by telling them what their employer wants. If the leaders are too far out of line, they can be removed. Ultimately the leaders know this. In even the most corrupt unions, in even the most undemocratic, leaders must make some show of responsiveness, must help satisfy the demands of at least one part of their constituents. While the pressures of the employers are felt by the union leaders every day and those of the members only occasionally, the latter are ultimately decisive in the leaders' keeping their positions.

Further, it is the militancy of the workers, their fighting capacity, their ability to engage in broad struggles, to link up with workers in other industries and trades, that strengthens the union side of the class compromise. Unions and labor movements whose leaders and members forget this (as much of the U.S. labor unions have in past decades) weaken their position within the class compromise and may even lose recognition by the capitalists as participants with whom it is necessary to compromise. Even the most conservative, privileged craft unions

10. Thus the saying that any union is better than no union. Even the most "liberal" employers often lack the simple sense of decency many times evinced by local leaders in even the most compromised unions. In 1980, at the University of Chicago, for example, an employee, several days after having been raped, showed disorientation and walked off the job. Local 743 of the Teamsters, an amalgamated local that has a reputation for neither militancy nor liberalism, successfully forced the University of Chicago (which first had fired the employee, later reinstating her merely as a new hire) to rehire this union member with her full seniority and pay for the time she was kept off the job. The university for a good while refused to budge on the case, even though their own rape counseling service testified that the victim was displaying normal reactions that were "almost predictable." See Lillian (1980).

must succumb to these imperatives at times. The destruction of union strength in the construction trades during the 1970s serves as a reminder of this point.

Thus, while unions have many conservative, narrow interest–oriented tendencies, they also provide a certain framework for broader social struggles.

Unions project, even if only embryonicly at times, class cohesion, confidence, fighting capacity, and working-class unity. When these characteristics are heightened in time of broad struggle and extended organization, all social movements of poor and oppressed people may gain. When they reach low levels—as in the United States today—these other constituents are usually less successful.

To achieve certain broader goals, but even to defend their narrow economic interests in times of crisis, unions must reach out and ally themselves with other constituencies. Their success often depends on it. While their tendency to take up the interests of these other constituencies is neither natural nor inevitable, there is a certain logic to it. Their reliance on numerical strength for greater economic and political leverage suggests such a course. Their overlapping interests and need for unity—most oppressed constituencies have representatives within the working class (e.g., nonwhites, women, youth) or close ties to the working class (the unemployed, the physically disabled)—often require it.

THE SIGNIFICANCE OF PRESENT TRADE UNION DECLINE

The above discussion, albeit of necessity somewhat abstract and perhaps seemingly distant from the current fate of trade unions, is in fact directly relevant to the questions posed at the beginning of the chapter. If one accepts the previous analysis, then one should view trade union development and growth as in some sense a natural development under capitalism. Its rises and falls are thus affected by the development of economic and social trends in a particular society. Hence, the present fate of U.S. unions may in part be a reflection of these trends. The decline of unions may be a sign that something fundamental is changing in the economic and social structure of the society at large.

While the development of unions may be a natural product of capitalist development, their fate, however, is also the product of ongoing class struggles. If the decline of unions is not the inevitable concomitant of capitalist economy, then the several-decades-long weakening of unions in this country may also be a reflection of a fundamental shift in the relation of class forces, having deep impact on our politics as a whole.

These explanations, of course, are not mutually exclusive. Both of them suggest fundamental changes in United States society. The political changes, whose significance few doubt, are already apparent.

The decline in strength of trade unions, rather than clearing the way for wider reform struggles or broader, more radical forms of class organization, only strengthens the hand of the capitalists, disorganizing and demoralizing those who seek concessions from them or the state. But even though the political right and business interests are the main beneficiaries, capitalists and their free market exponents do not receive unqualified benefits. Union organization seems to be coincident with higher productivity, lower turnover, more efficient corporate practices, as well as many other social gains.[11] Nevertheless in general it is the majority of the population, particularly workers and various oppressed strata, who suffer the most from trade union decline.

Diminished trade union organization gives a freer hand to the capitalists. It leads to declines in real wages and working conditions, to increased capital mobility, decreases in social welfare benefits, losses of civil rights and civil liberties, and more social inequality. Rather than opening the way for broader forms of activity, it leads to the demoralization of the working class, an upsurge of individualism, and the general loss of class identity.[12]

What is paradoxical is that the arguments presented here would suggest that those U.S. trade union leaders who have been the most cooperative in their relations with business and the state may bear a major responsibility for the current weakness of unions. Their accommodations in the form of long-term agreements, legalistic, slow grievance procedures, no-strike clauses, increased recognition of management "rights," and the acceptance of lessened local union representation in the workplace has helped pave the way for an accelerated pace of work, increases in

11. See Freeman and Medoff (1984a, pp. 162–80; and 1984b).
12. While trade unions often or potentially may play a broad progressive role, it would be foolish to argue that this is necessarily the case. Particularly when unions represent narrow, highly privileged groups (e.g., the present-day exclusively white trade unions in South Africa), they may more likely play an all-around reactionary role.

forced overtime, and more recently, lack of solidarity on the picket lines and lowered real wages.

In not wanting to "offend" their management counterparts, most unions, during the post–World War II period have participated in the racial and sexual "gentlemen's agreement." They have at best given only lip service to fighting discrimination against minorities and women, particularly in the workplace and in hiring. This orientation has played a key role in estranging unions from the upsurge of minorities, women, students, and antiwar protests of the 1960s, both weakening and deflating these movements and losing the full, enthusiastic support of valuable allies.

The decline of trade unions casts a pall on the quality of life for the country as a whole in the short run and weakens the forces struggling for a better society in general. Value judgments, perhaps, but flowing from an analysis of the structural role of trade unions under capitalism in general and in U.S. society in particular.

Thus unlike the disappearance of wagon-wheel makers and coopers or the contraction in the number of small farmers; unlike the disappearance of the Know Nothings, Populists, and Bull Moosers, the fate of trade unions in the United States determines fundamental aspects of the society and its politics.

5

The Components of Union Decline and the Importance of New Organizing

The Importance of New Union Organizing

The previous chapter has suggested that the decline of U.S. trade union strength is extremely important, that it has had and will continue to have a major impact on U.S. politics and on society in general. If one is convinced of the importance of the phenomenon, then it is likely that one will want to know its causes. As the next chapter will describe, there are myriad theories and proffered explanations. Before examining these, however, it is helpful to narrow the focus of our inquiry. In this chapter I will begin by arguing that a proper understanding of trade union decline must focus on the failures in new union organizing. In order to make this argument, we shall first look at the components of trade union growth and decline in the United States. One heuristic device for decomposing union growth is a simple accounting model, a stock flow model. The changes in union membership per year may be viewed as gains and losses:

Changes in Union Membership = Gains − Losses.

This relationship may be represented more formally by the following identity:

(1) $$\Delta U_t = O_t + \phi_1 U_t - \phi_2 U_t,$$

where U_t = union membership at time t; ΔU_t = the change in union membership from time $t - 1$ to time t; O_t = the net number of workers organized into unions in the previous time period (workers organized into bargaining units minus those lost through decertification and attrition); ϕ_1 = the rate of automatic increase in unionized jobs due to expansion of the work force in union shops; and ϕ_2 = the rate of automatic loss in unionized jobs due to layoffs, plant closures, runaway shops, and so on. A more extensive decomposition is indicated in figure 7.

If we let

(2) $$\phi = \phi_1 - \phi_2$$

represent the total rate of loss of union jobs due to economic causes, then equation 1 may be rewritten,

(3) $$\Delta U_t = \phi U_t + O_t.$$

Equation 3 may also be written as

(4) $$\Delta D_t = \frac{\Delta U_t}{L_t} = \frac{\phi U_t}{L_t} + \frac{O_t}{L_t},$$

where ΔD_t is the change in union density from time period $t - 1$ to time t, and L_t is the number of workers in the labor force at time t.

As can be seen from equation 3 union membership remains constant if $-\phi U_t$ is equal to O_t. In other words, union membership is stable if the net members lost due to economic factors are equal to the net members won through new organizing. In an economy where the work force is increasing, however, a constant union membership will lead to a decreasing union density. This can be easily seen by transforming equation 4 with two new identities:

(5) $$r_o = \frac{O_t}{L_t},$$

where r_o is the net organizing rate; and

(6) $$r_e = -\phi D_t,$$

where r_e is the rate of net loss of union density due to economic changes. Thus we have

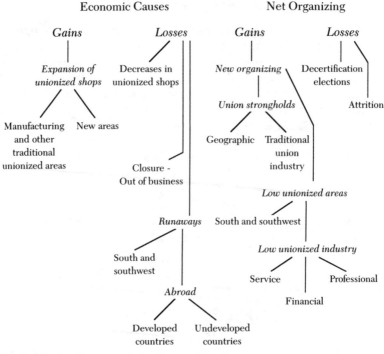

FIGURE 7.   Decomposition of union growth

(7) $$\Delta D_t = r_o - r_e.$$

In order for union density to remain constant, the rate of new organizing must equal the rate of loss due to economic changes, that is,

(8) $$r_o = r_e.$$

And since $r_o = O_t/L_t$, an increasing L_t requires an increasing O_t, if r_e remains constant and the identity is to hold.

An increase in union density requires

(9) $$r_o > r_e,$$

while a decrease in union density requires

(10) $$r_e > r_o.$$

In order to understand better the factors responsible for union growth and the decreasing union density over the past several decades, it is instructive to compare these two rates since World

War II. As discussed in part 1, the declines in U.S. trade union membership and density have taken place largely in the private sector, and it is here that r_o and r_e will be examined. I have calculated these rates for private sector organizing through the NLRB. The labor force is represented by the nonagricultural labor force, not including public sector and construction employees, the latter mainly organized outside the NLRB. Net organizing is the number of workers gained in elections won minus the number lost through decertification elections.[1] A relatively accurate calculation may be made for r_o using NLRB new organizing data and labor force data from the Bureau of Labor Statistics. The union membership figures used here are constructed by subtracting union members in construction from the total in the private sector; this may be estimated to a close degree of approximation. Thus union density may be calculated for our private sector segment. From here, r_e is easily computed from equation 6. Both rates have certain cyclical variations. In particular r_e has extensive variations seemingly coincident with the business cycle. While r_e occasionally varies by several percentage points for the period 1946–80, it averages between .5 and 1 percent. Subject to much less cyclical variation (rarely more than a few tenths of a percent), r_o shows a relatively steady decline from nearly 2 percent at its height in 1946 to 1.4 percent in 1953, dropping below 1 percent in 1954 (the year of the highest postwar union density) to less than .2 percent in 1981. Thus the steady decline in union density from 1954 to the present is almost totally explained by the slowing down of the rate of new organizing during this period.

New Organizing in the United States

While the above estimates suggest that the ultimate fate of union growth and shrinkage is tied to the success of union organizing, it is wrong to believe that these two phenomena travel together in the short run. This is the error made by certain econometricians of union growth who argue that new union organizing and union growth are "coincident indicators."[2]

1. This calculation biases O_t upward since many unions certified by the NLRB never establish themselves, either failing to obtain a first contract or disappearing during the first several years (Prosten 1978; Weiler 1984; Cooke 1985). This bias, however, if corrected for, would make the decline in organizing rates even steeper than I argue it is.

2. See Adams and Krislov (1974). This point will be discussed further in chapter 8.

Union growth is made up of two components, whose relative impact in different time periods varies. A look at table 11 in this chapter, for example, will show that new union organizing through the NLRB from the middle 1950s until 1981 has varied only slightly from year to year, declining gradually over the course of several decades. Examination of table 1, however, in chapter 1 will show that union growth often varies by a large amount in any particular year.

The largest drops in union density tend to occur during recessionary periods when many unionized members are dropped from the work force. Thus, during "normal" periods, at least since the middle 1950s, the sharpest variations in union density are not a result of new organizing, but rather of economic factors. On the other hand, during periods of rapid union growth, as in certain years from the late 1930s until the early 1950s, economic factors have played a relatively minor direct role; during these periods, union growth and new organizing are indeed "coincident." The view that they are always so in the short run, however, is wrong.

Despite this lack of coincidence between union growth and new organizing during periods of slow growth or attrition, new organizing is still, I would argue, central. The gaining of new recruits, not only for expansion, but for the replacement of lost union jobs, is crucial to the strength and ultimately the survival of the trade unions. New union organizing is the central aspect to isolate in any long-term study of union growth. Its failure or weakness is as much a part of the explanation as is its existence during periods of rapid growth. Thus the key phenomenon to study if one wants to understand the *decline* of union strength is their fate in new organizing.

UNION CERTIFICATION IN THE UNITED STATES

While I have argued that the analysis of private sector organizing through the NLRB is crucial to an understanding of union decline, it is worth looking at the other ways workers in the United States may gain official union recognition, and at the availability of data.

The Public Sector. Public sector or governmental unions operate at the federal, state, and local levels. The Federal Labor Relations Board handles certification elections for all federal employees. As indicated previously, there has been a large upsurge in federal employee union organizing since the early 1960s, involving a majority of the several million federal employees. This new growth runs counter to the general trend of union decline. The success of public sector union organizing serves to highlight union difficulties in the private sector. Unfortunately, while federal union membership data are publicly accessible, certification data are virtually unavailable, existing in file folders and other non-machine readable form in regional offices around the country.

Union certification of state and local public employees has also increased rapidly since the early 1960s. While it has taken place all around the country (witness the 1985 statewide teachers strike in Mississippi), it has been strongest in those areas of high union density—the Northeast, Midwest, and California. It should come as no surprise that public employees in New York City, Detroit, and San Francisco are virtually all organized. Detailed, accessible data, however, are not easy to come by. Unlike the federal level there is great variance from one area to the other, although some states do have "mini-NLRBs" patterned after the national board. Thus, with the exception of a few areas, there is less consistency to the information and even less availability of it than at the federal level.

The Private Sector. There are still *voluntary recognitions* by employers of unions that go through no official agency. These are nowhere tabulated or centrally recorded, although impressionistic evidence suggests they have decreased over the last decade and are now quite few in number. They have historically been very important in the construction industry, though here too, with the successful anti-union drive that began in the early 1970s, their importance has declined.

There are also *prehire agreements* between construction unions and employers, permitted under Taft-Hartley. For these again there are few data, although they too seem to be decreasing.

The National Mediation Board (NMB) handles all bargaining certification of airline, railroad, and some subsidiary trucking employees, administered under the 1926 and 1934 Railway Labor Act. Though the data are available, certification elections are small in number and generally among units, involving few employees. There were hardly 1 percent as many certifications under the NMB (fewer than a hundred elections per year) during the 1970s as there were under the NLRB.

The National Labor Relations Board is responsible for the certification of the vast majority of private sector employees. This certification is usually done on the basis of an election administered by the board. By law and by the nature of the NLRB process, the data are reasonably accurate, well kept, and centralized on a national basis.

The study of public sector union organizing presents difficult problems in the gathering of data. Fortunately, material on private sector organizing is more accessible. NLRB records provide a goldmine of information for our purposes. They reflect union organizing in all the heavily unionized manufacturing industries, in mining, trucking, service industries, some in construction, and in white-collar and technical occupations. In short, it is a good guide to the majority of those areas in the private sector that have been the backbone of union strength, and also to those areas where unions have been historically weakest.

THE CONTEXT OF NLRB ELECTIONS

In the previous chapter, the importance of the 1935 establishment of the NLRB was noted for the development of trade union legality in the United States. Labor laws themselves reflect the contradictory effects of the uneven acceptance of unions by major parts of the capitalist class, the impact of the strength of organized labor, and the continued need for orderly (even if curtailed) relations with the unions on the part of many of the largest capitalists.

The laws that signified the recognition of the rights of unions to organize, culminating in the establishment of the NLRB, were passed in a brief several-year period. It is useful to note them here:

1. The Norris–La Guardia (Anti-Injunction) Act, passed 23 March, 1932.[3]

2. The National Industrial Recovery Act (NIRA), signed 16

---

3. The Norris–La Guardia Act placed limits on the hitherto almost unlimited power of courts to issue injunctions against unions. It also declared illegal (and unenforceable) the "yellow-dog" contract, whereby an employer could require a worker both to agree not to join a union and to resign if he did so. See *Statutes at Large* of the U.S. Congress (1976) and the legal compilation published by the Senate Subcommittee on Labor (1979).

June 1933. Section 7(a) asserted the right of workers to join unions and engage in collective bargaining.

3. The National Labor Relations Act, signed 5 July 1935. Established the National Labor Relations Board.

Labor legislation after this period has been marked by two seemingly contradictory, although actually quite complementary, tendencies. First, the major pieces of legislation (4 and 5 below) were largely designed to limit the rights of unions and to enhance the position of employers, and they reflect the *political weakness* of U.S. trade unions vis-à-vis the capitalist class since the 1930s:

4. The Labor-Management Relations Act of 1947 (Taft-Hartley). Trade unions lobbied intensely against Taft-Hartley, calling it the "Slave Labor Act."[4] In spite of a veto by President Harry Truman, it was passed into law on 22 August 1947, when the veto was overridden by the Senate. Taft-Hartley banned wildcat strikes, allowing the courts to fine unions for damages in such strikes; it made secondary boycotts, sitdowns, slowdowns, and closed shops illegal; it increased the injunctive powers of the courts, Congress, and the president.

5. The 1959 Labor Management Reporting and Disclosure Act (Landrum-Griffin Act). This bill made it legally obligatory for labor unions to disclose a large degree of their internal functioning to public government review. It thus legalized further intervention into union affairs by the federal government.

Unions have totally failed in eliminating or softening even those particular sections of the Taft-Hartley and Landrum-Griffin bills they have considered most noxious.

The second trend in national labor policy is reflected in a series of laws and executive orders, seemingly antithetical to the above legislation, that extend NLRB and Federal Labor Relations coverage to additional sectors of the working class. Among the most significant of these are the following:

1. Executive Order 10988, issued in 1962. Authorized federal employees to organize and engage in collective bargaining.

---

4. It is likely that many conservative and anticommunist union officials saw positive aspects in Taft-Hartley, both in hampering Communist union leaders and in gaining greater control over rank-and-file initiatives. Such an evaluation may have limited the desire of certain union leaders to throw all their energy and resources into the early efforts to defeat the bill. There is little hard, though much suggestive, evidence for such a speculation. Yet by the time the bill came up for a final vote, virtually all union officials recognized that many of the provisions could only weaken the strength of the unions.

2. The Postal Reorganization Act of 1970. Brought postal workers under NLRB jurisdiction.

3. The Labor Law Reform Act, passed on 25 August 1974. Extended NLRB coverage to nonprofit hospital workers.

Last, there exists a variety of state and local legislation (including the establishment of rights for farmworkers in California) affecting new union organizing.

The above is a rough summary of U.S. labor laws and the partial acceptance of trade union legality that they reflect, that is, the context in which NLRB certification elections occur. The struggle between workers and their employers, unions and capitalists, has created this patchwork of laws. These laws determine the legal framework in which unions are organized through the NLRB.

THE PROCESS OF CERTIFICATION THROUGH THE NLRB

The process of union certification by the NLRB is codified in law and public policy; formally, it involves the following steps:

1. The union obtains the signatures of employees on cards, authorizing it to represent them in negotiating over wages, hours, and other working conditions. Legally, the union must gain signatures of 30 percent or more of the employees in the bargaining unit to force an election. In practice, unions often obtain well over 50 percent.[5]

2. The union then files with the board for an election. The board, usually in the person of its regional staff, determines (a) whether an election should be held, (b) the bounds of the bargaining unit, (c) the date of the election and other matters. An election may be set by varying degrees of mutual consent between the employer and union or may be ordered by the board. Either party may object to or appeal any aspect of the board's decision at this point.[6]

3. An election date is set and the campaign period begins. This period is from fifteen to thirty days and is governed by a strict set of rules for how the participants should act.[7]

5. Detroit political scientist James Jacobs informs me that his discussions with top UAW officials indicate that the UAW has changed its policy on the number of signatures it wants before demanding a certification election. Where formerly, 50 percent was considered sufficient, now they believe they require 60 percent or more.

6. For more detailed discussion of NLRB procedures, see McCulloch and Bornstein (1974) and the NLRB annual reports.

7. For extensive discussion of the campaign period, see Getman, Goldberg,

4. The election itself takes place.

5. The election may be appealed to the board, which may, on the basis of unfair labor practices, set the election aside. A rerun may even be ordered.

6. Either the union is certified as the bargaining agent and a bargaining order issued or the union is not certified.

7. Any repeat elections (in the case of a loss by the union) or attempts to decertify the union (in the case of a win by the union) must wait at least one year.

THE NLRB DATA

By law the NLRB must collect and maintain accurate records on all cases that it handles. It issues monthly, quarterly, and annual reports. For each certification election, the employer and union agree (sometimes after much haggling or by board imposition) upon the boundaries of the voting unit and the number of eligible voters. With the union and company watching over its shoulder, the NLRB ascertains the validity of and counts each vote. Each election is tabulated and classified by a number of categories. Unlike union membership data, one need not depend on a varying set of subjectively (and occasionally arbitrarily) applied criteria.

Thus both the yearly aggregated summary records and the individual summary election records may be taken as accurate and consistent. The yearly aggregated data set used in this study contains yearly totals for fiscal years 1935–84. The larger disaggregated data set consists of summary records from all of the approximately ninety thousand NLRB certification elections held from the beginning of fiscal year 1973 (i.e., July 1972) to the end of 1984.[8]

THE DEPENDENT VARIABLES

There has been some debate over the proper dependent variable to use in examining union success in NLRB elections.[9] In this

---

and Herman (1976); see also Lachman (1982).

8. See Appendix D for a further discussion of this data set and its analysis.

9. In my private conversations with Richard Freeman, he argues that the percentage of the unorganized work force actually organized (i.e., the percentage of the potentially organized constituency) is the key. Paula Voos (1982) and David Ellwood and Glenn Fine (1983), all of whom were at Harvard, also take a similar approach. Sandver (1982) and Sandver and Heneman (1981), on the other hand, see the margin of victory (or defeat) as most important.

study two dependent variables are examined: the percentage of valid votes cast in NLRB elections for the certification of a union and the likelihood of a union victory in a particular election (which is also the percentage of union victories). Below I discuss the pros and cons of these and other possible dependent variables, presenting some reasons why these particular variables have been chosen.

Among the potential weaknesses of these variables is that they do not control for the degree of organizing effort by the union. Thus it is conceivable that one union might not call an election until it had a large majority of cards signed and was very sure that it would win. Another union might call elections very early as part of its organizing campaign, expecting a high likelihood of losing the election, but reckoning that it would make victory in a subsequent election more likely. It has been suggested to me that the latter has been the approach of at least one union. Certain of these decisions may even be made at the organizer level and may be subject to the assessments of individual organizers.[10]

The percentage of union victories and the percentage of workers voting for unions in these elections do not measure several things. They do not reflect the number of elections called and the number of workers brought to election (a phenomenon whose importance increases especially after 1980). Further, they do not reflect the number of workers won by unions or the degree to which a potentially organizable constituency is being organized. As Voos (1982) quite correctly notes, there are actually two stages to the organizing process through the NLRB: (1) the campaign leading up to the calling of the NLRB election and (2) the campaign leading up to the NLRB election itself. The percentage of union victories and the rate of workers voting union measure the degree of success at the latter stage, while the number of eligible voters brought to election is one measure of the former. The potential weaknesses must be borne in mind when interpreting the NLRB data presented in this study.

Thus another potential candidate for the dependent variable

10. One union official has suggested to me that Hospital Union 1199 calls elections very early in the organizing process, even if the chances of winning are not overwhelming. Another experienced organizer relates to me that he believes there are differences between unions on how soon elections are called, often depending on whether the organizing staff is evaluated by the number of elections called or by the number of elections (or workers) actually won.

is the number of workers eligible to vote in certification elections (i.e., the number of workers brought to election) or this number as a percentage of the potentially organizable constituency, broken down where possible by economic sector, union, and geographic regions. Voos (1982) has argued that this variable is the most reliable measure of union effort. She has constructed such a variable and persuasively used it in certain of her models. Like all other variables, this one too has its problems. On a sheer technical level, the data themselves are not accurately available. There is no time series of union membership broken down by industry and geographic region. The data that do exist are very crude and their reliability is occasionally doubtful.[11] Nevertheless, even were the technical problems overcome, there would be reasons to question this variable. The notion of potentially organizable constituencies has problems. Statistical accuracy on a particular union's province is dubious. The UAW, for example, has been organizing clerical and government workers in Wayne County, Michigan, and more recently has been organizing university employees around the country. Some of the most dramatic breakthroughs in new organizing have traditionally been outside what seemed to be the natural constituency of a particular union.[12]

Thus the notion of natural constituency (particularly when it is based, as Voos's is, on the percentage of the organized work force already organized by a particular union) has an inherently conservative bent. More significantly, the number of workers eligible to vote in NLRB elections was relatively constant from the mid-1950s until 1980 (see table 11). Voos's model shows a small time-trend for this variable, but the trend appears to be based on the particular year that her model starts, rather than on a real pattern. While the number of workers brought to election as a percentage of the potentially organized has been declining (since the labor force has been gradually expanding over time), it

11. Beginning in 1973, the Bureau of Labor Statistics Current Population Survey began asking questions about union membership. Questions were often reformulated. The 1977 and 1980 surveys were the beginning of a consistently organized disaggregated time series. Presently, BLS union membership data is based on the CPS data, rather than on the previous union surveys. Prior to the addition of these questions on the CPS surveys, however, membership breakdowns were at best only rough estimates.

12. The Farm Equipment Workers Union, for example, among the most militant and radical of the CIO unions formed in the 1930s (and which originally organized International Harvester, John Deere, and Caterpillar), was at first a spin-off of the Steel Workers Organizing Committee.

TABLE 11   NLRB Election Results, 1935–1984

1 Year	2 Number Elections	3 Number Voters Eligible	4 Number Valid	5 Number Union Vote	6 Percentage Union Vote	7 Number Elections Won	8 Percentage Elections Won	9 Number Civilian Labor Force (in thousands)
1936	31	9,512	7,734	4,569	59.1%	18	58.1%	53,440
1937	265	181,424	164,207	113,488	69.1	214	80.8	54,000
1938	1,152	394,558	343,587	282,470	82.2	945	82.0	54,950
1939	746	207,597	177,215	138,032	77.9	574	76.9	55,230
1940	1,192	595,075	532,355	435,842	81.9	921	77.3	55,640
1941	2,568	n.a.	729,915	589,921	80.8	2,127	82.8	55,910
1942	4,212	1,296,567	1,067,037	895,254	83.9	3,636	86.3	56,410
1943	4,153	1,402,040	1,126,501	923,169	82.0	3,580	86.2	55,540
1944	4,712	1,322,225	1,072,594	828,583	77.3	3,983	84.5	54,630
1945	4,919	1,087,177	893,758	706,569	79.1	4,078	82.9	53,860
1946	5,589	846,431	698,812	529,847	75.8	4,446	79.5	57,520
1947	6,920	934,553	805,474	621,732	77.2	5,194	75.1	60,168
1948	3,222	384,565	333,900	256,935	77.0	2,337	72.5	60,621
1949	5,514	588,761	516,248	377,360	73.1	3,889	70.5	61,286
1950	5,619	890,374	781,382	649,432	83.1	4,186	74.5	62,208
1951	6,432	666,556	587,595	442,066	75.2	4,758	74.0	62,017
1953	6,050	737,998	639,739	497,286	77.7	4,350	71.9	63,015
1955	4,215	515,995	453,442	335,393	74.0	2,849	67.6	65,023
1956	4,946	462,712	414,568	268,531	64.8	3,230	65.3	66,552
1957	4,729	458,904	410,619	261,762	63.7	2,942	62.2	66,929
1958	4,337	351,217	315,428	190,558	60.4	2,636	60.8	67,639
1959	5,428	430,023	385,794	247,867	64.2	3,410	62.8	68,369

1963	6,871	489,365	441,969	264,727	59.9	4,052	59.0	71,833
1965	7,176	512,159	462,526	291,036	62.9	4,435	61.8	74,455
1967	7,496	592,309	526,809	324,276	61.6	4,552	60.7	77,347
1969	7,319	552,037	491,279	287,078	58.4	4,098	56.0	80,734
1971	7,543	546,632	480,119	268,489	55.9	4,157	55.1	84,382
1972	8,066	556,100	489,332	281,649	57.6	4,483	55.6	87,034
1973	8,526	506,289	450,032	228,017	50.7	4,501	52.8	89,429
1974	7,994	506,047	449,758	218,822	48.7	4,131	51.7	91,949
1975	7,729	533,576	471,933	234,159	49.6	3,900	50.4	93,775
1976	7,736	435,171	383,601	182,341	47.5	3,906	50.5	96,158
1977	8,308	519,102	460,300	222,979	48.4	4,056	48.8	99,009
1978	7,168	424,481	376,483	178,918	47.5	3,504	48.9	102,251
1979	7,026	528,798	465,183	227,075	48.8	3,363	47.9	104,962
1980	7,021	471,651	415,048	197,364	47.6	3,441	49.0	106,940
1981	6,429	395,573	346,523	163,853	47.3	2,972	46.2	108,670
1982	4,030	244,318	210,510	96,611	45.9	1,808	44.9	110,204
1983	3,241	164,907	142,343	73,321	51.5	1,616	49.9	111,550
1984	3,336	205,743	182,472	94,414	53.4	1,519	47.9	113,644

Source: Variables 2 through 8 are either taken from the NLRB annual report for the fiscal year or computed from material in these annual reports. Variable 9 is from the March 1982 issue of *Employment and Earnings* (see Appendix A). Variables 2 through 8 for 1982–84 were constructed from NLRB raw election data tapes. Owing to different methods of analysis and data cleaning, they may be as much as several tenths of a percent different from the final figures released by the NLRB. Variable 9 for 1981–84 is computed from figures in the January 1985 issue of *Employment and Earnings*.

is still not clear that this is the best variable to inform us about labor union decline.

The number of workers actually won in certification elections as a percentage of the potentially organized is another possible dependent variable. It has certain of the same problems as those mentioned above concerning eligibles.

Because of these difficulties, it is my belief that the number of workers brought to elections and the number of workers actually won are most useful as interpretive aids when viewing what I regard as the more compelling dependent variables. All the above variables, of course, have their merits and disadvantages. The percentage of victory and vote variables were chosen because they were felt to have the following advantages: First, their high degree of accuracy, particularly on a disaggregated level, was considered key. Second, they are available as time-series data. Third, they can be constructed purely from the NLRB data without resorting to outside (and potentially inconsistently coded) estimates. Fourth, and perhaps most important, they seem to reflect in their trend the general decline of unions over the past few decades, the primary factor we hope to understand.

To a certain degree, I would argue, union success rates in new organizing through the NLRB are a plausible surrogate for other aspects of the organizing process and for union growth in general.[13] As to their drawbacks, they must be kept in mind when analyzing the results, but it is my assessment that the drawbacks are secondary (the differences in union attitudes

---

13. As a check for this, I calculated a series of regressions to test the extent to which this surrogate relationship held. Thus

$$Y_t = \beta_o + \beta_1 X_t + U_t$$

where Y is the dependent variable, β_o is the intercept, β_1 is the coefficent, X_t is the surrogate variable being tested, and U is the stochastic term.

Preliminary results of these regressions were made for a wide variety of surrogate variables, including union density and number of workers gained in NLRB elections. Many of the models had high degrees of fit. Many, however, also had a large amount of first-order autocorrelation that could not be removed without going to the Cochrane-Orcutt techniques. Several surrogate relationships remained strong when these methods were applied. Though these results are not conclusive, they do suggest that the dependent variables chosen in this study capture important aspects of the union membership decline, at least up until 1980. It is also clear that the number of workers voting in NLRB elections dropped dramatically for the period 1981–84. Whether this is a permanent trend is difficult to tell.

toward elections are in general overrated, the exceptions being minor; more significant, victory rates in elections are not unrelated to the first part of organizing effort).

CONCLUSION

In this chapter, I have tried to place the question of new union organizing through the NLRB within the context of union growth. I have argued that analyzing new union organizing through the NLRB is a reasonable approach for understanding the long-term decline in union strength in the last several decades.

6

Possible Explanations for the Decline

Three main types of explanations are put forth to account for the trends in union membership decline.[1] The first, and by far the most popular, points to changes in the structure and composition of the labor force and will be called the "sociological explanation." This perspective traces declining union membership to the changing sociology of the work force, itself the result of at least five continuing trends in this country's economic development: (1) the move of population and industry from the industrial Midwest and Northeast (i.e., the Frostbelt) to the reputedly more union resistant Sunbelt; (2) the contraction of the work force in smokestack industries and the corresponding increases in the supposedly less hospitable service, financial, and governmental sectors; (3) the dwindling percentage of U.S. workers in the traditionally prounion blue-collar occupations; (4) other changes in the composition of the work force by race, sex, education, and age; and (5) the increasing tendency to smaller sizes of new plants. These changes allegedly have led both to automatic

1. It is also worth noting that some of these explanations purport to explain organized labor's accelerated decline during the 1970s, a trend that we have already called into question.

declines in trade union membership and to difficult prospects for increasing or even recouping lost members by new organizing in the emergent sectors. These arguments imply that the declining unionization of the U.S. labor force is perhaps the inevitable concomitant of economic development and the regional cultural/social structure of U.S. society.

Second, various cyclical economic, social, and political conditions are sometimes held responsible for labor union decline. These will be collectively referred to as the "cyclical explanations." Such conditions include (1) the tendency to growing unemployment in the United States; (2) other economic factors related to the business cycle; (3) the growing influence of Republicans at the national level since 1952; and (4) the supposed declines in militancy and class conflict in the United States. It is the rise and fall of these various "environmental" factors that has allegedly determined the cyclical tendencies in union growth and decline.[2]

A further set of hypotheses suggest the causes of U.S. trade union weakness lie in the changing nature and interrelation of class forces—workers, unions, employers, and the state. These will be called the "political explanations," since they rest on choices (whether rational or not) by actors or are the outcome of political development, pressure, or struggle. The components of the political explanations include (1) the workers themselves, who are supposedly less interested in unions than they were previously; (2) the capitalists, who have mounted an antilabor offensive during the last decade; (3) the state, which oversees and enforces a worsening legal situation for unions; (4) the unions, which have supposedly exhibited a lack of aggressiveness, displayed poor organizing strategies, and decreased the percentages of their budgets used for new organizing.

Not all these explanations are mutually exclusive, but I shall try to keep them sharply delineated for analytic purposes.[3]

2. Dunlop described the industrial relations system as the "product of its total environment" (1948, p. 176) or as influenced by its environment (1958). Kochan discusses Kerr's similar usage of "the external environment" and expands Dunlop's description to include those factors that I have labeled sociological (Kochran 1980, pp. 36–37).

3. Nor are these three divisions without any overlap or a degree of schematic arbitrariness. For example, worker militancy and even the party in the White House are not unrelated to the relation of class forces.

THE EXPLANATIONS SPELLED OUT

SOCIOLOGICAL EXPLANATIONS: STRUCTURAL CHANGES IN THE LABOR FORCE

GEOGRAPHIC SHIFTS

The most important variation of the accelerated decline thesis places the onus on regional differentials in unionization rates. A full summary of this argument might be as follows: Since the 1930s there has been a concentration of trade union membership in this country in the Midwest, Northeast, and in California. The South has, since the 1930s, been an area of far lower union density, as well as a region of the country where wages have been on average over 20 percent below the national average (Douty 1968). There have been large-scale population shifts in the last several decades in this country, away from the Northeast and Midwest to the South and Southwest (Rones 1980). Both new industries and "runaway" shops relocating in the Sunbelt have paved the way for this population shift (Bluestone and Harrison 1980, 1982). Almost universally it has been argued by union officials and others that it is harder to organize in the South.[4] This is a result of a supposed unreceptiveness and hostility of Southern workers to unions, a higher degree of employer resistance to them, and a general political and social hegemony by the capitalist class and their allies there.

As capitalists in the traditional industrial areas (particularly the Northeast and the Midwest—the North Central region) attempt to make greater profits (or remain competitive with foreign producers), they move their operations to areas of lower labor costs. This is the "runaway shop" theory.[5] The prototype is the textile industry, which many years ago abandoned its base in New England and moved the bulk of its operations south and more recently to the Mexican border and overseas. Today, it is argued, the same process is taking place in other industries. This trend is well documented, its contours being broadly described,

---

4. The argument may be found in "No Welcome Mat for Unions in the Sunbelt," a special report in *Business Week* (17 May 1976, p. 108). Riche (1981) expresses one version; Voos (1982, p. 41), following Dunlop (1958), puts forth another. Aronowitz (1983) states a similar position. See also the statement of Donald Ratajczak, director of the Economic Forecasting Project of Georgia State University, quoted in Bureau of National Affairs) 1985 (p. 14).

5. For a detailed analysis of the complicated phenomenon of private disinvestment, see Bluestone and Harrison (1980, 1982).

for example, by Peter L. Rones (1980) and by Kilpatrick Sale in his widely quoted *Power Shift* (1975).

In addition, many new industries have begun and expanded their operations in the Sunbelt. Since World War II, for example, a huge growth of "high tech" companies, heavily supported by the Department of Defense, has taken place in California and the Southwest.

Quite simply stated, the regional thesis is that organizing in Mississippi, Texas, and Virginia is more difficult than organizing in Detroit, Michigan, or New York City. The lower percentage of union victories in certification elections is in whole or part attributable to the new regional configuration. The thesis about the difficulties of organizing in the South is so widely accepted that it is usually presented without any documentation. The propositions appear eminently reasonable; they accord quite well with many Northern prejudices and stereotypes about the South, as well as with certain indubitable facts about regional unionization rates.[6] Anderson, Busman, and O'Reilly, for example, in a generally well-researched and well-documented article, state the following without reference:

Many unions and industrial relations theorists have indicated that it is substantially harder to organize workers in the South than in other areas of the country. (1979, p. 34)

Different commentators assign varying importance to the many components of the regional thesis. Some, like McConville, stress the increases in the firing of union activists in the South. McConville sees a " 'Southern Conspiracy,' as labor leaders refer to the combination of textile companies, police, politicians, local merchants and industrialists working together to keep unions out

---

6. The failure of the CIO to pursue successfully its stated goal of organizing the South after World War II (a point which will be mentioned again later) left the South the least organized part of the country. Virtually every state in the South is well below the national average for unionization (see U.S. Dept. of Labor, BLS 1980b, p. 414). To cite some examples: South Carolina has only 8.9 percent of its nonagricultural work force organized into trade unions and associations, North Carolina 10.7 percent, Florida 13.2 percent, Mississippi 15.0 percent, Virginia 15.3 percent, Georgia 15.8 percent, and Alabama has a high 24.6 percent, still over two points below the national average for 1978. At the other end of the spectrum there is New York at 41 percent, West Virginia 40.4 percent, Michigan 38.5 percent, Pennsylvania 37.3 percent, followed closely by such states as Illinois, Indiana, Washington, Ohio, Hawaii, Maryland, and Alaska, all over 30 percent. For more information on union density by state, see table 13 in chapter 7 and table 6 in chapter 1.

of the small Southern towns where most mills are located" (1980, p. 143). Others emphasize supposed anti-union attitudes of Southern workers, which they claim are a permanent part of Southern culture. As an article in *Business Week* dated 17 May 1976 asserts: "Southern culture remains inhospitable to unions" ("No Welcome Mat for Unions in the Sunbelt," p. 108).

When examining certification elections, *Business Week* views the South as one homogeneous aggregate: "In fiscal 1975, unions won 757, or 45%, of 1671 representation elections in the South, lower than the 48.2% national success rate" (p. 108). In this respect, *Business Week* is no different from other commentators, journalistic or scholarly, lumping the Southern and Southwestern states into one category.[7] As I will show later, disaggregation of this data will prove very informative.

Koeppel (1978) provides a broad overview for this whole theory. She sees the employer offensive, the flight of shops to the South, and the increasing attempts to keep workers nonunion as being dictated by the weakening position of U.S. business in the world economy. U.S. capitalists can no longer afford to make economic concessions to Northern unions, if they are to remain competitive with foreign firms. They "run away" to the South to obtain cheaper nonunion labor. Hence they will resist attempts to organize unions there with special vigor. One might thus expect to see less likelihood of union victories in NLRB certification elections in the states in the South and the Southwest.

A small minority have argued that the South is not as inhospitable to unions as has often been claimed. Ray Marshall (1967, 1968) argues that patterns of union organization in the South were similar to the rest of the country until 1935 (1968, p. 65). The lower degree of union density in the South is in part attributable to the failure of the post–World War II Southern organizing drives by the AFL and the CIO. Despite this failure, the union density in Southern manufacturing industries is not nearly so low as the figures for the states as a whole. Thus Marshall concludes that the lower union densities in the South are primarily due to the area's industrial composition, not to legal or social factors. Indeed, the 1970s have in general seen less loss in union density in Southern states than in the country as a whole (U.S. Dept. of Labor, BLS 1980, p. 414). More recently, investi-

7. For a more recent work that purports to examine regional differences but that does not attempt to disaggregate the South, see Sandver (1982).

gators have found that unorganized workers in the South are as likely to vote for unions in NLRB elections as workers in other parts of the country (Rose 1972; Sandver 1982; Goldfield 1982), and are about as supportive to unions in answers to survey questionnaires (Kochan 1979).

CHANGES IN INDUSTRIAL COMPOSITION: ECONOMIC
DYNAMISM AND INDUSTRIAL SHIFTS

One could make a plausible argument that unionization is often strongest in those industries that are expanding and gathering large profits. Such a case would certainly be strengthened by reference to the rise of the UAW in auto, aircraft, farm, and construction equipment, and to the strength of the Teamsters after World War II. One could also conceivably make an opposite argument based on references to such industries as steel and farm equipment at the turn of the century, when they enjoyed extensive monopoly profits but were able to keep unions out. Certainly the lack of unions at IBM, Texas Instruments, and other highly profitable computer companies today is another potential buttress for such a case. However, although numerous off-the-cuff remarks are made by various commentators, no one with whom I am familiar has done a careful empirical examination of this question.

More substantially, it is often argued that slow (or negative) growth in employment in heavily unionized industries, combined with relatively fast growth in low-unionized industries, makes union growth difficult during normal times. Since the massive union organizing of the 1930s, the most highly unionized industrial sectors have been manufacturing, mining, transportation, and construction—all, at least until very recently, having a majority of the manual workers organized. Some investigators (e.g., Bell 1953, 1954) have argued that these industries were "saturated" and that prospects in other sectors, including government, services, and finance, would be small.

During the last several decades, the industrial makeup of the U.S. has dramatically shifted. The labor force, in general, has grown most in the traditionally low-unionized industries of the economy. Thus many argue that the prospects for union growth and new organizing are not good. This argument is quite common. It appears in Roomkin and Juris 1978, in Freeman and Medoff 1976, and in Burton 1979. It is presented most articulately in Voos 1982:

In contrast to the periods of rapid expansion, the cross-sectional pattern of membership is typically stable in the normal periods of slow union growth, stagnation, or actual decline. In such periods, union growth is strongly related to changes in those environmental factors with which membership is highly correlated. (Voos 1982, p. 33; see also Dunlop 1958a, pp. 33–36)

Voos argues that the reasons for this are twofold: Union membership is affected first, by changes "in the number of jobs offered by employers who are already unionized," and second, "by making the remaining nonunion establishments easier or harder to organize" (1982, p. 34).

The industrial shifts in the past few decades have been quite unfavorable to unions, according to Voos. The heavily unionized industries (i.e., mining, manufacturing, construction, transportation, and utilities) have grown less quickly than the less unionized industries. In the twenty-five years between 1953 and 1978, these industries declined from 50 percent to 35 percent of total employment (Voos 1982, p. 37).

Voos concludes two things from this industrial shift. First, the slow employment growth in the heavily unionized industries means that few new jobs will automatically be union jobs. Second, new organizing may be more difficult in less unionized industries because of intrinsic factors (like employer opposition, lower degree of leverage) or because it is more difficult to organize in industries where there is a smaller initial percentage of union members. Thus, according to this thesis, industrial shifts have been a major factor in the decline of both union growth and union success in new organizing efforts.[8]

There are two relevant "facts" that should lead us to be cautious of accepting these claims unreservedly. First, similar industrial shifts have taken place in the countries of Western Europe, none of which seem to have impeded steady union growth during this same period (Bain and Price 1980). Second, attitudinal surveys indicate that workers in less organized industries do not tell interviewers that they are any less willing to support a union than do their counterparts in more organized industries (Kochan 1979).

8. Donald Ratajczak gives a further variant, citing the impact of growing competition from abroad on the "decaying industrial sector" (BNA 1985, p. 12).

CHANGES IN THE OCCUPATIONAL STRUCTURE

The most highly unionized occupational groups have always been blue-collar workers. In 1980, well over 40 percent of all blue-collar workers were unionized, compared to less than 20 percent in other occupational categories. Thus it is significant that white-collar occupational categories have increased substantially over the past several decades, while the percentage of blue-collar workers has declined (although there was no evidence of absolute declines up to 1980). Many have argued that this situation bodes ill for successful future organizing (Freeman and Medoff 1976; Roomkin and Juris 1978; Voos 1982). Again there is more to make us wary: (1) Similar occupational shifts have occurred in Western European countries where unions have succeeded in organizing these new constituencies. (2) More close to home, the most rapid recent growth in unionism in this country has been among public employees; even discounting school teachers, these new recruits have been overwhelmingly white-collar workers (Freeman 1984). (3) Finally, BLS occupational categories are notoriously crude; many numerical shifts supposedly hide newly proletarianized categories of workers (Kassalow 1961; Bagli 1980) or actual rises in manual labor categories (Levison 1974). There are even those who have argued that certain kinds of white-collar workers would be not only more likely to join unions, but more militant than the blue-collar proletarians (Gorz 1967, 1982).

CHANGING WORK FORCE COMPOSITION AND CHARACTER

Roomkin and Juris argue that declining union success in the recent period is, at least in part, a result of large-scale changes in the composition of the work force: "The changing nature of the work force has slowed union organizing. Women, the better educated, and younger workers traditionally have been more difficult to organize" (1979, p. 37).[9] Ratajczak sees the problem as especially acute with regard to women (Bureau of National Affairs 1985, p. 19).

---

9. Roomkin and Juris cite various references that supposedly substantiate this assertion, although they do qualify it slightly with respect to women (1979, p. 38 n. 5; see also Roomkin and Juris 1978). Riche gives a similar argument: "Many of the reasons for labor's decline are demographic. Unions have not adjusted fast enough to changes in the labor force, in occupations, in industry, and in the geographic location of jobs" (1981, p. 28).

The implicit argument is, of course, that traditional types of workers—male, less educated, older—are or have been more easily organized than the newer groups are today. Thus we might expect relatively constant union victory rates in those traditionally organized sectors (e.g., basic industry, skilled trades, and trucking) where there has not been a heavy influx of women, younger workers, and the better educated. In those sectors where there has been such an influx (e.g., social services, teaching, professions) we would expect a decline, or at least a lower than average union victory rate.

CYCLICAL EXPLANATIONS: CHANGES IN THE MACROECONOMIC, SOCIAL, AND POLITICAL ENVIRONMENT

UNEMPLOYMENT

There is widespread agreement that unemployment affects the working of the labor market. Marx argued in depth that unemployment created what he called a "reserve army of the unemployed."[10] When this army grows in numbers, there is greater competition among workers for scarce jobs, and reduced bargaining leverage by employed workers and their unions over wages and conditions.[11] Thus, with higher unemployment, unions are hypothesized to do less well than with lower unemployment. Unions with less bargaining leverage are therefore organizations with less to offer, with less ability to win new recruits. In addition, unemployment is often a sign of a downward turn in the economy. According to many, starting with Commons, it is at this time that unions do least well. Conversely, when the economy is in an upswing, unemployment drops, prices rise, and workers are anxious to organize and to struggle for better terms in the sale of their labor power (Commons 1958, p. 19).

10. Marx's theory of the labor market under capitalism is presented in *Capital* ([1867] 1979, vol. 1).
11. For an explanation that is not dissimilar, we can turn to Kochan:

> One of the most widely accepted hypotheses is that the bargaining power of unions increases as the business cycle moves towards full employment. Conversely, the power of unions is hypothesized to decline during periods of falling product demand and rising unemployment. The argument is that the costs of the strike are greatest to employers when product demand is high or increasing. During periods of slack demand, employers may, in fact, welcome a strike because it helps to work off inventories and may serve as a substitute for layoffs. (1980, p. 40)

By implication, the high and rising rates of unemployment over the last two decades might well help explain both the trends and the cyclical variations in union growth and in new organizing success rates in NLRB certification elections as well.[12] While not disagreeing with this assessment, there are also those who argue that severe widespread unemployment creates large-scale social dislocation, providing a context for massive spurts in union growth (Dunlop 1948; I. Bernstein 1953, 1954a).

OTHER CYCLICAL ECONOMIC FACTORS

Large numbers of investigators since Commons have argued that union growth and strength is procyclical. Thus general downward trends in growth rates, productivity, and other economic indicators would signify a weakened position for unions. This hypothesis will be developed and examined more fully in chapter 8.

REPUBLICANS IN THE WHITE HOUSE

Quite simply, Republicans are supposedly more anti-union than Democrats. While Republican domination in Congress may affect public policy related to labor unions, it is the dominance in the White House that affects the functioning of the NLRB. Control of the White House means control of new five-year appointments to the board itself. It also allows other methods of control over the NLRB, including approval of the budget, a power that has been used quite effectively by the Reagan administration.[13] Thus Republican control of the White House is believed to make the NLRB less sympathetic to unions.[14]

MILITANCY

Marx and Lenin both argued that union gains and growth were only possible by militant struggle. Lenin coined the aphorism "All reforms are only a by-product of revolutionary struggle."[15] Bell and other more conservative commentators also argued that

12. This, of course, is one of the direct possibilities that are implied in the Commons (1956), Ashenfelter-Pencavel (1969), and Bain-Elsheikh (1976) theories.

13. See, for example, the description of the effects of budget cuts on NLRB functioning by James Warren (1981b).

14. Considering the differences between the graphs of percentage of workers voting for unions and the percentage of election victories by unions over time, I hypothesized such an effect in an earlier study (Goldfield 1982).

15. See, among many places, "How Not to Write Resolutions" (March 1907; in Lenin 1963, 12:237).

unions would decline as the degree of strikes and class conflict declined. Thus the decline of union strength is hypothesized to bear a relation to a supposed decline in worker militancy. Others, however, like Crouch and Pizzorno (1978) have argued that strikes are a reflection of the lack of general strength of a union. Many point to Sweden as an example of a country with high union density (the highest of any capitalist country), large bargaining leverage, and a low strike rate, presumably because strikes are unnecessary (Korpi and Shalev 1979, 1980).

POLITICAL EXPLANATIONS: THE CHANGING RELATION OF CLASS FORCES

The analysis of the nature of trade unions under capitalism presented in chapter 4 implicitly offers a series of hypotheses about trade union growth and decline. It suggests that trade unions are a natural development of the emergence of capitalism. Thus, while the economic structure and social composition of the work force might change, while cyclical factors might provide its ups and downs, the relation of class forces will be the major determinant of the strength of workers' organizations. Chapter 4 argues that the relations between workers and their organizations and capitalists and their organizations are the key determinants of the strength of working-class organizations. To this relation might be added the state, which has been variously described as an agency for capitalist domination, a reflection and arbiter of class conflict, and an autonomous structure largely concerned with its own functioning and preservation.

A focus on the relation of class forces is, of course, certainly not confined to Marxists. Those who argue that societal development will moderate class conflict and even eventually elimi-nate the need for unions often pinpoint changes in the nature of class actors or the nature of the state. This is certainly true of those who view the changing attitudes of workers as the main reason for union decline.

THE CHANGING ATTITUDES OF WORKERS

A number of sources argue, not merely that the composition of the work force has changed, but that there is a "new worker" in traditional blue-collar jobs, one who is less receptive to the concept of unionism. The view that workers have grown more conservative is not a new one. Bell, for example, argued that workers were becoming less radical over three decades ago.

The middle-class aspirations of U.S. workers, the desire and ability to own a house, a car, and other essential luxuries of middle-class living, have led to an acceptance of the capitalist system and its technology. (1953, p. 121)

Bell (1960), Lipset (1960), and others argued further that not only the more radical forms of class and union consciousness, but traditional union allegiances would gradually diminish among workers. Such a view has again become quite popular.

One researcher presents a vivid and descriptive version of this thesis to explain the decline of unions in the recent period. Peter J. Pestillo sees the twin development of a "new worker" and a "new capitalist." He mentions the "dismal record at the polls of the workplace. Organized labor can't even win half the elections it forces." According to Pestillo (1979) there is a "new worker," who

comes from greater affluence, is better educated, and does easier work for shorter periods. In sum, he hasn't got it as tough. His isn't a class struggle. More likely, his is a struggle for recognition, for independence, for individuality. Unions can't help toward achieving these aims. (p. 33)

The young worker thinks primarily of himself. We are experiencing the cult of the individual, and labor is taking a beating preaching the comfort of coalition. (p. 33)

To whom is the new, individualistic worker able to turn? Pestillo suggests that there are new benevolent capitalists. As vice president for industrial relations at B. F. Goodrich Company, he writes: "At B. F. Goodrich, we tell our managers to treat their people as they want to be treated; it's that simple" (1979, p. 34).[16]

UNFAVORABLE LABOR LAWS AND PUBLIC POLICIES

Many have argued that private sector labor law in this country is highly unfavorable to new organizing (e.g., Barkin 1961; Baker 1977; Klare 1978; Ferro 1982; Weiler 1983; Houseman 1985). Most of the unfavorable policies stem from the passage of the Taft-Hartley Act in 1947: (1) it banned secondary boycotts and mass picketing, two tactics used quite successfully in new organizing by the CIO during the 1930s and 1940s; (2) it gave employers the right to "free speech" during NLRB certification election campaigns; (3) it strengthened the injunctive powers of the courts and increased the severity of the penalties that could

16. Pestillo now holds a similar position at Ford.

be imposed on unions, while giving minimum punishments for violations by companies.[17]

It has also been argued that the U.S. government has become increasingly antilabor in the last several decades, making it more difficult for unions to organize in the private sector.[18] It is useful to separate the worsening legal situation for union organizing in the United States, the failure to close loopholes used by corporations to avoid the intent of labor relations laws, the growing conservatism of the courts and the NLRB, and the overt anti-union activities of the government itself.

From 1935 to 1947, the NLRB acted to a large degree as an advocate of unions among employees; its explicit legal purpose was to ascertain whether employees wanted unions and to protect their rights in such expression (Gross 1974, 1981). The passage of the Taft-Hartley Act in 1947 is generally recognized as a major setback to unions in their ability to organize and to struggle against their employers.[19]

Taft-Hartley banned wildcats, making unions liable for damages. It made "economic" strikers ineligible to vote in certification elections, while allowing their replacements (i.e., "scabs") voting rights. It banned sit-downs, slow-downs, and closed shops. Section 14b of Taft-Hartley, which allowed states the right to ban union shops, not only put unions in a more difficult situation, but provided a vehicle for the mounting of enormous anti-union campaigns at the state level. Most significant was the granting to employers of the right to campaign vigorously against unions (Kistler 1977). Many of the effects of Taft-Hartley were not felt for a number of years. Some, like employer campaigning and the decertification election, have become much more heavily used since the early 1970s.

The passage of the Landrum-Griffin Act in 1959 had additional serious effects on unions' organizing, eliminating some of

17. There are, of course, many other aspects of Taft-Hartley that make difficulties for unions, including the right of states to pass "right-to-work" laws.

18. Gross (1974, 1981) sees this trend developing in the 1940s. Barkin (1961, p. 19) sees the trend emerging strongly in the 1950s. Kistler (1977) and Prosten (1978) view it as especially strong in the 1970s. Others, of course, cite the 1980s under the Reagan presidency.

19. While some might argue that Taft-Hartley merely redressed the balance that was weighted too heavily against business, few would deny that the bill constrained labor unions. Besides Barkin, who says that "the Taft-Hartley Act, and the NLRB interpreting it, have provided employers with a springboard for overt counterattacks" (1961, p. 19), see Ferro (1982) and Baker (1977).

the most powerful weapons at their disposal.[20] These included secondary boycotts and "hot cargo" agreements, whereby one employer agreed not to handle products of another, recalcitrant employer involved in a dispute with the union. Certain econometricians regard the act as so important that they create a separate variable to capture its effect in their time-series models (Shalev 1980).

The net effect of these legal barriers to union organizing has, according to some, been significant. Freeman, for example, sees the legal situation as a prime factor in holding back union growth in the private sector in this country (1980, p. 369). By way of comparison, he notes the positive growth in union density in Canada during the same period it was declining in the United States; the Canadian private sector has many of the same unions and firms confronting each other as in this country.

During the 1970s, there has been an increase in the use of what some would consider loopholes in labor relations laws. These include, not only the aforementioned increased employer campaigning, but extreme legal maneuvering solely for the purpose of delay and a greater willingness of employers to accept the negligible penalties for large-scale violations of the law. The 1978 Labor Law Reform Act, as initially drafted, was to increase penalties on employers for violations and to eliminate most of the delays in the holding of certification elections. Its failure to pass was in part a green light to those who would continue to use the various loopholes.

The NLRB itself seems to have grown continually more conservative over time. Gross (1974) sees this process beginning in 1940 after the Smith Committee hearings had begun. Barkin (1961) sees the trend as greatly accelerated after the 1952 election. Others have pointed to growing conservatism since the Nixon administration took office in 1968. The board has always been excessively concerned with legal precedents and the views of the courts. The growing conservatism of the Supreme Court since the arrival of the Nixon appointees has made the board

20. The Landrum-Griffin Act did give a partial remedy to the complete disenfranchisement of economic strikers. However, while it made them eligible to vote in NLRB elections for one year, it also allowed their substitutes ("scabs") the right to vote. As a consequence, certain strikes in which the employer is attempting to break the union are often dragged on past the year mark in order to disenfranchise the strikers (see, e.g., Howard 1982).

even more cautious (Ferro 1982). As one would expect, this process has not improved under Reagan.[21]

Other government agencies in addition to the NLRB have added to the problems in union organizing. One small example was the 1982 decision by the Health Care Financing Agency reversing a long-standing policy. After the 1982 decision hospitals became reimbursable under Medicare for the costs of trying to keep out unions, including the payments of high fees to anti-union consulting firms (American Nurses' Association 1982). This decision was only recently reversed. Of course, little comment is necessary about the Reagan administration's firing of the twelve thousand members of the air controllers union and the government's successful attempt to decertify the union as the legally recognized bargaining agent. Thus one might hypothesize that the growing overt opposition of the state to unions is a major factor helping to explain their decline.

These laws, unfavorable to labor unions, are rooted in the Taft-Hartley Act, which has been on the books in relatively unchanged form for almost forty years. Some have argued that the policy implementations of these laws (as determined by the NLRB and by court interpretations) have been tilting more and more toward employers, although it is not clear that the changes have been overwhelming (Lachman 1982). What is most significant is the degree to which employers have been able to make use of provisions and loopholes in these long-standing laws to undermine union growth and stability. In response, unions have been unable to force the government to tighten the loopholes and provisions (viz., the defeat of the highly limited 1978 Labor Law Reform Act) or to devise tactics to challenge employers' use of them. Thus the question of the independent importance of labor laws, including their interpretation and enforcement, as a central cause of trade union decline must be examined.

21. For example, the NLRB ruled in a three-to-two decision that the union had no basis for seeking an appeal of an election in which the employer had made illegal and false charges against the union. This decision overruled the previous precedent set by the board (*Chicago Sun Times*, 10 August 1982). Since the Reagan majority gained control in 1983, there have been numerous other reversals. See, for example the following testimonies from the 1985 hearings of the House Subcommittee on Labor-Management Relations: Kane (pp. 108–9), Klare (pp. 773–82), Levy (pp. 598–632), and Gould (pp. 82–87).

THE CAPITALIST OFFENSIVE

It is almost universally acknowledged that the past decade has seen a large-scale employer offensive against unions.[22] A. H. Raskin, for example, sees labor's difficulties as a result of "employee apathy and of savvy employer resistance" (1979, p. 34). Numerous reports attest to the rise of a thriving new industry of antilabor management consulting firms, whose business, according to the *Economist,* had reached over 100 million dollars a year by 1979 (over half a billion dollars according to more recent estimates).[23] Many of their activities are widely reported in the business press (e.g., in the *Wall Street Journal*) and also in many labor publications.[24]

Overt attempts by companies to break unions take place with increasing regularity. The newspapers of virtually every large international U.S. union are filled with stories of workers fighting for union recognition or, upon getting it, engaging in many-month-long strikes to achieve their first contracts. The tactics of J. P. Stevens received widespread publicity. What is especially characteristic of the present period are the attempts to break more established unions. We have already mentioned the successful attempt by the Reagan administrationto break PATCO, the air traffic controllers organization. Earlier there was the less well-known and unsuccessful attempt by the International Harvester Company to break the union representing its employees (UAW), one of the strongest unions in any industry (Goldfield 1980b; "Louisville Workers Win Strike," 1978). Paradoxically, the six-month strike forced on the union by Harvester's aggressive management was a major factor in the later insolvency and eventual reorganization of the company.

There have been other attempts to break the power of established unions, affecting both their new organizing and existing

22. Among those who mention the trend are Koeppel (1978); McConville (1975, 1980); Prosten (1979); Ferguson and Rogers (1979a, 1979b); and Anderson, Busman, and O'Reilly (1979). See also "U.S. Union Buster," an editorial in the *Nation* (19 April 1980), and the following articles from *Business Week*: "No Welcome Mat for Unions" (17 May 1976), "The Mixed Results of Labor Law Reform" (7 Nov. 1977), and "Do Representation Elections Need the NLRB?" (21 March 1977).

23. See "American Union Busting" (*Economist,* 17 Nov. 1979, p. 50) for the lower estimate, and Georgine (1979) and Freeman and Medoff (1983) for the higher figures.

24. Two regular AFL-CIO publications are filled with such information: the *Report on Union Busting (RUB)* and the *Statistical and Tactical Information Report (STIR).*

membership. Perhaps the most stark example is the activity of the Business Roundtable in undoing the dominance of old-line construction unions. This assault is described as a "burgeoning open shop movement" by J. C. Turner (1979), the general president of the International Union of Operating Engineers. Robert A. Georgine, president of the Building and Construction Trades Department of the AFL-CIO, in a lengthy testimony before a congressional committee, describes it as an attack by a "guerilla army dressed in three piece suits" (Georgine 1979).

Large-scale employer offensives are, of course, not new in the United States or in capitalist countries in general, Yet the current offensive is the most widespread since the unionization of mass production industries by the CIO in the late 1930s and early 1940s. Various factors have been said to constitute the most effective forms of employer resistance. The AFL-CIO has stressed the importance of employer-initiated election delays.

Richard Prosten has done a study of employer-initiated delays in certification elections. His impressive research examines over 130,000 NLRB elections closed between 1 January 1962 and 31 December 1977. He argues that business resistance to unions is reflected in the astronomical rise in election delays during this period. Further, he argues that there is a close correlation between the amount of delay and the percentage of units won by unions. There is a 12.5 percent dropoff in percentage of victories by unions when the election is held five months or more after the date of filing for the election rather than during the first month of filing. The loss, according to Prosten, is remarkably continuous over time: "the average dropoff in union victories is 2.5% per month through the first 6 months of delay" (Prosten 1979, p. 39). Thus Prosten not only argues that the employer resistance is directly responsible for the decline in the percentage of union victories since 1962, but that one tactic (election delays) is largely the cause.

Some have argued that the increase of other activities has slowed new organizing, registering in part in the rise in decertification attempts. Others cite the vast increase over the last three decades in unfair labor practices committed by employers (*Wall Street Journal*, 21 Oct. 1982). A number of studies claim that these illegal tactics have a significant negative effect on union success in NLRB elections (Dickens 1980, 1983), while others argue that illegal employer interventions in organizing campaigns have little effect on election outcomes. Among the few commentators who discount the effect of employer resistance on certification election outcomes are Getman, Goldberg, and Herman in their highly controversial *Union Representation Elections: Law and Reality* (1976). Their argument is that even illegal actions by employers or by the union during the campaign period have little effect on the outcome of the elections. Thus the effect of employer resistance on union difficulties in new organizing must be tested empirically. It should perhaps be mentioned that there are also those who argue that union difficulties are the result of *more* cooperative management activities (Pestillo 1979; see also the remarks by Bernie Trimbull, executive director of the National Association for Manufacturers' Committee for a Union-Free Environment in BNA 1985, p. 13). Although it is hard to take such statements as being made in good faith, they too will be examined.

THE UNION RESPONSE

Almost continually since the end of World War II, a steady stream of writers have argued that unions and their leaders have become or are becoming highly bureaucratic, unaggressive, and conservative, sooner or later lowering the strength of union organization (Mills 1948; Bell 1953; Lens 1949, 1959; Barkin 1961; Jacobs 1963; Widick 1975). Others have argued that union leadership has been doing quite well (Dunlop 1980; Kistler 1977). The validity of this hypothesis too must be determined.

UNION DYNAMISM

Although some commentators maintain that union leadership has been doing quite well, since the end of World War II, it has also been common to argue that unions and their leaders (or at least the majority of them) have become bureaucratized, placid, unaggressive—in short, business unions.[25] This is often stated as the reason for their increased failures in winning union certification elections. Virtually no effort has been made to examine such claims empirically. This argument comes in a large variety of flavors, sometimes put forth coherently, sometimes based merely on impressionistic evidence.[26]

25. The argument that the weakness of contemporary unions is in part a result of their bureaucratization is a common one among radicals. For a nonradical argument, see Widick (1975b).

26. Those putting it forth include Barkin (1961), Lester (1958), Shister (1953), Lens (1949, 1959), Glaberman (1962), James (1958).

In addition, numerous off-the-cuff remarks are made about the comparative success rates of various unions. Although it is fairly simple to find out how a union did in NLRB elections for a particular year and compare it with other unions, some commentators make ill-informed statements even at this elementary level. James Warren (1981), for example, states that the Teamsters "win more often than other unions," which is not at all true on a percentage basis. Myths about the Teamsters die hard. The Bureau of National Affairs (1985, p. 6) includes them in its list of unions that have "posted unusually high organizing rates." No commentators, to my knowledge, analyze and compare the success rates of unions over time.

SUMMARY

With the arguments laid out, the issues should be reasonably clear: Are the problems of unions permanent and likely to worsen, or are they only temporary, perhaps even based on unfavorable cyclical trends that are likely to reverse? Are U.S. trade union difficulties a result of irreversible structural changes in U.S. society? Are they the result of changes in the relation of class forces, and if so, are these changes reversible or not? It is with the goal of shedding some small amount of light on these questions that the discussion will proceed.

In the next three chapters, the preceding hypotheses will be examined. In chapter 7, I will subject what is perhaps the most common argument for union decline—the changing composition and structure of the labor force—to a sustained analysis.

Part 3
Reasons Behind the Trade Union Decline

7

The Interrogation of the First Suspect: Changes in the Economic Structure and Social Composition of the Work Force

The sociological explanations for trade union membership decline and union organizing failures place a strong emphasis on changes in the economic structure and social composition of the labor force. These theories begin with a number of observations. High membership in U.S. trade unions is associated with certain industrial, occupational, geographical, and social characteristics. Various other factors seem to be associated with lower union densities. Those factors associated with union strength (certain regions of the country, traditionally unionized industries, certain occupations, for example) seem to have decreased in relative importance in this country. Those factors associated with union weakness seem to have increased proportionately.

On the basis of the above assertions, one might reasonably conclude (1) that relatively fewer new union members would be recruited as the *automatic* result of work force expansion in the already unionized economic sectors; and (2) that there would be a relatively larger growth in the *automatically* nonunion jobs because of the more rapid growth in the unorganized sectors.

In addition, the rapidly growing sectors are more likely to be resistant to new union organizing. Those groups whose numbers are expanding most quickly in the labor force (e.g., women, youth, the educated) are supposedly more difficult to organize. Those parts of the country and those industries that have been traditionally nonunion (or have low union density) will probably be more resistant to unionism: the social structure will be less receptive, the employers will be more antagonistic, and the workers themselves will be less likely to be interested (having less personal experience of unions, fewer relatives and friends in unions, etc.). The unions, having less leverage because of lower unionization rates, will themselves have less to offer. The industry itself may be highly resistant to unionization. There may, of course, be several different reasons why such might be the case. It might be that those unorganized industries were intrinsically harder to organize—the workers have less economic leverage or a dispersed social situation makes communication difficult. It could also be that employers are more resistant because they feel that competition from nonunion rivals is difficult to match. Ceteris paribus, such changes in the economic structure and social composition of the labor force will lead to a decline (or slower rates) in union growth, and to greater difficulties in new organizing.

Some initial distinctions are warranted before embarking on a detailed examination of our subject matter. First, as we noted in chapter 5, the factors affecting union growth need not be the same as those affecting new organizing. New organizing is, of course, always a component of union growth. Thus all that affects new union organizing of necessity has an impact on union growth. Difficulties in new union organizing (e.g., in Southern textile industries) may have a great effect on the low union density in an industry or region. Yet union growth may be affected in ways that have little direct impact on new organizing. Declines in the employment of highly unionized industries (e.g., automobiles) have a great effect on union membership and hence on union growth. They need have no direct effect, however, on organizing successes, for example, of the United Auto Workers or any other union.

Additionally, we want to keep clear about the relation between the cross-sectional differences in union density and the causal reasons for union decline. The fact that a high-density sector is losing its constituency while a low-density sector is increasing in number is not prima facie evidence of a sufficient cause for a decline in total union density or membership. Declines in the percentage of workers employed in highly unionized states (e.g., New York) and rises in the percentage of workers employed in less unionized states (e.g., Mississippi) do not necessarily entail a decline in the total union membership or union density in this country.[1] Even were the decreases in the populations of highly unionized sectors to be accompanied by general national declines in union membership or union density, the two need not be directly related. It might be the case that the national declines are merely a reflection of declines in union density in the highly unionized areas. Thus one must be wary of jumping to conclusions.

My approach here will be, first, to look at the strengths and weaknesses of unions by cross-section; second, to trace the shifts in the economic structure and social composition of the labor force; third, to summarize those arguments that have an initial plausibility; fourth, to see whether the hypotheses are borne out with respect to new organizing by examining NLRB union certification election results and other types of data.

WHERE ARE UNIONS STRONG? WHERE ARE UNIONS WEAK?

U.S. union membership, examined cross-sectionally, shows the following characteristics.

1. Geographic Characteristics. Both the distribution of union membership and its density are highly uneven in the United States. Particularly, they are uneven geographically. The vast majority of union membership and states with high union density are, with the exception of California, concentrated in the Northeast, Middle Atlantic, and Midwest (the so-called Frostbelt). In 1980, the two most populous states, New York and California, accounted for one-fourth of all union members with 2.792 million and 2.661 million members respectively.[2] Seven Midwestern states—Illinois (1.487 million), Ohio (1.376 million), Michigan (1.284 million), Indiana (.554 million), Wisconsin (.554 million), Missouri (.544 million), and Minnesota (.463 million)— possess almost one-third of U.S. union membership. Still another 20 percent are accounted for by Pennsylvania (1.644 million), New Jersey (.784 million), Massachusetts (.660 million), Mary-

1. In fact Mississippi, to take our example, might be increasing in union membership faster than New York is decreasing—for a net gain in membership.
2. See Bureau of National Affairs 1982 for 1980 figures. Figures for prior years may be found in the *Directory of National Unions and Employee Associations* (published biennially by the Dept. of Labor, BLS) and in BLS 1980b.

land (including the District of Columbia, .527 million), and Connecticut (.327 million). These states also have high union densities. Other states with high percentages of workers organized include West Virginia, Washington, and Alaska.

Those states with the lowest union densities are either in the South and Southwest or are small and largely rural. These cross-sectional results are summarized in table 12 below.

TABLE 12   Union Density by State, 1980

Highest Densities		Lowest Densities	
New York	38.8%	South Carolina	7.8%
Michigan	37.3	North Carolina	9.6
Pennsylvania	34.6	Texas	11.4
Washington	34.4	Florida	11.8
West Virginia	34.4	South Dakota	14.8
Alaska	33.7	Virginia	15.0
Ohio	31.3	Georgia	15.1
Illinois	30.4	Oklahoma	15.3
Indiana	30.4	Kansas	15.4
Montana	29.2	New Hampshire	15.8
Wisconsin	28.5	Arkansas	16.0
Rhode Island	28.3	Arizona	16.0
Hawaii	28.0	Mississippi	16.2
Missouri	27.6	Louisiana	16.4
California	27.0	North Dakota	17.1
Minnesota	26.2	Utah	17.7
Oregon	26.1	Vermont	18.0
New Jersey	25.7	Nebraska	18.1
Delaware	25.2	Colorado	18.1
Massachusetts	24.9	Idaho	18.4
Maine	24.1	Wyoming	18.9
Kentucky	24.0	Tennessee	19.3
Nevada	23.8	New Mexico	19.0
Connecticut	23.0	Alabama	21.8
Maryland/D.C.	22.8	Iowa	22.2

Source: BNA 1982 (p. 68)

In addition, union members tend to be more heavily concentrated in large urban areas, SMSA's (Standard Metropolitan Statistical Areas), as defined by the Bureau of the Census. Union density is lowest in rural areas and small towns.

The general trend of population growth over the past several decades, with some notable exceptions (California being the most significant), has been away from those areas of high union concentration to those with low levels of union density. These population shifts are summarized in figures 8 and 9. It is these trends that provide much of the fuel for the theories of union decline based upon population shifts.

One word of caution might be introduced so that we do not reach precipitous conclusions. While the union densities in most highly unionized states have been dropping over the last decade (U.S. Dept. of Labor, BLS 1980b, p. 414; Bureau of National Affairs 1982, p. 68), those in many of the less heavily unionized states in the South and Southwest have risen or are holding firm (even in the face of large population increases).[3]

2. *Industrial Characteristics.* The distribution of union members by industry is also highly uneven in this country. Since the CIO organizing drives of the 1930s, the traditionally highly unionized sectors of the economy have consisted until recently of mining, construction, manufacturing, transportation, and public utilities. Also appropriate to add to this grouping today are communication workers, state, local, and federal government employees (including postal workers). By 1980, two-thirds of all federal employees were covered by union contracts.[4] The agricultural, service, finance, and trade sectors have historically been the least organized. State and local government, formerly among the least organized, is today highly unionized. These results are summarized in table 13.

Two trends are apparent in looking at figures 10–12. First, certain industries, particularly in manufacturing, have increased their operation in states of low union density (viz., the Sunbelt) and decreased their activities in the areas of high union density. Second, except for the continuing decline in percentage and absolute number of agricultural employment and increases in state and local government employment, all major employment shifts by industrial sector have been away from the traditional union strongholds toward the less unionized sectors.

3. See Marshall (1968) for an analysis of the 1939–64 period. He argues that the drop in union density for the country as a whole from 1954 to 1964 was not paralleled in the South. A similar case, I believe, could be made for the more recent period. Data for the past decade may be found in BLS 1980c.

4. See U.S. Office of Personnel Management (1981). See also Freeman (1984).

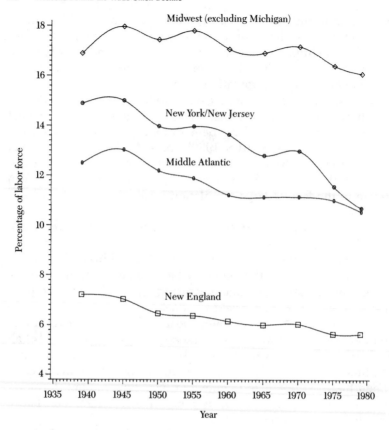

Source: U.S. Dept. of Labor, BLS 1979c, 1981d.

FIGURE 8.   Percentage of nonagricultural workers by region by year

3. *Occupational Characteristics.* Unions have traditionally been strongest in this country among blue-collar workers. In 1980, according to Current Population Survey (CPS) data, 41.4 percent of all blue-collar workers were members of trade unions, while only 18.5 percent of white-collar workers and 18.4 percent of service workers were members (U.S. Dept. of Labor, BLS 1981e, pp. 6–7). A detailed breakdown of union membership percentages by occupation is given in table 14.

As is generally known, the changes in the occupational structure are toward lesser percentages of blue-collar workers (although up to 1980, there was little indication of absolute declines; from 1980 to 1985, there were declines, particularly in

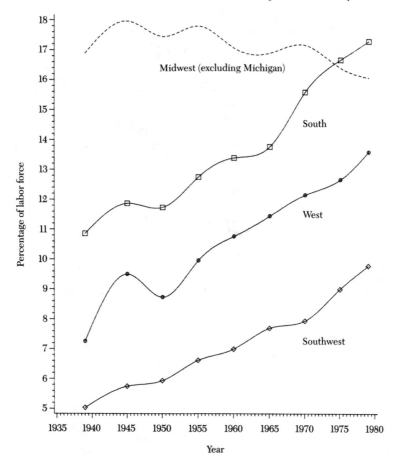

Source: U.S. Dept. of Labor, BLS 1979c, 1981d.

FIGURE 9.   Percentage of nonagricultural workers by region by year
                (continued)

manufacturing), and toward greater percentages of white-collar
and service workers.[5] In addition, there has been a sharp increase in the percentage of supervisory workers in manufacturing (summarized in figure 13).

Occupational categories are notoriously crude, particularly in
their ability to capture the changing nature of work. Many

5. For pre-1980 figures, see table 17. For breakdowns on the losses of
approximately two million workers from manufacturing employment from 1979
to 1985, see BLS (1985c).

TABLE 13   Union Organization by Industrial Sector, 1980

Industry	Organized Workers	Number Employed	Percentage Organized
	(in thousands)		(Wage & Salary)
Agriculture	51	1,455	3.5%
Mining	286	892	32.1
Construction	1,574	4,982	31.6
Total Manufacturing	6,771	20,976	32.3
Durable Goods	4,366	12,546	34.8
Primary Metals	686	1,176	58.4
Auto	582	951	61.2
Lumber	103	539	19.1
Instruments	79	622	12.6
Nondurable goods	2,405	8,430	28.5
Textile	117	786	14.9
Paper	369	751	49.1
Transportation, utilities	2,903	6,048	48.0
Railroads	474	579	81.8
Communication	714	1,447	49.7
Trade	1,753	17,401	10.1
Finance, Insur., Real Est.	190	5,152	3.7
Services	4,743	26,121	18.9
Professional Services	4,086	18,451	22.1
Hospitals	692	3,901	17.7
Educational	2,767	8,062	34.3
Public Administration	1,812	5,364	33.8
Federal (except postal)	347	1,795	19.3
Postal	509	691	73.7
State	253	972	26.0
Local	703	1,906	36.9

Source: U.S. Dept. of Labor, BLS 1981e (p. 4).

Note: 1984 figures, which in general indicate minor downward changes from 1980, are available in BLS 1985. They are, however, more limited than the above; they are also only roughly compatible owing to changes in classification definitions.

service occupations, for example, have become manual, hardly differentiated in any meaningful way from many types of blue-collar occupations. Certain white-collar jobs are not so different from small assembly work.[6] Nevertheless, certain general trends are worth noting. These are summarized in tables 14 and 15 below.

6. For a discussion of the proletarianization of postal work, see Bagli (1980).

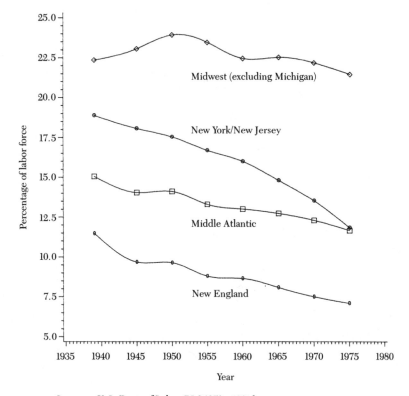

Source: U.S. Dept. of Labor, BLS 1979c, 1981d.

FIGURE 10.   Percentage of manufacturing workers by region by year

4. Racial Composition. Blacks and other nonwhite workers have
become increasingly more organized than white workers over
the last decade. In 1980, 32.1 percent of nonwhite workers were
organized compared to 24.9 percent of white workers (25.7
percent overall), according to CPS figures (U.S. Dept. of Labor,
BLS 1981e, p. 6). Occupational breakdowns for these figures are
given in table 16.

Most striking is the disparity of unionization rates between
black women and white women, 27.4 percent compared to 17.5
percent respectively. Many of these differences may in fact be
due to the crude occupational classifications that hide the location of nonwhites at the bottom of various categories, often ones
that are more likely to be unionized. A good part of the rise in
black unionization rates is often attributed, not to new organiz-

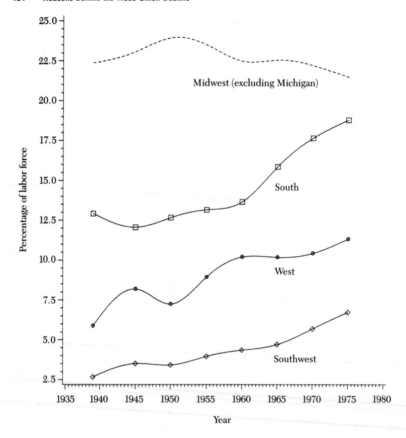

Source: U.S. Dept. of Labor, BLS 1979c, 1981d.

FIGURE 11.   Percentage of manufacturing workers by region by year
(continued)

ing, but to the movement of black workers in large numbers into
highly unionized basic industry.

It has been a common argument that black workers might be
more resistant to union organizing than white workers because of
the explicit or implicit support of discriminatory practices by
most unions.[7]

7. There has, of course, been a traditional argument that black workers were
at one time anti-union, often breaking strikes. They supposedly broke strikes
since that was the only way they could obtain employment in otherwise racially
exclusionary employment markets. Even Irving Bernstein refers to "the firm
establishment of the Negro in the role of strikebreaker" (1966, p. 108, also p. 126).
This view is criticized by Foner (1964, pp. 243–44), Nyden (1974), and Meier and
Rudnick (1979).

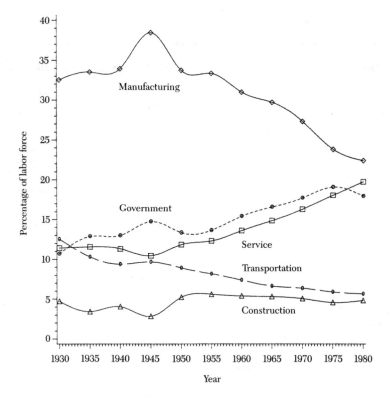

Source: U.S. Dept. of Labor, BLS 1979b, 1982e.

FIGURE 12.   Percentage of nonagricultural workers by industrial sector by
year

The trends are complicated and multidimensional. On the one
hand, the disparity between white and nonwhite unionization
rates is not large, especially when we take into account the
disproportionate number of nonwhites in blue-collar and other
more organized categories. The nonwhite population is growing
at a faster rate than that of whites, a highly pronounced trend
among the age group just entering the labor force. The extremely
large and growing unemployment among young nonwhites and
the declines in those traditionally unionized sectors where
nonwhites are disproportionately employed (like auto and steel),
however, do nothing to suggest that there will be rapid increases
(not to mention automatic ones) in black unionization rates as
compared to white ones.

TABLE 14   Employed Union and Association Members by Occupation, 1980

Occupation	Number (in thousands)	Percentage Organized
Blue-collar	11,763	41.4%
Craft and kindred	4,571	41.2
Carpenters	284	33.9
Construction (except carpenters)	1,116	50.4
Machinists	397	56.9
Auto Mechanics	223	24.0
Operatives (except transport)	4,229	42.4
Motor Vehicles	315	85.8
Transport Equipment	1,514	46.9
Service Workers	2,221	18.4
Private Household	4	.4
Cleaning	644	27.8
Food	426	9.7
Personal	164	15.1
Health	363	19.4
Protective	621	43.9
White-collar	8,483	18.5
Professional, technical	3,997	27.7
Engineers	148	10.6
Health workers (except doctors)	418	20.1
Teachers (except college)	2,022	61.8
Technicians	252	22.7
Managers and administrators	868	9.7
Clerical and kindred	3,365	19.2
Sales workers	253	5.0

Source: BLS 1981e.

5. Women. According to CPS data, 18.9 percent of employed women belonged to labor organizations in 1980 compared to 31 percent of men (U.S. Dept. of Labor, BLS 1981e, p. 7). The percentage of women in unions has increased substantially since 1954 (see tables 17 and 18). The percentage of women in the work force, however, has also risen dramatically. Rates of participation in the labor force of females over twenty years of age increased from 35.5 percent in 1961 (30.7 percent in 1948) to 51.1 percent in 1979 (U.S. Dept. of Labor, BLS 1980b, p. 45). Thus there has been a virtual explosion in the percentage of the labor force of one group traditionally regarded as less open to unions (see table 19). My best guess is that the percentage of women in

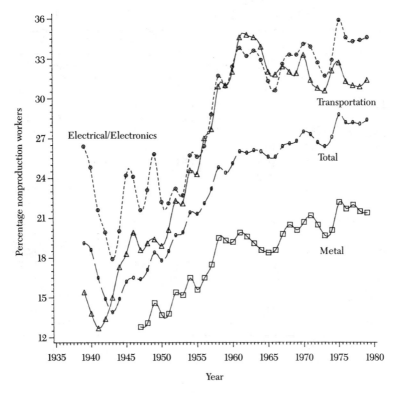

Source: U.S. Dept. of Labor, BLS 1979b, 1982e.

FIGURE 13.   Percentage of nonproduction workers in manufacturing in selected industrial groups

the labor force who are in unions has increased slightly from
1960 to 1980. No reliable figures are available for breakdowns by
sex (or race) prior to the 1973 CPS surveys; thus this judgment is
by no means easily extrapolated from the data.

6. *Education.* There is no publicly published time-series information for the average educational levels of union and nonunion
workers (although it is possible to extract post-1973 information
from Current Population Survey tapes). CPS data for 1977,
however, indicate that a disproportionately large number of
union members have only a high school or less than high school
education, while a disproportionately large number of nonunion
members have some post–high school education (Freeman and
Medoff 1984a, p. 27). It is generally assumed that union members are less educated than nonunion members (U.S. Dept. of

TABLE 15   Distribution of Employed Workers by Occupation, 1960–1981

	White-collar				Blue-collar			Service
Year	Total	Prof.	Manag.	Sales	Cleric.	Total	Craft.	Oper.	Total
1960	43.4%	11.4%	10.7%	6.4%	14.8%	36.6%	13.0%	18.2%	12.2%
1962	44.4	12.0	11.1	6.2	15.1	36.1	13.0	18.0	12.6
1964	44.5	12.3	10.7	6.1	15.3	36.6	13.0	18.6	12.8
1966	45.4	12.8	10.1	6.1	16.2	37.0	13.2	19.0	12.6
1968	46.8	13.6	10.2	6.1	16.9	36.3	13.2	18.4	12.4
1970	48.3	14.2	10.5	6.2	17.4	35.3	12.9	17.7	12.4
1971	48.3	14.0	11.0	6.4	17.0	34.4	12.9	16.4	13.5
1972	47.8	14.0	9.8	6.6	17.4	35.0	13.2	16.6	13.4
1973	47.8	14.0	10.2	6.4	17.2	34.4	13.4	16.9	13.2
1974	48.6	14.4	10.4	6.3	17.5	34.6	13.4	16.2	13.2
1975	49.8	15.0	10.5	6.4	17.8	33.0	12.9	15.2	13.7
1976	50.0	15.2	10.6	6.3	17.8	33.1	12.9	15.3	13.7
1977	49.9	15.1	10.7	6.3	17.8	33.4	13.1	15.3	13.7
1978	50.0	15.1	10.7	6.3	17.9	33.4	13.1	15.3	13.6
1979	50.9	15.5	10.8	6.4	18.2	33.1	13.3	15.0	13.2
1980	52.2	16.1	11.2	6.3	18.6	31.7	12.9	14.2	13.3
1981	52.7	16.4	11.5	6.4	18.5	31.1	12.6	14.0	13.4

Source: Unpublished BLS data.

Labor, BLS 1980b, p. 141). The concentration of organized workers in blue-collar occupations and the lower unionization rates among more highly educated administrative, professional, and technical workers are undoubtedly the basis for this belief. Thus, if the changing occupational structure were to require higher educational levels among the more rapidly growing occupations, this could conceivably decrease the percentage of the work force most readily open to unionization.

The trend to higher levels of education in the labor force has been a steady one for more than one hundred years (U.S. Bureau of the Census 1975, 1: 380; 1982, p. 143; Kochan 1980, p. 73). Various studies confirm that since World War II ended in 1945, there has been a large increase in the median number of years of schooling completed by workers in this country. This trend will most likely continue unabated. As many have noted, however, the number of years of schooling does not mean that the real educational level of the labor force will be higher, considering the generally acknowledged lower quality of education that seems to have affected all spheres of society.

TABLE 16   Occupational Distribution of Nonwhites, 1959–1981

Year	White-collar					Blue-collar			Service
	Total	Prof.	Manag.	Sales.	Cleric.	Total	Craft	Oper.	Total
1959	14.4%	4.6%	2.5%	1.3%	6.1%	41.2%	5.9%	19.9%	31.8%
1960	16.1	4.8	2.6	1.5	7.3	40.1	6.0	20.4	31.7
1962	16.8	5.3	2.7	1.5	7.3	39.7	6.1	20.1	32.8
1964	18.8	6.8	2.6	1.7	7.7	40.6	7.1	20.5	32.2
1966	20.9	7.0	2.6	1.8	9.5	41.9	7.6	22.6	31.4
1968	24.4	7.8	2.8	1.9	11.8	42.4	8.0	23.6	28.3
1970	27.9	9.1	3.5	2.1	13.2	42.2	8.2	23.7	26.0
1971	29.1	9.0	4.1	2.3	13.7	39.9	7.9	21.7	27.6
1972	29.8	9.5	3.7	2.2	14.4	39.9	8.7	21.3	27.2
1973	31.1	9.9	4.1	2.3	14.9	40.8	8.9	22.2	25.3
1974	32.0	10.4	4.1	2.3	15.2	40.2	9.4	21.9	25.1
1975	34.2	11.4	4.4	2.7	15.7	37.4	8.8	20.0	25.8
1976	34.6	11.7	4.4	2.5	16.1	37.6	8.7	20.6	25.4
1977	35.3	11.8	4.8	2.6	16.1	37.6	9.0	20.3	25.0
1978	36.2	11.7	4.8	2.8	16.9	37.2	8.8	20.5	24.1
1979	37.9	12.2	5.2	2.8	17.7	36.7	9.4	19.9	23.2
1980	39.2	12.7	5.2	2.9	18.4	35.8	9.6	19.4	23.1
1981	41.1	13.9	5.8	3.0	18.4	35.8	9.2	19.2	22.4

Source: Unpublished BLS data.

7. *Age.* The median age of members of labor organizations is considerably higher than the median age of unorganized workers, according to CPS estimates. In 1980, the median age of organized workers was 37.7 years, and only 33.8 years for unorganized workers (U.S. Dept. of Labor, BLS 1981e, pp. 33–64, tables 12–15).

The average age of the labor force, on the other hand, has been steadily declining since the 1950s (U.S. Bureau of the Census 1975, 1: 131; 1982, p. 379; U.S. Dept. of Labor, BLS 1981e, p. 33). As Thomas Kochan notes, the effects of the post–World War II "baby boom" were felt in full during the 1970s, as the labor force grew at unprecedented rates.[8] The median age of the labor force dropped from 39.6 years in 1970 to 34.9 years in 1980. Thus there are increasing numbers of younger workers at a time when the "natural" constituency of unions appears to be among older workers.

8. See BLS special labor force reports for further details. (2.3 percent increase per year in the first half of the seventies, 1.9 percent in the second).

TABLE 17   Female Membership of Unions and Associations, 1954–1978

Year	Number (in thousands)	Percentage of Total Membership
	Unions and Associations	
1970	5,398	23.9%
1972	5,736	24.9
1974	6,038	25.0
1976	6,438	26.7
1978	6,857	28.1
	Unions	
1954	2,950	16.6
1956	3,400	18.6
1958	3,274	18.2
1960	3,304	18.3
1962	3,272	18.6
1964	3,413	19.0
1966	3,689	19.3
1968	3,940	19.5
1970	4,282	20.7
1972	4,524	21.7
1974	4,600	21.3
1976	4,648	22.0
1978	5,267	24.2

Source: BLS 1980a (p. 62).

TABLE 18   Female Union Members, 1973–1980

Year	Total Members (in thousands)	Percentage of Women Workers	Percentage of Organized Workers
1973	4,184	13.9%	23.1%
1974	4,268	13.8	23.4
1975	4,187	13.5	25.0
1976	4,431	13.6	25.5
1977	5,329	15.7	27.6
1978	5,499	15.3	28.1
1979	6,156	16.6	29.3
1980	6,056	15.9	30.1

Source: BLS, CPS; BNA 1982 (p. 3).

TABLE 19   Percentage of Women in Labor Force, 1947–1979

Year	Percentage
1947	31.8%
1950	33.9
1955	35.7
1960	37.8
1965	39.3
1970	43.4
1972	43.9
1974	45.7
1976	47.4
1978	50.1
1979	51.1

Source: BLS 1980b (p. 6).

8. *Unit Size.* Larger workplace units have traditionally been the strongholds of unions. In all countries they have generally been the first organized; only later, if at all, are smaller units more systematically unionized. Such has certainly been the case in this country. One of the buttresses of the "saturationist" arguments in the 1950s was that the most likely places (i.e., the large workplace units in the traditional union sectors) were all organized, while the unorganized places tended to be the more difficult-to-organize smaller ones (Bell 1953, 1954). One contemporary analyst even ascribes the difficulties of new organizing in New England to unit size:

The lowest rate of representation elections won in 1979 was not in the Sunbelt, as one might have thought, but in New England. The best explanation seems to be that unions were going for smaller firms in New England than elsewhere. (Riche 1981, p. 30)

In examining the sizes of workplace units, we find there has been a decided trend during the past two decades toward a decreasing average number of employees. The decreases appear to be largely among new installations. Klein (1982) finds, in examining the U.S. Census Bureau's County Business Patterns surveys, that the proportion of workers employed in firms of over five hundred employees peaked in 1967 at 27.6 percent, then dropped steadily to 22.4 percent in 1979. The same pattern holds for workers in manufacturing. A compilation of results for 1947–82 is given below in table 20.

TABLE 20   Number of Large Manufacturing Establishments by Year

Year	Total Number Estabs.	Total Number Workers	Number of Large Establishments by Size				
			2,500+	1000–2,499	500–999	250–499	100–249
1947	241,000	14,294,304	504	1,431	2,729	5,555	14,323
1954	286,000	15,651,000	535	1,473	2,837	6,042	15,647
1958	298,000	15,393,000	498	1,363	2,757	6,240	16,132
1963	306,000	16,234,000	544	1,375	2,942	6,639	17,614
1967	305,000	18,492,000	674	1,639	3,450	7,749	19,762
1972	312,000	18,032,000	582	1,527	3,481	8,032	20,800
1977	350,000	18,515,000	581	1,480	3,677	8,364	21,546
1982	348,385	17,818,000	482	1,388	3,323	7,874	21,281

Source: U.S. Bureau of the Census, Census of Manufacturers, 1947–82 (vol. 1: Summary Statistics).

These figures suggest that few very large manufacturing plants are being built. Since most of those that already exist are organized, unions must look for their new members in smaller units. This, as Voos argues, could create potential difficulties:

Since it is likely that there are economies of scale in organizing, small plants are both more difficult and more expensive to organize; exacerbating this trend, they are increasingly located at dispersed sites in small towns. (1982, p. 56)

Each of the above eight factors supposedly has an impact on both union growth and new organizing. First, they reduce (or in some few cases increase) the "pro-union share" that automatically will become union. Second, they make more difficult (or in some few cases easier) new union organizing because the fastest growing unorganized constituencies are those least likely to be organized into unions.

There are various levels on which one may try to assess how important each of these changes is on the development of labor organizations in this country. Freeman and Medoff (1976, 1984a) estimate that approximately 55 to 60 percent of the decline in union membership may be accounted for by these structural and compositional changes. They also assign relative importance to many of the various factors: .5 percent decrease in union density to geographic shifts, 1.2 percent drop to industrial shifts, 2.3 percent drop to occupational shifts, and 2.3 percent decline to all of the compositional (or personal) characteristics taken together (i.e., race, age, sex, and education). Based on these figures, Freeman and Medoff make the following argument (1984a): Even were one to accept the claim of those who take the structural and compositional changes as having causal significance, there would still be 40–45 percent of the decline in union density left to explain. Presumably included in this category would be (1) declines in traditional union strongholds, for example, construction and New England manufacturing, (2) declines among the percentage of blue-collar workers organized, and (3) the relative stability (and even in some cases rise) of union densities in the South.

The assumption by those who argue for the importance of structural and compositional changes is, of course, that unions will continue to grow and organize in the same proportions as they have in the past. This, as Freeman and Medoff point out, is a very large assumption:

Indeed, even if nearly all of the observed decline were attributable to structural changes, the story of the decline in unionism would not be complete, for like other organizations, unions might be expected to take steps to alter their services to appeal to growing sectors of the market. (1984a, p. 4)

There are a number of reasons, I believe, why one might expect union growth not to become mired in its past cross-sectional propensities. The development of public sector unionism is a concrete example of why it is inappropriate to assume that unions will continue to gain members most readily in those areas where they have previously been strong. During the 1950s, the saturationists argued that the public sector was not an area where unions were likely to gain strength. Their arguments, many of them quite persuasive, made a key unwarranted assumption: since union growth had been slow there in the past, it would continue to be slow there in the future. The opposite has proven to be the case.

In addition, many of the changes in the structure and composition of the labor force have been paralleled by similar changes in other countries. Canada, France, Britain, and other economically developed capitalist countries have had industrial and occupational shifts, similar changes in the proportion of highly educated, younger, and female workers entering the labor force. In these other countries, unions have succeeded in altering their appeal, gaining new strength in many of those areas where they had previously not been strong.

In many ways, it is sophistic to claim that changes in the structure and composition of the labor force are the ultimate (rather than the immediate) reason for the failure of union growth. In a growing, dynamic economy, such changes will be continually taking place. Growth in labor organization has always been characterized by organizing among sectors of the population where previous organization and collective action have been weak. It is not primarily the lack of automatic growth that has hurt labor organizations in this country, but the lack of success in new union organizing. Thus what is most important for us here is to evaluate the degree to which union prospects for organizing successes are related to their current cross-sectional patterns of organization. In this regard, I will first discuss the questions of the personal characteristics (or composition) of the labor force. One reason for beginning with these is that they are, in my opinion, the least convincing.

RACE

Nonwhite workers (85 percent of whom are black) are, as has been noted, a growing sector of the population and increasingly more heavily unionized than their white counterparts. Some researchers have suggested that black workers may be becoming less receptive to unions because of the discriminatory practices of the unions themselves. Attitudinal data from a number of sources indicate that black workers, despite such practices, are far more receptive to joining unions than are white workers. In a large 1977 survey of nonunion workers, 30 percent indicated they would vote for a union if an election were held at their workplace. Sixty-seven percent of the black and other minority workers gave such a preference (Kochan 1979, p. 25). Unionization has been found to raise the average wage of workers in a unit (to cause an upward shift in the mean of earnings distribution). It has also been found to reduce the dispersion of wages (i.e., the range between the highest and the lowest paid). Thus unionization provides special economic advantages for workers at the bottom of the pay structure (Farber and Saks 1980, p. 352). Blacks are, of course, heavily concentrated in these lower positions. Even when one controls for their position, however, survey data accumulated during NLRB election campaigns find black workers "significantly more likely" to vote for union representation:

This suggests that blacks perceive that unions will provide more benefits to them than to similarly situated whites. One possibility is that blacks gain more than whites from the imposition of the quasi-legal framework for handling grievances that often accompanies unionization. Such a framework may be valuable in protecting blacks from certain aspects of discrimination on the job. (Farber and Saks 1980, p. 365)

The high degree of pro-union sentiments among unorganized black workers does not explain the slightly higher degree of union organization among black workers today. Black workers have not become heavily unionized mainly because of new organizing efforts. Rather it has been the result of their large-scale movement into highly unionized industries, including auto, steel, and transportation. The question that really needs to be explained is why black workers are not more highly union-ized today, given their clearly expressed preferences. Many unorganized black and other nonwhite workers, of course, con-stitute small minorities in predominantly white units. Many others, however, work in low-wage sectors where they constitute a substantial proportion of the work force. One reason for the failure to organize may be the high degree of resistance among employers (as has certainly been the case in the textile industry). Whatever the ultimate reason for the failure of unions to cash in on the willingness of black workers to unionize, one thing is clear: while none of the data can prove conclusively that the increase in th black population and its higher unionization rates will necessarily lead to higher degrees of new union organizing, there is certainly no basis for saying that these trends among black workers help explain declines in new organizing suc-cesses.

WOMEN

As already indicated, women are less highly organized than men and constitute a rapidly increasing segment of the labor force. Many industrial relations researchers (including Bell and Dun-lop) have argued that women are inherently less likely to join unions than men. Such arguments are presented with much vehemence by many orthodox commentators. Dunlop, writing just after World War II, relates this to their lack of commitment: "One of the problems of organizing women arises from the fact that they expect only a short working life and then plan to retire to the more arduous duties of the household" (1948, p. 84). Bell seems to concur with this view (1954, p. 235). Bok and Dunlop, even in an era when the relation of women to work has changed substantially, go a step further:

To some extent, the difference is explained by the heavy employment of women in clerical and sales occupations and in service industries, where unions have traditionally made little headway. . . . In general, however, women outside the professions appear not to place the importance men do on matters connected with employment; they frequently do not conceive of themselves as remaining in a job for a working lifetime. (Bok and Dunlop 1970, p. 44)

A large number of other pluralist writers go still further. Jack Barbash, for example, writes, "Women workers, with notable exceptions, are not the material out of which strong unions are typically built" (1964, p. 105). Such views are repeated by many others, including Seidman (1954) and Shister (1967).[9] Even in 1985, one widely used labor economics textbook found the rising percentage of women in the work force to be a major factor explaining decreasing union membership (Ehrenberg and Smith 1985, p. 373). One surprising exception is Irving Bernstein, who argues:

In fact, we know nothing about the comparative propensity of men and women to join unions. In the abstract there is no reason to anticipate a difference, because the economic and social forces that shape the decision work on both sexes. Women, that is, tend to be as indifferent or as militant as men. The difference in the membership rate, rather, is to be explained largely by the fact that women work primarily in industries and occupations into which unions have not made a deep penetration, primarily office, sales, and services. In those areas both sexes are relatively unorganized. (1961, p. 150)

Attitudinal and other data on the propensities and desires of women workers to join labor organizations do not support the assertions that women are less "organizable" than men. Kochan (1979) finds that among nonunionized workers, women are significantly more likely to say they would vote for union representation than men. Forty percent of all unorganized women, as opposed to 30 percent of all the unorganized workers surveyed, said they would favor unionization. Other studies either have supported this finding or have found that male/ female differentials were insignificant when other factors were controlled. Antos, Chandler, and Mellow (1980) report in their

9. For additional references, see the notes on page 116 of Voos 1982.

study of 1976 CPS data that controlling for differences in occupation, industry, and wage dispersion eliminates the most significant determinants of the lower cross-sectional unionization rates for females. Hirsch likewise finds union membership differences between males and females are "generally not significant when industry structure variables are included" (1980, p. 155). Farber and Saks, in their analysis of survey data accumulated during NLRB election campaigns, find little difference in pro-union tendencies of males and females when other factors are controlled for. In the same work unit, however, they find women *more* likely to vote for unions than men, "just because females are more likely to be located in the bottom part of the intrafirm earnings distributions" (Farber and Saks 1980, p. 365).

Thus it is only reasonable to conclude that the greater entry of women into the work force is not a significant barrier to unionization. It may be, however, that certain unions with older male organizing staffs will have to learn to relate to new constituencies whose values and interests do not totally coincide with their own.

AGE

As noted earlier, the average age of union members in the labor force is considerably older than the average age of the nonunion worker. This fact is somewhat less compelling than evidence about sex and race because the median age of workers in a union shop is not a significant reflection of the median age of the workers in that shop when it was organized.[10] In fact, given the well-known stability of union compared to nonunion shops, one could probably have predicted that the average age in unionized workplaces would increase over time after the initial organizing.

When various other factors are taken into account (including occupation, industry, race, and sex), several researchers have found little actual variation in the importance of age as a cross-sectional characteristic of union membership (Antos, Chandler, and Mellow 1980; Hirsch 1980). Attitudinal data reported by Kochan (1979) indicate that younger blue-collar workers not in unions are somewhat more ready to join them than their older counterparts. After controlling for various factors, including wage rates, Farber and Saks found that older workers participat-

10. Freeman and Medoff (1976, 1984b) in their otherwise penetrating analysis fail to take this into account, actually ascribing the changing age of the work force as a potential liability for unions.

ing in NLRB certification elections were much less likely to vote for union representation. They explain this by saying that this result "is in accord with views that older workers are more 'conservative' and reluctant to join new organizations which will have an uncertain impact on their jobs" (1980, p. 366).

It is reasonable to conclude that the increasing age of the average union member and the decreasing age of the labor force do not provide fertile soil for even a partial explanation of the declining union density of U.S. labor organizations.

EDUCATION

Many writers in the past have suggested that more educated workers are less likely to join unions that their less educated counterparts. This view is widely accepted even today. As Martha Farnsworth Riche writes: "The labor force of the 1970s grew rapidly in several directions unfavorable to unions: more women, more youths, more educated workers" (1981, p. 28).

Average education of union membership is lower than that of the work force as a whole. Education, however, does not appear significant even by cross-section when other factors (particularly occupation) are controlled (Antos, Chandler, and Mellow 1980). Most attitudinal studies have found the educational level to be among the least consequential of variables. Kochan's analysis of the 1977 Quality of Work survey data found union attitudes of nonunion workers to have no significant differences based on their educational attainments; he did find, however, that higher education correlated with a higher approval rating for unions (Kochan 1979, p. 24). Farber and Saks found that education had no "significant impact on the vote" of workers participating in NLRB certification elections (1980, p. 365).

Despite the prevalence of the view that more highly educated workers are less likely to vote for unions than less educated workers, there is no compelling evidence to support such a contention.

Those who suggest that compositional changes in the labor force will make organizing most difficult are most likely wrong. A more highly educated and more heavily female labor force seems to present no insurmountable difficulties. An imaginative leadership might even be able to have greater success among women workers if it geared itself to their special grievances and their recently emerging independent political attitudes. The changing age and national composition of the labor force, taken as independent factors, both seem to present greater possibilities for success in organizing for unions instead of the reverse.

Rather than explaining labor union decline, the focus on the compositional changes raises the question of why unions have not been more successful in light of these changes, which, if anything, have largely been in their favor.

GEOGRAPHY

As discussed earlier, the past several decades have been accompanied by major shifts of population from the more heavily unionized states in the Northeast, Middle Atlantic, and Midwest regions to the less unionized states in the South and Southwest. Much evidence exists on the high degree of opposition to unions in the Sunbelt by employers and by politicians. This stance is in part reflected in the lower rates of unionization there.

In addition, small-town and rural areas have traditionally suffered from low unionization rates. The South and Southwest (with the exception of California) have until recently been disproportionately rural and small-town. Now, of course, urbanization and industrialization in these areas are catching up with the rest of the country. Yet certain commentators have suggested that it is precisely for this reason that workers in the Sunbelt are less receptive to unions. Hirsch, for example, argues:

Unionization is expected to be lower in those SMSAs showing the most rapid population growth. These labor markets will tend to have labor-force members who are relatively more mobile and have less permanent job attachment; the effect will be decreased demand for unionization and increased organizing costs. The secular decline in private sector unionism also implies that SMSAs with recent rapid growth will have a lower percentage of their labor force organized. For instance, lower unionization in the South and the West than in the country as a whole may be the result, in part, of the recent rapid growth in those areas (1980, p. 151).[11]

This argument is both counterfactual as well as unreasonable. The South and Southwest have been among the least unionized parts of the country at least since the CIO organizing drives of the middle and late 1930s succeeded in organizing the bulk of manufacturing employees in the North, Midwest, and West. But

11. This is the neoclassical welfare paradigm of cost-benefit analysis carried to a rather bizarre extreme.

one may see from looking at table 21 that states in the Sunbelt have maintained or increased their union densities during the recent period while more heavily unionized states have in general decreased. This would indicate that, if anything, the population shifts have aided new union organizing in those areas of most rapidly growing population.

TABLE 21   Union Density by State, 1970–1978

State	1970	1972	1974	1976	1978
Alabama	22.6%	21.2%	23.9%	24.0%	24.6%
Arkansas	19.4	17.7	18.1	18.5	17.6
Mississippi	14.9	14.0	13.3	13.2	15.0
North Carolina	9.4	10.4	9.8	11.1	10.7
Louisiana	19.4	18.0	17.7	17.6	16.9
Maryland/D.C.	24.5	25.0	25.5	25.4	25.0
California	35.7	34.5	33.3	32.2	28.8
Illinois	37.3	37.8	37.1	34.3	33.4
Michigan	43.5	42.6	42.4	36.6	38.5
Minnesota	31.9	31.6	28.3	28.7	27.6
New Jersey	31.2	32.7	32.3	29.9	27.3
Ohio	38.9	37.7	36.4	35.8	33.6
West Virginia	46.8	45.4	41.9	42.6	40.4

Source: BLS 1980b (p. 414).

It is only recently that researchers have begun to question seriously the opinion that it is more difficult for unions to win certification elections in the South and Southwest. Yet there have been some small pieces of research that suggest that the picture is not as one-sided as the vast majority of commentators view it. Joseph Rose, for example, in his study of one thousand NLRB elections between March and September of 1966, concludes that there are only "slight variations in election results among geographic regions ... with even a slightly higher percentage of union triumphs in the South" (1972, p. 57). This is a relatively minor point in Rose's article and has obviously been disregarded by most commentators.

Other studies, while not dealing directly with certification results, call into question certain of the assumptions of those who argue about the resistance of Southern workers to unions. Of special interest is Thomas Kochan's 1979 investigation, which summarizes both his own research and material from the 1977

Quality of Life survey conducted by the University of Michigan's Survey Center:

In general, findings concerning the demographic characteristics suggest there are *no specific subgroups in the population that are consistently unwilling to join a union* if their job conditions warrant unionization. At the same time, there were no specific subgroups, *with the exception of nonwhite workers,* that appeared willing to join unions as a matter of course. (Kochan 1979, p. 27; emphasis mine)

Moreover, in breaking his data down by region, Kochan found that

including regional variables in the analysis also provided somewhat surprising results. Although it has often been argued that Southern workers are less interested in joining unions than their Northern counterparts, the negative coefficient on the Southern variable was significant only for white collar workers. (1979, p. 28)

This, as Kochan points out, means that blue-collar workers in the South are no less organizable than those in the North. The argument about the resistance of Southern culture to unions is not as simple, or as obviously true, as many would have us believe.

These attitudinal data suggest that unorganized workers in the Sunbelt are at least as ready to join unions as their Northern counterparts. Analysis of the survey data from the 1977 Quality of Work study indicates that 35 percent of nonunion workers in the South compared to 29 percent of those in the country as a whole would vote for unions in a union certification election (Kochan 1979, p. 25). This study suggests some differences between blue- and white-collar workers in the South (as Kochan notes above), the latter being slightly less likely to vote for unions than their nonunion counterparts nationally. The most significant regional effect in this study, however, was the stronger anti-union sentiment among unorganized workers, both blue- and white-collar, in the North Central (or Midwestern) part of the country. This and the Southern pro-union sentiment are the two most surprising results of this study.

Cross-tabulation of NLRB victory rates by state shows similarly unexpected results. States in the Southwest have significantly higher victory rates in NLRB union certification elections for the period 1972–84 than do other regions of the country. These results are listed below in table 22. Further, the victory rates have in general been rising during this period, having been

TABLE 22   Union Victories by State in the Southwest, 1972–1984

State	Number	Average Rate	Trend
All	89,634	49.1%	Declining
Arizona	932	54.6	Steady
Colorado	1,200	52.6	Rising
New Mexico	455	54.7	Varying
Texas	2,566	50.2	Steady
California	10,589	51.2	Steady

lower than the national average for the first several years. Victory rates in the South are, as reported in Goldfield 1982, highly uneven, which underscores the importance of not merely aggregating the states in the South in one category and leaving it at that. Of special importance are the rates near the national average for Mississippi and Alabama, the heartland of the Deep South.[12] Virginia, and not surprisingly, West Virginia (not really a Southern state) also have high victory rates (see table 23). Aggregating these states with Florida, Georgia, and North Carolina clearly leaves something to be desired.

Of additional significance is the almost doubled average size of the election units in the South (this pattern does not hold at all in the Southwest). For all states during this period, the average size of election units is 64.2. The figures for states in the South are given below in table 24. As will be discussed later, a doubling of the size, say, from 65 to 130, may account for as much as a 6 percent lesser chance of success, all other factors being equal. These figures give us added reason to suspect that the difficulties in new organizing in the South, while real, may not be as detrimental to successful unionization as many have suggested.

The cross-tabulations presented above do not control for other factors, including industry, occupation, size, union, and employer resistance. Such control has been sought using a cross-sectional regression model, viewing elections both by year, and also without respect to the year in which they were held,[13]

12. These states are generally regarded as those most historically resistant to integration and, as a consequence, to unionism.

13. Since this model is used to test hypotheses discussed in chapter 9 as well as ones discussed in this chapter, I have relegated its full discussion to Appendix B.

TABLE 23   Union Victories by State in the South, 1972–1984

State	Number	Average Rate	Trend
Alabama	1,243	47.1%	Rising to 51.6% in 1980
Arkansas	639	45.6	Varying
Florida	1,777	40.9	Steady
Georgia	1,630	41.6	Declining
Louisiana	1,229	43.3	Declining
Mississippi	592	50.7	Rising
North Carolina	1,014	38.1	Varying
South Carolina	417	44.7	Varying
Tennessee	1,778	45.2	Declining
Virginia	956	50.8	Steady
West Virginia	713	55.4	Steady

jointly testing variables relevant to both the political and sociological hypotheses. The initial model appears thus:

$$Y = \beta_o + \beta_1 REG + \beta_2 TRAD + \beta_3 BLUE + \beta_4 TEAM + \beta_5 ELIG + \beta_6 DELAY + \beta_7 MULT + U,$$

where Y is the dependent variable, percentage of union victories, or percentage of union votes; β_o is the intercept; REG is the state or region of the country; TRAD is the traditionally unionized sectors; BLUE is for blue-collar employees; TEAM is if the union is the Teamsters; ELIG is the number of workers eligible to vote in the unit; DELAY is the number of months preelection

TABLE 24   Average Election Unit Size by State, 1972–1984

State	Size	State	Size
Alabama	108	Arizona	54
Arkansas	105	Colorado	56
Florida	68	New Mexico	49
Georgia	101	Texas	86
Kentucky	86		
Louisiana	75	New York	60
Mississippi	130	California	51
North Carolina	155	Missouri	52
South Carolina	151	District of Columbia	79
Tennessee	107	Illinois	63
Virginia	143	Hawaii	43
		Puerto Rico	86
		Minnesota	42

delay; and MULT is for multiunion elections, and U is the error term. When this model was estimated, the variable for the South as a whole was not significant, while that for the Southwest was in fact positively significant.

In order to obtain results that give appropriate weight to each of the factors that seemed important and also to gain some measure of understanding of the trends over time, I developed a pooled cross-section time-series model.[14] When this model is estimated, one finds a slightly positive effect for both the South and the Southwest. When the model is estimated using regional variables for Mississippi, Alabama, and Virginia, each state registers a strong positive effect. These results indicate that the South does not, when other variables are taken into account, show lower rates of organizing success than other parts of the country.

There is little to substantiate the claim that union growth and new union organizing has reached a dead end because of the migration of population and industry to the unorganized South. Certainly the picture of the monolithic union-resistant South, whose recent population and industrial growth present an immovable wall to major organizing—and is a fundamental cause of present-day trade union decline—must be judged too simple.

INDUSTRIAL CHANGES

The past several decades have witnessed major employment changes in the industrial structure of the U.S. economy. The percentage of the labor force employed in manufacturing, construction, mining, transportation, and federal government—all highly unionized—has declined. Rapid growth (with larger percentage shares of the labor force) has taken place in those sectors that have traditionally had low union densities, namely trade, finance, service, and state and local government. Many have suggested that this is one of the major reasons for trade union decline in the past decades.

Cross-sectional analysis of union data does find that the industrial grouping is strongly associated with the degree of union membership it possesses, even when all other factors are taken into account (Moore and Newman 1975). Other types of data, however, suggest that the industrial concentrations of

14. The details of this model and its results are discussed in Appendix C, since it, like the previous model, is also used to test hypotheses examined in chapter 9.

union membership are not necessarily good predictors of union organizing successes.

Attitudinal data, for example, indicate that in areas of low union strength, nonunion workers are not less ready to support union certification than in other industrial sectors. What is suggested by these studies, however, is that nonunion workers in two high unionization sectors—construction and mining—are less likely to vote for unions (Freeman and Medoff 1984a).

Disaggregation of NLRB certification election results by industry indicates that union organizing in rapidly growing sectors of the economy is not less successful than in the more slowly growing traditional union sectors. Various service industries seem to have quite high victory rates. Finance and trade do not appear to do worse than other industries. Table 25 gives the average victory rates for a large number of industries.

The disaggregated results have the advantage of giving very detailed figures by industry. They have the disadvantage of not taking into account other factors that might influence the results in particular industries, including size, region of the country, occupation. When examined by the cross-section regression model, it was found that there was a small positive coefficient for traditionally unionized industries.[15] When the pooled cross-section time-series models were estimated, it was discovered that industry had only a marginal impact on the decline in union success rates in NLRB certification results. These results are summarized in Appendix C.

We may conclude the following: Although the changing industrial structure of the U.S. economy is currently having a devastating effect on union membership (note the dramatic absolute declines in membership in the auto and steel unions, for example), it is not clear that those growing (or less rapidly shrinking) sectors are impervious to concerted organizing drives by labor organizations.

OCCUPATION

Many have suggested that the changing occupational structure is a major cause of declining union strength in this country. Blue-collar jobs (the most heavily unionized) have declined as a percentage of occupations, while white-collar and service jobs (the least organized) have risen as a percentage of the labor force.

15. This model and its results are discussed in Appendix B.

TABLE 25   Union Victories in NLRB Elections in Selected Industries, 1972–1984

Industry	Number	Average Rate	Trend
Health Services	6,691	56.4%	Stable
Education Services	898	61.9	Rising
Social Services	390	72.2	Rising
Membership Organizations	222	71.1	Varying
Legal Services	105	84.8	Varying
Amusement	397	49.5	Varying
Motion Pictures	286	64.1	Rising
Misc. Repair	368	49.9	Varying
Auto Repair	1,385	50.5	Varying
Business Services	3,396	54.9	Stable
Personal Services	618	54.4	Stable
Hotels and Lodging	1,234	41.7	Varying
Real Estate	514	63.4	Rising
Insurance Agents	110	53.6	Varying
Insurance	639	47.7	Varying
Credit Agencies	169	61.3	Stable
Banking	162	37.0	Varying
Retail Stores	1,160	44.8	Varying
Eating and Drinking Places	1,916	45.8	Stable
Auto and Gas	2,524	46.2	Rising
Food Stores	2,270	56.6	Stable
Nondurable Wholesale	3,397	47.6	Stable
Durable Wholesale	3,737	47.7	Varying
Gas and Sanitary Services	1,507	52.7	Varying
Communication	2,492	57.3	Varying
Transportation Equipment	2,648	46.4	Declining
Electronic Equipment	2,642	41.0	Stable
Other Equipment	4,253	43.2	Declining
Metal Fabricating	4,028	45.9	Declining
Primary Metals	2,380	50.4	Stable
Stone, clay, glass, concrete	1,787	51.1	Stable
Rubber and Plastic	2,042	44.7	Declining
Chemicals	2,186	44.8	Declining
Printing	2,621	49.9	Declining
Textile	817	38.4	Varying
Food Products	4,645	48.9	Varying
Trade Contractors	1,354	50.8	Varying
General Contractors	646	56.1	Stable
Bituminous Coal	344	52.6	Stable

Even when controlling for other factors (including region, industry, and education), unionization is found to be negatively related to white-collar occupations in cross-sectional regression analyses (Hirsch 1980, p. 155; Antos, Chandler, and Mellow 1980, pp. 165–66). Thus the effect of the changing occupational structure on union membership, ceteris paribus, does appear to be negative. Increasing percentages of supervisory and technical workers in enterprises where they are not organized (and where blue-collar workers are organized) automatically decrease the percentage of union members in that unit. The effects of such changes on new organizing possibilities are, however, less clear.

Looking at the attitudinal data on nonunion workers taken in 1977, one finds that 39 percent of blue-collar workers compared to only 29 percent of white-collar workers are disposed to vote for unions in certification elections. The data also indicate that unionism has different appeals for each of the two groupings. While both blue- and white-collar employees view bread-and-butter issues as very important, white-collar workers were far more concerned with issues of dissatisfaction over the content of their jobs than their blue-collar nonunion counterparts:

Pro-union white-collar workers were (1) more concerned with pay inequities and fringe benefit problems than with the absolute levels of their wages, (2) more interested in participation in decision making, (3) more likely to support unionization when dissatisfied with the content of their jobs, and (4) less likely to avoid unionization because they hold a negative image of the labor movement. Female white-collar workers were more likely to support unionization than were their male counterparts. Blue-collar workers, however, were most likely to turn to unions when dissatisfied with wages, benefits, and health and safety hazards on their jobs. Younger blue-collar workers were somewhat more willing to join unions than were older blue-collar workers. (Kochan 1979, p. 28)

Farber and Saks (1980), examining survey data from twenty-nine NLRB certification election campaigns, found that position in the wage structure of a firm is relevant in determining the likelihood that an individual will vote for a union. Because of the real and perceived effect of unions in equalizing wage scales, those at the lower end of the wage scale are likely to gain more economically from unionization than will those at the upper end of the wage scale. Farber and Saks found that the workers at the lower end of the wage scale were more likely to vote union and attributed it to this latter effect. They further note that the white-collar/blue-collar wage differentials are also reduced within unionized firms.

TABLE 26   Union Victories by Occupational Classification, 1972–1984

Unit Type	Number	Average Rate
All	89,632	49.1%
Industrial	44,807	45.0
Craft	1,880	56.4
Departmental	3,672	51.7
Guards	973	62.6
Profession/Tech.	4,529	60.6
Prof./Tech./White-collar	359	49.9
Truck Drivers	9,168	49.3
Office, Clerical	7,680	51.4
All Others	16,531	53.5

Given the seeming importance of location in the wage structure of the firm, we may conclude that at least some of the attitudinal differences may be based on the particular location of white-collar workers. This would also help to explain, at least in part, why female white-collar workers are more prounion than their male counterparts, given the predominance of women in the lower-wage white-collar occupations.

Cross-tabulating NLRB union certification victory rates by occupational grouping gives the results shown in tables 26 and 27. White-collar and service workers do not appear to do worse than blue-collar workers. Still these results cannot be taken at face value since the two lowest occupational groupings have far higher unit sizes than the rest (see table 28).

Cross-sectional regression analyses confirms this suspicion. Blue-collar election units give positive coefficients, indicating that if the unit is made up of blue-collar employees, it is slightly more likely to vote union, all other factors being equal. When the data are estimated in our pooled cross-section time-series regression model, however, it is found in all variations of the model that blue-collar occupations are negatively correlated with the likelihood of victory. This means that declines in blue-collar victories (not the difficulty in the organization of white-collar units) bear a share of the responsibility for the declining victory rates by unions in NLRB certification elections over the last decade.[16]

16. For two early articles discussing the changing nature of white-collar and service jobs see Kassalow (1961, 1965).

TABLE 27   Union Victories for Industrial Units by Year

Year	Number	Average Rate
1972–84	44,807	45.0%
1972	2,698	48.6
1973	4,889	48.7
1974	4,571	46.1
1975	4,000	46.8
1976	4,556	45.2
1977	5,602	44.7
1978	3,661	45.4
1979	3,378	41.5
1980	4,016	39.8
1981	2,616	39.9
1982	1,499	45.0
1983	1,530	46.7
1984	1,791	46.2

UNIT SIZE

One of the most controversial factors is unit size. It is a generally acknowledged fact that union density is highest among larger representational units (more than five hundred employees). In this country, the larger shop units have been the backbone of union strength and organizing. The huge General Motors plants in Flint, Michigan, the big Chrysler plants in Detroit, and the immense Ford complex in River Rouge, Michigan, have been the basis of UAW strength and militancy in the auto industry. Similar things can be said about the large West Coast aircraft plants and the Chicago International Harvester plants, the larg-

TABLE 28   Union Victories by Election Unit Size, 1972–1984

Unit Type	Number	Average Unit Size
All	89,632	64.2
Industrial	44,807	86.7
Craft	1,880	25.7
Departmental	3,672	36.5
Guards	973	54.6
Prof./Tech.	4,529	65.3
Prof./Tech./White-collar	359	92.8
Truck Drivers	9,168	23.6
Office/Clerical	7,680	41.8
All Others	16,531	46.5

est of which, McCormick Works, was a byword of labor militancy in this country for almost a century before its closing in 1961. The examples abound in every industry: the large iron ore mines in the Mesabi Range, the large coal mines in Appalachia, the ports in New York City and the San Francisco Bay area, the immense General Electric plants, the large rail and trucking centers in Chicago. Large nonunion shops, like the R. R. Donnelly printing complex in Chicago, are the exceptions that prove the rule.[17]

Daniel Bell (1954), like Lenin, considers the largest workplace units to be easy organizing targets. With the disappearance of these readily unionized places, smaller units offer more difficult, slimmer pickings. Arguments about the reasons why larger units are easier to organize have included the impersonal nature of large firms, lower per capita organizing costs (since certain fixed costs are virtually the same for all units), greater economic leverage, and greater possibilities for developing class solidarity.

The question of the degree to which such large units have become "union saturated" is a difficult one to answer. It is certainly significant, however, that saturation variables in various functional forms have never given statistically significant results.[18] Further, NLRB figures make clear that a significant percentage of workers voting in certification elections each year are in units of over five hundred employees. Thus I tend to discount the importance of saturation for union organizing in the United States.

Attitudinal findings, not nearly as reliable as other forms of data, show that nonunion workers in units of less than ten or

17. Lenin, in his classic studies of Russian strike statistics, analyzes the key role played by workers in large units in the Russian labor movement. He shows convincingly that workers in larger units tend to strike sooner in reaction to political events, stay out longer, and put forth more far-reaching economic and political demands. He notes this tendency in his writings in 1907 (see, e.g., *Collected Works* [Lenin 1963, 12:65, 67]) and analyzes the strike statistics systematically in later years. Among the articles where he discusses these questions are the following: "Strike Statistics in Russia" ([1910] 1963, 16:395); "Economic and Political Strikes" ([1912] 1963, 18:83); "Factory Owners on Workers' Strikes" ([1913] 1963, 19:125); "The Results of Strikes in 1912 as compared with Those of the Past" ([1913] 1963, 19:213); "Metalworkers Strikes in 1912" ([1913] 1963, 19:311); and "Strikes in Russia" ([1913] 1963, 19:534). Lenin summarizes his conclusions concisely in the first part of his "Lectures on the 1905 Revolution" ([1917] 1963, 23:236).

18. See, for example, the model developed by Adams and Krislov (1974), discussed briefly in chapter 8.

more than a thousand are less likely to vote union, while those in unit sizes in between are somewhat more likely.

These results may reflect the close interpersonal relationship between workers and employers in the very small organizations and the effectiveness of the very large nonunion employers in reducing the incentives to join unions by paying higher wages and benefits and by using sophisticated personnel techniques and policies. (Kochan 1979, p. 28)

The 1972–84 NLRB data confirm the reports by other commentators that there is an inverse correlation between unit size and union success in certification elections (see table 29). The NLRB results are consistent with results found by Rose (1972; summarized in Goldfield 1982) for his 1966 sample, and by Chaison (1973) for all elections held between 1966 and 1970. Chaison tried a variety of breakdowns, all with the same general conclusions.

TABLE 29   Success Rate by Size of Bargaining Unit, 1972–1984

Size	Number of Elections	Mean Victory Rate	Trend
1–9	20,341	60.2%	Stable
10–19	19,509	53.2	Stable
20–39	18,665	48.1	Stable
40–99	17,883	43.3	Stable
100–199	7,402	38.1	Declining
200–499	4,445	31.2	Declining
500 and over	1,395	30.9	Varying

The unit size variable is also significant in the cross-sectional model. This means, as the cross-tabulations suggest, that all other things being equal, greater unit sizes mean a lesser likelihood of success.

I know of no simple answers to explain the anomaly of low union success rates in larger units. Chaison (1973) cites the possibility that many smaller units may actually be craft or clerical subsets of larger units, although even he does not offer this as a full explanation, only something that must be checked. Rose shows that large units having repeat elections (where a prior certification election was held and lost by a union) show a much higher rate of success, 61.2 percent compared to "less than half in larger units of firms without prior experience" (Rose 1972,

p. 51; see also Czarnecki 1969). Thus there may be an initial difficulty in organizing larger units, even when they eventually are organized into staunch union strongholds. Descriptions of initial organizing during the period of union illegitimacy tend to support such a view.[19] After the first breakthroughs, other large units have tended to fall into the union fold rather quickly. Those that did not soon were given many of the union benefits without a union. This and employer resistance may have made them more difficult to organize at a later period.[20]

Paula Voos argues that much of the problem is a dispute over how to define organizing success.

One must also realize that even though union victory rates are higher in small units, it does not follow by necessity that unions which dispro-portionately organize small units will succeed in unionizing a larger portion of their potential jurisdiction. A 30 percent likelihood of win-ning a unit of 200 people will net the union more additional members in a repeated number of attempts than a 75 percent likelihood of winning a 20 person unit. (1982, p. 194)

These are only speculations. A complete understanding of these contradictory results undoubtedly requires a fuller analy-sis.

CONCLUSION

In reviewing the effect of changes in the structure and composition of the labor force on the increasing union difficulties in new organizing, we have found (1) that compositional changes seem to have had little negative bearing, and (2) that changes in economic structure, while certainly having some immediate negative effects, cannot be accepted as a primary cause of the long-range declines. In our search for the real culprits, we now shift our attention to the larger economic, social, and political cyclical variables.

19. Mortimer, in *Organize* (1971), describes this phenomenon in the initial organizing of White Motors in 1932. Ozanne's *A Century of Labor-Management Relations at McCormick and International Harvester* (1967) documents the many failures and the eventual successful organization of International Harvest-er's McCormick Works. It should be noted that the defeat of Debs's 150,000-plus-member American Railway Union in the 1894 Pullman strike, despite its many-decades-long influence on U.S. labor, would have been recorded as a loss if NLRB statistics had been kept at the time, since the ARU was, in fact, not certified.

20. Richard Freeman suggests in a private communication that larger employ-ers may be devoting more per capita resources to resisting unions, particularly in expenditures on consultants.

8

A Preliminary Investigation into Cyclical Trends in New Union Organizing

Among neoclassical economists, the most popular explanations for long-term trends in union growth and new union organizing have followed the theories of John Commons, described briefly in chapter 4. These theories root the growth of union membership in variations in the economic business cycle. Other investigators have tried to tie decreasing union fortunes to various social and political cyclical phenomena, including variations in strike rates, turnovers in national political administrations, and major changes in U.S. labor law. In this chapter, the degree to which these factors might be associated with both long-term trends and short-term cyclical variations in union victory rates in NLRB certification elections will be investigated. I develop here several econometric models, all of which use aggregated national annual data.

My strategy for the construction of the econometric models will be as follows. First, a critical examination will be made of some of the recent literature on NLRB certification and decertification elections. Second, a number of hypotheses about the large economic, social, and political factors that influence union success will be discussed. Third, an attempt will be made to identify certain variables that capture (or reflect) these factors.

Fourth, several full models will be specified. Fifth, the results for these models will be discussed.

In chapter 4, it was argued that the ultimate cause of union growth and decline was to be found by studying new union organizing. Many econometric modelers who study union growth, however, have been conceptually confused. They have often lumped together effects on union growth that were most likely due to new organizing with effects that were most likely related to other factors. It is important to separate these factors. A study of union growth per se does not give us direct evidence about the state of union organizing, recruitment drives, and union effort in this arena. To obtain such information, we must focus specifically on new union organizing itself.

Even the focus on new union organizing through the NLRB, it should be noted, does not completely isolate the efforts of the unions from other factors. It should be clear that if economic growth in this country had favored the rapid increase in new automobile and steel plants (particularly in the Northeast and Midwest) and large increases in construction and trucking—in short, large rises in the number of unorganized workers in new units in traditional union sectors, occupations, and parts of the country—union organizing would most likely have been more successful. Inversely, the growth in nontraditional areas has most likely made new union organizing through the NLRB more difficult. Such factors are, in part, independent of the effort of unions and their organizers.

NLRB LITERATURE

I begin by examining the literature on new union growth through the NLRB. The earliest published econometric model is that of Adams and Krislov (1974), based on the union growth model of Ashenfelter and Pencavel (1969). In addition, a variety of other models view noneconomic variables. Some of these models have already been mentioned in previous chapters.[1]

1. Voos (1982) attempts to model new union organizing on the basis of union organizing expenditures, using one economic variable—unemployment. Prosten (1978), on the other hand, examines union success rates in NLRB elections as they are correlated with election delays. Other commentators, including Sandver (1982), use cross-sectional models. The time periods and dependent variables for each of these models are different. Finally, there are a number of articles that attempt to model decertification elections. A partial survey of this literature may be found in Heneman and Sandver 1983.

THE ADAMS-KRISLOV MODEL AND ITS WEAKNESSES

The model most relevant to our purposes here is that of Adams and Krislov. Although their work is based upon that of Ashenfelter and Pencavel, they make certain slight modifications that attempt to clear up one or two obvious weaknesses.[2] It is worth beginning with the initial specification of the Adams and Krislov model before discussing its general conceptual weaknesses. Some of the criticisms that follow have appeared in the econometric literature in various critiques of the Ashenfelter and Pencavel model, but few have dealt explicitly with the Adams and Krislov model. Certain of the other problems have not been raised at all.

Their model is as follows:

$$L_t = \beta_0 + \beta_1 \Delta P_t + \sum_{i=0}^{n} \beta_{2i} \Delta E_{t-i} + \beta_3 \ g(U_t^P, t-\theta)$$
$$+ \ \beta_4 (T/E)_{t-i} + \beta_5 D_t + e_t$$

where L_t is the number of workers voting for unions in NLRB elections, ΔP_t is annual rate of change in prices, ΔE_t is change in employment in the nonagricultural private sector, U_t is unemployment, $(T/E)_t$ is the proportion of employment in union sectors that is organized, and D_t is the percentage of Democrats in the House of Representatives.

The Adams and Krislov model sees the number of workers voting for unions in NLRB elections as (1) equivalent to the number of workers gained in union growth owing to new organizing and (2) "correlated with the ability of unions to retain existing membership." Thus successful new organizing and total union membership growth are assumed to be "coincident indicators" (Adams and Krislov 1974, p. 304). The number of workers voting for unions each year is seen to be dependent on the yearly change in the level of prices (ΔP), a moving average of the changes in employment in the private sector $(\Sigma \ \Delta E_{t-i})$, a decaying function of the level of the past peak of unemployment, the union density, and the number of Democrats in Congress.

2. Mancke (1971) argues that Ashenfelter and Pencavel use a misspecified (i.e., bogus) variable in their model, the percentage change in the traditionally unionized sectors of the economy. He argues that it is "uninteresting" that this variable has positive coefficients. The increase in employment in these sectors would quite naturally increase union membership because of the large number of shop agreements there. Adams and Krislov attempt to deflect Mancke's objections by using employment figures for all of the private sector.

Unlike Ashenfelter and Pencavel, Adams and Krislov found that the union density (which is meant to test the saturation hypothesis) and the number of Democratic congressmen (meant to serve as a gauge of prolabor public opinion) were not significant (1974, p. 310).

As has been noted by Mancke (1971) and Bain and Elsheikh (1976) in their comments on the Ashenfelter and Pencavel model, the variable for changes in employment is a confused one. It measures a number of effects rather than just the one it is supposed to capture. Supposedly, it shows the increase in potential union members available for new organizing. Mancke and Bain and Elsheikh found this variable deficient for union growth, although not necessarily for new organizing. But the variable has even more problems for new organizing. First, it does not merely indicate potential members available. Certain of these new (or lost) jobs may, in fact, represent increases (or decreases) in already unionized units, thus representing increases (or decreases) in actual, rather than potential, union members. This difference would be especially significant in a year of rapid economic growth or in a year of recovery from recession, where hard-hit union manufacturing plants, for example, would presumably have large increases in employment. A further problem is that the variable not only reflects two factors—actual and potential increases—as it tries to measure the number of potential members, but it may also reflect a changing labor market in which potential union members have greater leverage in selling their services. As Bain and Elsheikh note correctly, this effect would have been better captured by an unemployment variable. Moreover, when looking at the change in the number of private sector jobs available, it is not clear which of the above effects is being measured, or even the number of potential, in contrast to actual, union jobs that were created. Such is not the characteristic one wants from an explanatory variable in a model.

Bain and Elsheikh's criticism of the step function that measures the previous low of unemployment, as it is used by Ashenfelter and Pencavel, applies with equal validity to Adams and Krislov. The last low point in unemployment is supposed to represent "labor's stock of grievances," but as Bain and Elsheikh aptly note:

What exactly are these grievances and by what process do they result in workers' joining trade unions? Do they represent anything more than dissatisfaction with rising prices and falling employment, factors which are already taken into account in the model . . . ? If they do, then why are these additional factors which cause "worker discontent" not spelt out more precisely? In short, as specified by Ashenfelter and Pencavel, U_p is simply a rag bag which may contain everything or nothing. As such, its effect is extremely difficult to interpret. (1976, p. 40)

The union density variable and the Democratic congressmen variable have also been criticized heavily in the Ashenfelter and Pencavel model. Since Adams and Krislov did not find them significant, little will be said about them here. An important result of the Adams and Krislov model, however, consistent with the facts stated in chapter 7 about the declines in union coverage in traditionally organized areas, is that saturation is not a significant influence on union organizing through the NLRB at this time.

The final variable is the one that denotes the changes in prices. This variable is highly significant. It has been an uncritically accepted mainstay of all previous econometric analyses of union growth (including that by Bain and Eisheikh). What it specifies, however, is not totally clear. It supposedly captures a variety of effects from decreases in real wages to increases in economic activity. Thus it would seem to be another one of those variables that capture "everything and nothing." As Hobsbawm has noted, we know that union activity, union organizing, and union growth all prosper when economic conditions are favorable and decline when they are less so. Price changes, however, no longer seem a good indication of business cycle activity. If the "stagflation" of the 1970s has shown economists nothing else, it is that rising prices are not necessarily the bellwether of improving economic indicators and economic growth. The key variable used in these models must be judged highly dubious.

There are still further problems with the Adams and Krislov model in its dependent variable and other assumptions. It assumes that the number of voters selecting unions represents new growth. This is a crude assumption; there is occasionally a good deal of variation between the two. Also, it is an unnecessary assumption since the NLRB provides data for the number of workers covered by new bargaining agreements in addition to those who voted for unions.

A further indication that the model is misconceived is contained in an assumption that is far too simplistic. Adams and Krislov believe that "successful organizing is correlated with the ability of unions to retain existing membership" (1974, p. 304). This is true, I would agree, over the long run. In the short run, however, ability to retain membership depends in large part on the lack of layoffs and plant closures among unionized workers. Only a small percentage of members are lost through decertifications (there does not seem to be a high relation between slow-growth unions and decertifications), and virtually none through workers quitting the union. Rather, most losses in membership in the current period fall into one of two categories. Either they are the result of decreases in employment in the industry, as illustrated by the huge recent losses suffered by such unions as the UAW, Steelworkers, Rubber Workers, and Teamsters, or they result from out-and-out union busting. As noted in chapter 5, for the period covered by Adams and Krislov (1949–70), the number of workers voting union has varied slightly by year with a small downward trend after the early 1950s until 1970. The number of union members gained each year during this period has varied immensely from very little (occasionally negative) to well over a million, largely because of the economic fluctuations already mentioned. Thus to see the two as "coincident indicators" is certainly incorrect.

Adams and Krislov also attempt to justify their time period as some type of ideal choice. Nineteen forty-nine is, of course, a reasonable choice for the stability of labor union organizations.[3] It is also after the shift in government policy that followed from and was symbolized by Taft-Hartley. Yet to argue that there were no major shifts ("radical shifts," as Adams and Krislov argue) is simple-minded. We do not care whether the shifts were radical or not (some observers did not even find that the Bolshevik Revolution made a radical shift in the functioning of the Czarist bureaucracy), but whether the shifts in policy were statistically significant in terms of the model. Here the passage of the Landrum-Griffin Act and even policy changes in switches between Democratic and Republican administrations cannot be dismissed so blithely.

In conclusion, I would argue that the Adams and Krislov model is wrong in two fundamental respects: (1) it incorporates

3. It was also after the more militant and radical leaders of the CIO unions had been purged. The removal of the left, which had played such an important role in the massive organizing in the decade-and-a-half previously, assured that growth patterns would be less spectacular. For detailed descriptions of this purge, see Cochran (1977).

errors already existing in the Ashenfelter-Pencavel model; (2) it assumes a too direct short-term relation between union organizing and union growth.

DECERTIFICATION ELECTIONS

Study of decertification election results was almost nil until recently. During the past decade, however, there has been a virtual downpour, much of it rich and suggestive.[4]

In various regression models of decertifications, which take union success rates as the dependent variable, only the size of the unit is generally agreed to be significant. Here, in exactly the opposite relation we discovered with certification elections, larger units are found less likely to be decertified than smaller ones. Attempts in general by investigators to duplicate or modify the Ashenfelter and Pencavel model or the Adams and Krislov model for decertification elections have been in the main unsuccessful. One is struck, moreover, by the abstractness of much of the work, its removal from the real situations faced by workers and the unions representing them.[5]

4. Among the recent academic articles are those by Krislov (1979), Dworkin and Extejt (1979a, 1979b), Anderson, Busman, and O'Reilly (1980, 1982), and Elliott and Hawkins (1982). Also of interest are Lublin's discussion (1982) and something of a reply by the AFL-CIO in *STIR* (Oct. 1982). Virtually none of these articles are conclusive, claiming to be merely exploratory.

5. Dworkin and Extejt (1979a) talk about decertifications and have some interesting preliminary findings. Their discussion, however, shows that they regard each loss by an incumbent union as a decertification, neglecting the other possibility, that a union is decertified and replaced by another. Anderson, Busman, and O'Reilly (1979, 1980) recognize that decertification results contain the switching of unions, and they even add a political variable to control for Landrum-Griffin (although their specification of it for just three years—1959–61—is clumsily explained, except that it fits the data). Yet they show little sense of awareness of how union jobs are filled (and replaced) when a worker quits: "Total union growth would also include individual decisions to move from union to nonunion establishments and vice versa" (p. 104).

While the number of Nobel Prize winners in the physics department at a university might be an inelastic commodity, observers since Marx have generally noted that the functioning of the labor market under capitalism provides many soldiers in the reserve army of the unemployed ready to fill a union or nonunion job as it is quit by any particular worker. Thus these individual decisions count for very little in the aggregate statistics.

Anderson, Busman, and O'Reilly (1982), in an interesting study of California that includes in-depth studies of various decertification campaigns, attempt to evaluate the militancy of the union leadership as it affects the chances of decertification. They rely on survey information from union and company officials, however, and do not mention the militancy of the work force itself.

Finally, Elliot and Hawkins (1982) attempt to frame the decertification decision in the context of cost-benefit analysis.

Virtually all the econometric models of union growth, new union organizing, and decertifications are based on various microeconomic assumptions of neoclassical welfare economics. Of those who model decertification election results, perhaps Elliot and Hawkins (1982) are the most explicit about these assumptions. Ashenfelter and Pencavel, and their offspring Adams and Krislov, are also explicit in placing their analysis within this context. In particular, they speak the language of cost-benefit analysis.[6] For Ashenfelter and Pencavel, the worker is an individual consumer, weighing the costs and benefits of purchasing the union service from the union. While this model does capture certain elements of the decision to join a union and engage in union activity, it is deficient in a number of respects.

First, it takes the preferences of the worker out of their historical and social context, erroneously assuming that they are mainly the result of a purely "rational," goods-maximizing decision.[7] Thus, among other things, this perspective ignores, or at

6. See Layard 1980 for a collection of articles that lay out the contours of cost-benefit analysis. For a clear and informative general survey, see Prest and Turvey's essay "The Main Questions" (1965) within the Layard volume. For a limited critique, dealing with the weakness of the neoclassical assumptions about individuals' invariant preference structures, see Gintis (1972). For a broader, yet more technical critique, Campen (1976) is highly useful. And if one is interested in an extended philosophical critique of neoclassical assumptions about modern society, MacPherson (1962) is insightful.

7. Karl Marx and Howard Raiffa both make this point in quite different ways. Raiffa (1982, p. 85) describes the "both-pay escalation game" that he tried with two fellow professors from the Harvard Business School. Raiffa was the auctioneer of a one dollar bill. The bidding started at 10¢; each bidder was allowed to raise the other 10¢ or drop out. Both loser and winner paid their last bid, the dollar going to the highest bidder. With various pauses at critical points, the bidding quickly escalated to several dollars, each professor refusing to quit. When Raiffa stopped the game at $3.10, his colleagues were mad, not for his snookering them out of their money, but for refusing to let them finish the game! Rational calculations cannot be taken out of their social context.

Marx notes that the rational, calculating, preference-maximizing individual is the product of a long historical development, only acting that way under particular social circumstances:

> Individuals producing in a society, and hence the socially determined production of individuals, is of course the point of departure. The solitary and isolated hunter or fisherman, who serves Adam Smith and Ricardo as a starting point, is one of the unimaginative fantasies of eighteenth-century romances à la Robinson Crusoe. . . . It is, on the contrary, the anticipation of "bourgeois society." . . . The individual in this society of free competition seems to be rid of natural ties, etc., which made him an appurtenance of particular, limited aggregation of human beings in previous epochs. The prophets of the eighteenth century . . . saw this individual not as an historical result, but as the starting point of history; not as something evolving in the course of history, but posited by nature, because for them this individual was

least does not provide a framework for highlighting, the degree of national, racial, ethnic, and ultimately class influence (some might say peer-group pressure or coercion) on the formation and expression of workers' preferences.[8] Second, it fails to account for the role of other class actors with tremendous influence on the expression of "preferences" of the workers for a union. Among these actors, I would include the unions and their organizers, the companies, and the state, all of whom make significant efforts at various times toward affecting the outcomes of union certification elections.

It is possible that a broad tautological framework, such as neoclassical microeconomics, could conceivably accommodate certain of the above factors about the real world. It is, however, no accident that adherents of this model usually do not take such things into account. In general, cost-benefit analysis leads to an exaggeration of the importance of the financial gains and benefits accruing (or not) to an individual worker who is considering joining a new union. Neoclassical cost-benefit analysis, like Freudian psychology, always has a retort.[9]

It is not my purpose here to criticize in detail the assumptions of neoclassical welfare economics and its cost-benefit subset. Yet it is important to understand the general framework hidden behind the majority of econometric studies of union growth and new union organizing. A discussion of those factors that determine union success rates may fruitfully begin with some indica-

---

in conformity with nature, in keeping with their idea of human nature. . .

Man . . . is not only a social animal, but an animal that can be individualized only within society (Marx [1857] 1970, pp. 189–90).

Marx and Raiffa might even agree. Change the social context and the expectations somewhat and *homus calculus* takes an unexcused break.

8. The May 1981 AFL-CIO *Statistical and Tactical Information Report* notes the following:

UAW International Representative Carl Shier used the Gdansk Accord, reproducing it in its entirety for the employees of Beardsley-Piper Company in Illinois. A substantial number of the employees were of Polish origin and the accord must have had some impact because UAW won the election by a better than 2 to 1 vote and beat one of the toughest union busting consultants in the process—Pope, Ballard, Shephard and Fowle.

9. As Paula Voos perceptively notes, "People who vote for unionization in a representation election always may be said to have done so because they had a higher subjective expected utility for the union than the nonunion situation" (1982, p. 134). Thus there is no phenomenon that could possibly serve as a refutation of the theory, no possibility of "falsifiability," to use Popper's criterion, or even a possibility of damaging, problematic data.

tions of what I believe are the weaknesses of much of the union growth (as well as the new organizing and decertification) literature. Fundamentally, the main analysts all pose the questions of union growth and union organizing within too narrow a context. A universal characteristic of the econometric literature on union growth and union organizing is to omit certain variables or to give vague specifications or justifications for others.

All the general models of union growth and union organizing, for example, omit any variables that might capture worker militancy, an indicator of collective working-class behavior and propensities. Militancy of the work force as measured by strike statistics, however, turns out to be a strong predictor of union success rates in NLRB elections. The reason that modelers neglect this variable is that none of them sees union growth or union organizing in the United States of America as part of an intense class struggle going on between workers and capitalists.

Further, none of the traditional econometricians take full cognizance of the role of the government apparatus in influencing union growth. Ashenfelter and Pencavel are far more insensitive to this than are Bain and Elsheikh, who at least recognize that 1937 to 1947 was a period in this country when the government was less obstructive to union organizing. Neither Ashenfelter and Pencavel nor Bain and Elsheikh, however, attempt to introduce dynamic variables to capture changes in the administration of national labor public policy or changes in political control of the administrative institutions. Ashenfelter and Pencavel are also vague in the specification of a number of variables, including prices (which capture changes in workers' costs of living) and number of Democrats in Congress (which supposedly captures the extent of prolabor public opinion). Both of these loose specifications have been criticized elsewhere (e.g., by Bain and Elsheikh) and will not be discussed here.

The model used here—a class-conflict model (whose assumptions are discussed in chapter 4)—sees three (and occasionally four) actors in the struggle for union recognition.[10] There are the workers and their unions (occasionally distinguishable as separate entities in this context), who have varying degrees of leverage against the capitalists, more or less cohesiveness and militancy, and lesser or greater grievances. Opposing them

---

10. Freeman and Medoff (1976, 1984a) are able to incorporate certain of the same criticisms of the neoclassical framework into their "exit-voice" model.

(either explicitly or implicitly) are the capitalists, who themselves have varying degrees of leverage, more or less power vis-a-vis the workers, greater or lesser capabilities for making profits, and hence greater or lesser abilities for granting concessions, and greater or lesser desire to do so without interruptions in production. In between, but hardly neutral, is the government, which provides greater or lesser degrees of legal and administrative opposition to new organizing.

Having briefly sketched my differences with the neoclassical models, I will specify the variables to be used in the models to be presented here.[11] The discussion will begin with the dependent variables and then proceed to the independent variables. In each case, I will discuss what each variable attempts to capture, its expected influence and sign, potential problems with the variable, and why it is preferable (if this is so) to some other variable or variables that might have served in its stead.

THE DEPENDENT VARIABLES

Two different, but related, dependent variables are used here. One is the likelihood of a union victory in any particular NLRB certification election (EW), which may also be interpreted as the union victory rate. This variable is dependent on, but not coincident with, the second dependent variable, the percentage of workers voting for union certification (UV). This second variable is formed by dividing the number of workers voting for a union by the number of workers actually voting. The lack of coincidence of these two percentages has several causes. The most obvious is that an overwhelming win or loss in a very large unit affects the second dependent variable greatly, but the first hardly at all. Of greater interest, however, is the impact the NLRB apparatus may have on appeals of close elections. Using both dependent variables may help us to gain some insight into the effect of different political administrations on the application of U.S. labor public policy.[12]

THE INDEPENDENT VARIABLES

The following factors were hypothesized to be potentially significant as independent variables.

11. The sources for the data used with each variable are disucssed in Appendix D.
12. This suggestion was made in Goldfield 1982, based upon the cyclical differences in the two dependent variables.

1. Unemployment. Unemployment, as many commentators have noted since Marx, has a great effect on the leverage unions have with employers. When unemployment is low, the job market is tight and employers are more reluctant to fire or to provoke their employees. On the other hand, when unemployment is high, the competition in the job market is more intense. Both workers and employers know that it is easier, at this time, to replace a particular worker with another with commensurate skills. Thus one may hypothesize that union activists, members, and potential members will run greater risks in expressing their pro-union preferences when unemployment is higher. Further, because the unions have more leverage in dealing with the companies when unemployment is lower, unions are more attractive to workers at this time. In general, it is hypothesized that the absolute level of unemployment (as a percentage of the workforce) is most critical. We note, however, that changes in the level of unemployment often signal a growing trend, thus promising greater future leverage for one side or the other. It is not surprising that certain of the econometricians of union growth have found unemployment in this functional form to be significant.

It is further hypothesized that the level of unemployment will affect long-term, as well as short-term, trends in union organizing.

2. Militancy and Cohesiveness of the Working Class. It is hypothesized that a relationship exists between the militancy and cohesiveness of the working class and its pro-union sentiment and hence between working-class militancy and the ability of unions to win NLRB union certification elections. There are many who argue that there is an inverse relationship between the strength and support of the trade unions and the quantity of strikes (Crouch and Pizzorno 1978; Korpi and Shalev 1979, 1980). I disagree, in general, with this assessment, but the difference is perhaps especially stark for the United States.

There are a number of measures of work stoppages in this country. They include the number of stoppages per year, the average duration of each stoppage, the number of workers on strike during a particular year, and the percentage of total working time lost during the year. The most significant of these variables for our purposes is the number of work stoppages in a year. An official union strike (e.g., of auto workers against

General Motors or the United Mine Workers against the coal operators) contributes to and reflects a certain degree of militancy and unity among at least one segment of the working class. Official strikes, however, often involve workers for a whole company or industry, are usually well-organized, and may last a long period of time. Their weight as to average duration, number of workers involved, and percentage of total work time lost is quite disproportionate to their value as an indicator of working-class militancy and unity. This is especially true of the last several decades when many official strikes have been almost businesslike affairs. It is the assessment here, for example, that several dozen wildcat strikes in mining are far more indicative of labor militancy than a small number of official strikes. Unfortunately, U.S. strike data in this form have not been gathered since 1981, thus limiting the time period of the model.

3. Workers' Economic Grievances. Many econometricians have tied workers' economic grievances to rises in prices, especially in the United States. They believe that price increases somehow capture both the rising profitability of industry (as well as general economic upward trends) and the declining real wages of the workers. Whatever the correlation prices may have had with union growth and success, the justification for them as an indicator is suspect. If nothing else, the "stagflation" of the 1970s should put to rest the claim that inflation and prosperity are coextensive. If one is interested in real wages and their trends, one should use real wages. The latter has been done in the model presented here. Changes in real wages each year are used as a variable despite some deficiencies. This variable is meant to capture directly the economic grievances that workers have and, hence, their desire for economic retribution. One may hypothesize that workers whose real wages are declining will be more open to joining a union, and to fighting for higher wages, than workers whose real wages are increasing, stable, or declining less than previously. Thus the expected sign of this variable is negative. Unfortunately, an accurate data series for real wages was only found to be available for the postwar period. This variable is therefore used only in the post-1948 model.

4. The General Health of the Economy. Rather than use prices to capture the rise or decline in prosperity, GNP is used. Positive increases in the size of the GNP are taken to indicate an expanding, prospering economy. Decreases in the size of the GNP are taken to indicate a declining, contracting economy. Thus one would expect a positive sign on the coefficient of this variable.[13]

5. *Control of the NLRB Administrative Apparatus.* It is hypothesized that there will be a difference in the functioning of the NLRB, depending on whether the presidency is controlled by Democrats or Republicans. The party in the White House has direct influence and control over the NLRB, through its appointments to the national five-member board, by its ability to replace NLRB personnel around the country during its four or more years in office, and by its control over the NLRB budget. Some of this influence over the NLRB is effective immediately after inauguration, while other aspects take a while to assert. My own experience in the early 1970s indicates that there were sharp changes at the lower level of the NLRB administrative apparatus during the course of the Nixon administration. Pressure at the top tends to be felt relatively quickly. Those NLRB employees who want to keep their jobs understand that the power of the new president can only increase as he begins to appoint new board members. His budgetary authority, as Ronald Reagan has shown, may be exercised immediately. The lower levels often take much longer to change. In Chicago, in late 1970 and early 1971, many of the examining officers (who started during the Kennedy-Johnson years) seemed quite sympathetic to unions.[14] By 1972, there was little evidence of these attitudes (or of the same personnel).

In addition, as noted in Goldfield 1982, there is a slight difference in the graphs of the percentage of workers voting union and the percentage of union victories in NLRB elections. The percentage of workers seems to follow a straight line, with possible rises or falls at election time, while that of union victories has a staircase effect, possibly along lines of the party in the White House. My hypothesis about the effect of the party in the White House is as follows. First, there will be an impact at election time (or rather in the year following the election). This

13. For a discussion of the biases in GNP calculations, see Block 1985 and Block and Burns 1985.
14. They were in my view "Peace Corp" types. One even bragged to me that he had spent a summer during law school working in the Mahwah, New Jersey, Ford plant, at that time a center of black worker radicalism.

initial impact will most likely be psychological. Second, there will be an impact based upon who has controlled the White House, and hence, the NLRB apparatus, over the previous four years, the effect being dynamic.[15]

6. *Profitability of Industry.* When profits are high the capitalists have more resources. This might suggest, at first glance, that they are better able to fight against union organizing. This has, of course, been true at times, especially when a particular industrial group (e.g., U.S. Steel and International Harvester during the first several decades of this century) had a monopoly in its industry. On the other hand, the taking of high profits may mean that capitalists are less likely to want to create conflicts, less likely to oppose the demands for small economic gains or for new organizational forms by their workers. This would seem to be the case when the companies are in a competitive environment and do not have an assured dominance of their particular market. I believe that this latter effect will tend to dominate, but I leave open for now the expected sign. Profits as a variable, however, have certain significant problems. First, there are real questions as to its accuracy, given its relation to taxes paid by large corporations. Second, these inaccuracies are not likely to be consistent given the many changes in corporate tax laws over the last decades.[16] Thus my model experiments with the National Income and Products Accounts (NIPA) profits series, but also attempts to use final sales to capture the "profit" effect. Final sales are not always coincident with profits (particularly at the firm level).[17] On an aggregate level, however, they would seem to be a reasonable surrogate, have in general a high correlation with after-tax profits, and are a far more accurate and consistent series. Unfortunately, an adequate series was only available for the postwar era, so this variable is only included in the model for the post-1948 series.

15. There is, of course, no suggestion that the Democrats are not probusiness, or that they are somehow more fully in labor's camp than the Republicans. They usually, however, have more political debts to pay to the unions, who have generally supported them.

16. This is one conclusion argued quite convincingly by Richard Jankowski (1984).

17. Such a disjunction is apparent in the comparison, for example, of the reported final sales and profits of Caterpillar and International Harvester companies through the decade of the 1960s and most of the 1970s. Harvester had several times the sales of Caterpillar, but less total profits.

7. The Intensity of Work and the Degree of Control by the Capitalists. Increases in output per hour hurt unions and workers in their short-run bargaining position. When the increases are due to rises in the pace and intensity of work (which must be sustained over a period of time to be reflected in aggregate output), they mark a defeat for workers and their unions—a loss in their struggle to conserve their bodies and effort for a given rate of pay. When the increases in output are largely technologically related, this is often marked by a decrease in the leverage of the union and a decline in its potential membership, particularly its unskilled segments. Whichever of the two phenomena is the cause of a rise in output per hour, the result is a weakened position for the union in the short run. This is the hypothesis I propose to test by including a variable for output per hour. Productivity data have been kept in a consistent manner by the Bureau of Labor Statistics since 1947. Although there have been attempts to develop productivity series beginning in earlier periods,[18] none of them were sufficiently reliable to include in the model for the 1935–47 period. As has been suggested, the expected sign of this variable is negative.

8. The Start-up Period. A dummy variable was added for the start-up period from 1935 to 1937. Although the National Labor Relations Act was passed in 1935, it was often ignored and flouted by many employers until its validity was upheld by the Supreme Court in 1937. It is hypothesized that this period will be less favorable, ceteris paribus, than the period after 1937. The expected sign of this variable is thus negative.

9. The Taft-Hartley Act. The passage of the Taft-Hartley Act in 1947 marked a significant shift in the legal rights of unions. A dummy variable is added for the period after its passage; it is hypothesized that its sign will be negative after 1948.

SPECIFICATION OF THE MODELS AND THE VARIABLES

The functional forms and lag structures of the variables to be included in the models are discussed briefly below.

1. Dummy Variables. There are three dummy variables. They are S, for the start-up period, set to 1 for the years 1935 through

18. See, for example, Kendrick 1973.

1937, and 0 thereafter; *TH*, for Taft-Hartley, set to 0 prior to 1948 and 1 thereafter; and *P*, for party in the White House, set to 1 if the president is a Democrat, and 0 if a Republican. For the election year (i.e., leap years), the variable is coded for the party in office up to the election in November. Thus the first year of a term is considered the inaugural year.

For the later time series (beginning in 1948), *S* and *TH* are obviously not included, because they are not relevant.

2. *Linear Variables.* The number of work stoppages per year *(W)*, final sales or profits *(F)*, and output per hour *(O)* are all represented by their actual values. Output per hour is also used in its differenced form. Several variables, however, represent a percentage of change from the previous year.

G, standing for percentage change in GNP from the previous year is calculated as follows:

$$G = \frac{GNP_t - GNP_{t-1}}{GNP_t} \times 100$$

R, standing for the percentage change in real wages (RW) from the previous year is calculated as follows:

$$R = \frac{RW_t - RW_{t-1}}{RW_t} \times 100$$

ΔO, the percentage change in output per year is defined as

$$\Delta O = \frac{O_t - O_{t-1}}{O_t} \times 100$$

3. *Unemployment.* The earlier conjecture suggests that unemployment should be initially coded as the percentage of the labor force unemployed (U_t). Tested in the models are U_t, U_{t-1}, ΔU_t, and both U_{t-1} and ΔU_t together. ΔU_t is calculated as follows:

$$\Delta U_t = U_t - U_{t-1}$$

It was the joint use of terms for both U_{t-1} and ΔU_t that gave the most fruitful results. Although ΔU_t contains U_{t-1}, and thus might appear as partially redundant, it was felt that the variable made sense analytically and was therefore preferred.

4. *Party in the White House.* The party in the White House, denoted by γ, was the variable with the most complex functional form. It was estimated that there were two effects: (1) A psycho-

logical effect, based on the party in control of the White House during the current year (which would be captured most sharply by the dependent variable *UV* and reflecting the percentage of workers voting for unions), and (2) an administrative effect, based on changes in the NLRB administration that might take as long as four years to be felt (more strongly captured in the dependent variable *EW*, reflecting the percentage of elections won by unions).

Preliminary regressions on the yearly lags of the party variable suggested an AR(2) function, although AR(1) was not definitely ruled out.[19] The structure and initial parameters for γ were estimated through nonlinear techniques. The most statistically significant results were obtained by regarding γ as a Box-Jenkins (or ARIMA) transfer (or intervention) function.[20] When the model was detrended and the rest of the variables' effects were whitened out, both AR(2) and AR(1) seemed to give statistically significant results. This is unusual, but it is important to note (and this will be discussed later) that the fits for the AR(1) models were firmer for the full series (1935–80) while the AR(2) models seemed slightly better for the later series (1948–80).

Because of the potential instability of the γ function, a variety of other alternative functional forms were experimented with. These included a simple ramp function, designed to test for the administrative effect,

$$\gamma_1 = P_t + P_{t-1} + P_{t-2} + P_{t-3} + P_{t-4};$$

a function designed to capture both the psychological effect and the seeming lag structure of the administrative effect,

$$\gamma_2 = P_t + P_{t-1}/4 + P_{t-2}/4 + P_{t-3} + P_{t-4}/2;$$

and a function similar to γ_2 except that it embodies the assumption that the psychological effect occurs only the year following an election (coding positives only for the present year if it is the year following an election). There is also an administrative effect, coded as 1 only for the second and third lags. Thus if the year is the one following an election,

---

19. AR stands for autoregressive, the number in parentheses standing for the order of the function. Simple explanations of autoregressive functions may be found in McCleary and Hay 1980.

20. Transfer functions are discussed in detail in Box and Jenkins 1976. A simpler explanation, along with more specific social-science-type examples, may be found in McCleary and Hay 1980.

$$\gamma_3 = P_t + P_{t-2} + P_{t-3}.$$

Otherwise,

$$\gamma_3 = P_{t-2} + P_{t-3}.$$

THE FULL MODEL

The following is the model that appeared to be the most reasonable and the most statistically significant for the full series:

$$DEP_t = \beta_1 S_t + \beta_2 TH_t + \beta_3 U_{t-1} + \beta_4 \Delta U_t + B_5 R_t + \beta_6 \gamma_t + \beta_7 G_t + \beta_8 O_t + e_t,$$

where DEP is the dependent variable either of likelihood of a union victory in a particular election (percentage of elections won) or of percentage of workers voting for unions, and e_t is the error term. All other variables are as described previously.

THE RESULTS

With eight variables, we expect a certain amount of multicollinearity. Though this may weaken our model, it should not cause any biases.[21] It is expected that there will be no serial autocorrelation of the residuals or error terms. The standard Durbin-Watson statistic is used to test for first-order serial autocorrelation.[22]

1. Party in the White House. For the full series γ_t was best fitted with a first-order autoregressive function (a Markov process) in the following form:

$$\gamma_t = P_t + \phi P_{t-1} + \phi^2 P_{t-2} + \phi^3 P_{t-3} + \ldots$$

The parameter ϕ was estimated using the nonlinear Box-Jenkins techniques mentioned previously. The estimation was done for both dependent variables EW (likelihood of an election victory) and UV (percentage of votes for the union). The behavior of γ_t in the full model seems to confirm the initial hypotheses:

21. This point is emphasized in Bain and Elsheikh 1976; it is also discussed in Kmenta 1971 and Johnson 1972.
22. A clear description of many of the regression techniques and statistical tests normally used in econometric models is presented in the appendixes of Bain and Elsheikh 1976. These appendixes are highly recommended for those who are not familiar with econometric modeling.

a. The variable is among the most significant in the whole model.

b. The value of ϕ when *EW* is the dependent variable is .89. When *UV* is the dependent variable, the value is only .52. On the other hand, the coefficient of γ_t in the model using *UV* as the dependent variable is higher than that of γ_t when *EW* is the dependent variable. This indicates sharply that the length of time a party has been in the White House is more important for elections won (suggesting an administration effect) than for pro-union votes. However, the party winning is more important for votes in the election year than for elections won.

c. The effects seem to be quite real, although the importance of the variable should not be overemphasized. Control of the NLRB would seem to be worth on the average two to three percentage points. The differential impact of the two effects on the two dependent variables thus represents a fraction of a percent, enough, it might be added, to account to a large degree for the differences in the two graphs.

2. Work Stoppages. The number of work stoppages is among the most stable variables for the whole model. Both its *t*-statistic and its coefficient only varied slightly among the full range of models with which I experimented. Increases in the number of work stoppages by 500 seem to be worth a little less than a 1 percent increase in union victories and a little more for union votes.

3. Output per Hour. Output per hour has the expected sign (negative) and is significant statistically. A 10 percent rise in output per hour is associated with approximately a 1 percent decline in percentage of union victories or votes. This variable appears to pick up a large amount of the time trend.[23] It fortuitously appears quite strong and allows the model to fit the

23. A series of preliminary checks were made to determine whether this was in fact the case. The omission of this variable, for example, significantly lowered the coefficient of determination, that is, *R*-squared. The differencing of the variable, eliminating its time trend, greatly diminished the impact of this factor and thus confirms the above statement. The variable was kept in the model, since this was deemed preferable to establishing a pseudovariable to account for the time trend. Such time-trend variables generally serve to explain nothing, capturing only what one already needs to explain. A further indication of the problematic nature of the strength of this variable is that output per hour has steadily increased for more than a century, while union growth and organizing successes during this time have had many significant ups and downs.

data more closely than is reasonably the case, a point to be discussed more fully later.

4. *Unemployment.* The percentage of the work force unemployed *(U)* is a significant variable and has the correct sign when its first lag is used. This follows the suggestion of Bain and Elsheikh. A 5 percent higher level of unemployment coincides with a 1 percent drop in union victories or votes. Such a finding is interesting although not momentous. Some of the effects of unemployment are also highly correlated with other variables, especially work stoppages. In any case, the significance and the sign are as expected. Somewhat surprisingly, a change in the level of unemployment seems to be accompanied by higher percentages of union victories and prounion votes. The statistical significance is low, but we might speculate on the possibilities. It is conceivable that sharp increases in unemployment give an initial boost to prounion sentiment, but that the maintenance of higher levels of unemployment demoralizes the workers, giving unions less leverage against the capitalists. A 4 percent rise in unemployment seems to be accompanied by an initial 1 percent rise in the union victory rate and the pro-union vote.

5. *Other Variables.* The start-up period *(S)* is significant, but this should come as no surprise, since we knew from the graphic representations and from the gross statistics themselves that the start-up period did not fit the general trend. Taft-Hartley is highly significant for the *EW* dependent variable, but has the wrong sign and is not statistically significant for the *UV* variable. The problems with the model involving the latter variable may be attributed to multicollinearity, particularly with unemployment and (negatively) with output. The *EW* equation seems most reasonable, that is, Taft-Hartley correlates with a general loss of over 7 percent in union victory rates, but there is little surety in this assertion.

THE POST-1948 PERIOD

For the period 1948–80, a more detailed model was estimated, dropping the *S* and *TH* dummy variables. The most adequate model appeared to be

$$DEP = \beta_0 + \beta_1 U_{t-1} + \beta_2 \Delta U_t + \beta_3 W_t + \beta_4 \gamma_t + \beta_5 G_t$$
$$+ \beta_6 O_t + \beta_7 F_t + \beta_8 R_t + e_t.$$

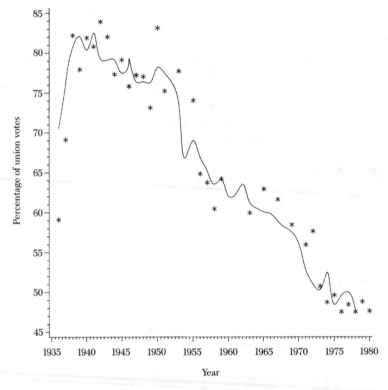

Symbol * represents the actual values.

FIGURE 14.   Percentage of union votes in NLRB elections by year: Actual values with least square fit

This model yielded highly interesting preliminary results, suggesting that certain of the hypotheses concerning the new variables (as well as the ones used in the full model) were correct. Nevertheless, the Durbin-Watson statistics indicate that there are serious problems of autocorrelation of the error terms. The employment of generalized least squares techniques (GLS or Cochrane-Orcutt) is probably ill-advised in this case. My reasoning, based on various suggestions from Theil (1972) and general considerations, is as follows. The first-order serial autocorrelation of the residuals indicated by the Durbin-Watson statistics suggest, not merely biases in the estimators, but problems with the model. Many modelers turn too quickly to Cochrane-Orcutt in order to eliminate these biases, rather than trying to figure out how the model itself may be made more adequate. Although I tried GLS techniques on this model, I concluded that more work was needed on the model. This may be done in the future. Since a large number of variations were tried, however, it is more likely that the model used for the full period 1935–80 is in fact the better model.

TEST STATISTICS

The model for the full period has extremely high coefficients of determination, testing goodness of fit for both dependent variables. The *EW* model "explains" over 98 percent of the variation of *EW,* while the *UV* model explains over 97 percent of the variation of *UV.* These are impressive statistics (e.g., Ashenfelter and Pencavel's model "explains" 72 percent of the variation and is deemed adequate) but should not be overemphasized. With a higher number of variables, one expects a tighter fit. Of importance for the unbiased nature of our estimated coefficients, the Durbin-Watson statistics for the model using both dependent variables indicate no significant first-order autocorrelation of residuals. The model seems fairly robust, performing well for the 1948–80 period as well. This is a reasonably good test that the model charts a single trend.[24]

A series of experiments were tried to see the degree to which this model captured the declines in union victory rates (and worker support for unions) in NLRB elections. The above models were differenced, with the result that the estimated coefficients appeared to remain stable and significant, thus indicating that the model was a good one. However, preliminary differencing of only those variables that seem to have spuriously "captured" the time trend (e.g., output per hour) greatly reduced *R*-squared and occasionally the statistical significance of the variables themselves. The dropping of output per hour, the most significant variable, reduced the *R*-square from .98 to .72.

The model as a whole has certain strengths and weaknesses, certain things that it helps explain and certain things for which it is superficially misleading. It is undoubtedly arguable that I should have recast the model presented in this chapter in a form that was not at all misleading. An unambiguous remodeling, however, is not always possible. I have chosen not to do this. The model

24. One common test (the Chow test) was deemed less valuable in this particular case, since it was hypothesized that the passage of Taft-Hartley (among other things) made a profound difference in the position of organized labor in this country after 1948.

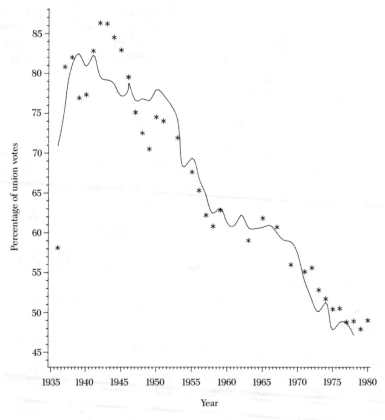

Symbol * represents the actual values.

FIGURE 15.   Percentage of union victories in NLRB electionsby year: Actual
values with least square fit

has been kept in its presnt form to underscore a point known to
some econometricians, but blatantly ignored by most modelers:
"Models are to be used but not to be believed" (Theil 1971, p. vi).

This is what I believe the model presented here does and
does not "explain." The model does appear to capture a large
amount of the variation around the general trend line of the
union victory rates. This is not an insubstantial finding; changes
in various cyclical variables have a strong relation to the ups and
downs of these success rates around the general trend line. The
model, however, has certain fatal flaws in its ability to adequately "explain" the long-term decline in union victory rates in
NLRB certification elections. This is so despite the high coeffi-

TABLE 30   Econometric Models of NLRB Certification Elections, 1935–1980

Model Year	1 1935–80	2 1935–80	3 1948–80	4 1948–80
DEP	Elections	Votes	Elections	Votes
Intercept	87.67 (45.7)	88.67 (40.5)	79.16 (42.16)	88.27 (36.56)
S	−1.98 (−1.33)	−11.0 (−6.12)		
TH		−7.21 (−7.22)		
U_{t-1}	−.21 (−2.27)	.07 (.75)	−.21 (−.694)	−.50 (−1.38)
ΔU	.27 (1.03)	.336 (1.10)	.99 (2.54)	1.67 (3.11)
W	.0016 (4.40)	.0024 (5.54)	.0015 (4.51)	.0023 (4.65)
γ	1.02 (5.68)	1.78 (4.49)	1.01 (5.61)	1.61 (3.95)
G	.41 (4.41)	.23 (2.23)	.69 (3.09)	.96 (3.30)
O	−.09	−.12	−.09	−.12
(all inds)	(−20.5)	(−30.1)	(−20.5)	(−19.5)
γ-form	AR(1)	AR(1)	AR(1)	AR(1)
ϕ_1	.89	.52 (3.63)	.89 (1.17)	.52
R^2	.985	.976	.9808	.976
R^2 adj.	.981	.972	.976	.971
Durbin-Watson	1.89	1.66	1.46	1.89

Note: t-statistics are in parentheses.

cient of determination. This point must be underscored. Only one variable has an estimated coefficient high enough to account for the trend. That variable is output per hour. Output per hour, or productivity, has generally risen steadily in this country for over a century. Union fortunes, however, have varied dramatically during this period. It is thus entirely fortuitous that union organizing prospects have declined steadily since the early 1950s as productivity has steadily increased. It is this fortuitous relationship that is largely "captured" in the close fit of the model's trend to that of the data. None of the other estimators have sufficiently high values to explain a substantial amount of the decline, although they appear, as is indicated in figures 14 and 15, to explain a good bit of the cyclical variations.

TABLE 31   Econometric Models of NLRB Elections, 1948–1980

Model Year	5 1948–80	6 1948–80
DEP	Elections	Votes
Intercept	91.97 (17.7)	82.34 (15.9)
U_{t-1}	−1.10 (−2.16)	−.37 (−.72)
ΔU	1.44 (1.83)	1.95 (2.49)
W	.0018 (2.27)	.0025 (3.35)
γ	.86 (1.83)	.88 (3.15)
G	1.21 (3.03)	1.20 (2.99)
O (manufact)	−.52 (−1.84)	−1.15 (−4.12)
R	.19 (.45)	.85 (2.0)
F	.11 (.50)	.55 (2.43)
γ-form	AR(2)	AR(2)
ϕ_1	1.04 (6.02)	1.45 (14.02)
ϕ_2	−.79 (7.42)	−.99 (8.07)
R^2	.957	.932
R^2 adj.	.910	.943
Durbin-Watson	.945	1.27

Note: *t*-statistics are in parentheses.

To put it another way, the close fit of the model to the data only indicates the possibility that the model might explain the phenomenon. The model does appear to capture the cyclical variations in union victory rates. The ability of the model, however, to capture the whole downward trend, while it has an initial appeal, falls apart when one looks at the most "significant" variable. This is not an unusual result of careful analysis of an econometric model. The models are usually at best heuristic devices; it is a mistake to reify them into embodiments of truth. Their importance as heuristic devices is great, but nevertheless their status should not be confused.

Thus my conclusion is that the variables in this model explain to a considerable extent the cyclical variations in union success by year, yet they ultimately fail to explain the bulk of the decline over the past several decades. Suspect number two is guilty of a misdemeanor, but not the main perpetrator of the felony itself.

9

The Continuing Search For the Real Culprits: The Relation of Class Forces

Though I have tried to examine carefully the first two sets of hypotheses presented in chapter 6, the attentive reader will note that the results of my inquiries are not wholly inconsistent with the analysis presented in chapter 4. Both sets of hypotheses fail to serve as primary explanations for U.S. trade union decline. The results of chapters 7 and 8 are thus largely negative; they serve to clear the ground for more adequate explanations. Our search for the causes of trade union decline in this country (particularly the increasing failures of unions in new organizing) leads us to an examination of what chapter 4 suggests is a more likely candidate: the changes in the relation of class forces. These forces include

1. The workers, who ultimately decide to join or not to join a union, who decide to provide or not to provide the energy and face the risks that are necessary to form a union.

2. The government, which maintains the legal framework in which labor organizing in this country takes place, which interprets this framework through its various agencies and courts, and which enforces it to greater and lesser extents.

3. The capitalists, who individually and collectively offer more or less resistance to union organizing in their workplaces,

who do so with varying degrees of threat, intimidation, and illegal activity.

4. The unions, which are generally quite distinguishable from the rank-and-file workers (except in those rare cases where they did not exist prior to the workers' self-organization). Unions offer more or less representation and ability to gain better working conditions, varying levels of benefits and appeal, and they possess greater or lesser militancy and willingness to lead struggles. In addition they provide organizers and resources that may be critical to a successful organizing campaign.

Most theories of union growth and new union organizing adopt a neoclassical microeconomic orientation, focusing on the economic decision of the workers to join or not to join a union. While this explanatory framework is, in my opinion, not totally devoid of merit, it is inadequate in accounting for key aspects of the reality of the union organizing situations. In contrast, the approach sketched in chapter 4 places the questions of new union organizing within the context of a more general struggle between workers and employers, one in which the government is also far from being a neutral participant. The typical neoclassical formulation of the worker as a consumer and the union as a purveyor of services does possess an element of truth. It fails, however, to conceptualize adequately other key aspects. To take an example from the traditional industrial relations literature: McKersie and Brown (1963) describe a hospital organizing campaign where a large majority of the workers not merely joined the union, but supported it in a strike. They were defeated in their struggle for recognition, however, by an obstinate management. The assumption that the organizing of a union mainly requires the expression of a pro-union "preference" by a majority of workers is naive, to say the least. This general point about the failure of neoclassical models of union growth and union organizing to account for the importance of labor-management conflict may be contrasted not only with the Marxist class-struggle standpoint, but also with that of certain traditional liberal pluralist followers of John Dunlop (Dunlop 1948; Freeman and Medoff 1984b).

THE WORKERS

The question about the attitudes of unorganized workers toward unions was discussed extensively in chapter 7. The data indicated that no large segment of unorganized workers, with the exception of nonwhite workers, were ready, in the majority, to join unions as a matter of course. This seems to be in contrast to the way that workers approached unions in the late 1930s. One does find, however, significant minorities of workers in the most unorganized sectors of the economy, in the least organized regions of the country, and whose social characteristics reflect relatively low organization who are ready and willing to join unions. By various other criteria also, the most important of which are strike statistics, one finds that U.S. rank-and-file workers since World War II do not seem to have lost their combativeness or general ability for self-organization.[1]

The question thus arises again why more unorganized workers are not forming unions. Although many of them are in shops where they constitute a minority, it is probable that there are also many in situations where they constitute a majority. A substantial number of other unorganized workers most likely have working conditions that would lead them to join their automatically pro-union coworkers.

The view that the faltering fortunes of unions are due to anti-unionism among nonunion workers is hardly convincing. Although around election time there is often much journalistic speculation based on some solid facts (as the opinion polls cited in chapter 3 indicate) that workers are alienated from union leaders, there is very little hard evidence that they are opposed to unions per se. The question remains why more workers are not joining, voting for, and successfully organizing unions.

THE GOVERNMENTAL AND LEGAL FRAMEWORK: THE STATE

The state has always played a central role in defining the context in which new union organizing takes place. In much of the nineteenth century and at times in the twentieth century, capitalists in this country have used the legal system and the courts to prevent worker organization; even violent means have been

1. This assessment is also reflected in certain more radical activities of U.S. workers. Montgomery (1979), for example, in his studies of the historical recurrence of struggles for workers' control of production in this country, finds these themes at least as important in the 1970s as in earlier periods. The short-lived League of Revolutionary Black Workers, which emerged in Detroit in the late 1960s and grew very rapidly (see Georgakas and Surkin 1975 and Geschwender 1977 for descriptive material), was the precursor for hundreds of explicitly anticapitalist black caucus movements as well as many more not so directly political organizations. Similarly, the less explicitly radical efforts of the farmworkers, coal miners, and large numbers of automobile wildcatters throughout the 1970s offer little to convince us that U.S. workers have become quiescent.

used by the state to stifle unions.[2] At certain times in this century, however, the state has provided a legal and public policy context in which new union organizing has been decidedly easier. It has generally done this in order to contain massive labor struggle; as the struggle has subsided (or the need to limit it has diminished), the rights and protections granted labor unions have been withdrawn. During both world wars (and their aftermaths), unions were given great protections in return for relinquishing the right to strike.[3]

The past several decades may be characterized as ones in which the legal rights of unions in the private sector have been diminished; public policy (via laws, court interpretations, NLRB rulings, and decisions by other federal or state bodies) has become less favorable to unions, at least in the private sector. The withdrawal of support by the state may be viewed in contrast to the last period when the state gave greater support to new union organizing.

A harbinger for this period was the passage of the Norris–La Guardia (Anti-Injunction) Act of 23 March 1932. Norris–La Guardia asserted the rights of workers to join and act through unions; it declared yellow-dog contracts illegal.[4] It severely limited the rights of courts to issue injunctions against unions involved in labor disputes. Though establishing certain principles, the Norris–La Guardia Act had few teeth. The next several years, 1933–35, saw massive labor struggles for union recognition, the most important of which were openly led by leftists.[5] These struggles spurred the passage of the National Labor

2. Trade union illegality existed in the United States during the nineteenth century and well into the twentieth century. During much of the nineteenth century, membership in trade unions and participation in strikes were often grounds for being charged with criminal conspiracy. Trade unions barely had a legal existence. Dramatic events—the conviction and hanging of the Chicago labor leaders after the "Haymarket Affair" (1886), the bloody suppression of Eugene Debs's American Railway Union (1894), the conspiracy and sedition trials of labor leaders during World War I, and the Memorial Day Massacre of striking steelworkers at Republic Steel by Chicago police (1937, almost two years after the passage of the National Labor Relations Act)—serve to highlight this situation.

3. Some argue that public employee organizing may be a partial exception to this pattern, their legal rights being granted without the threat of impending upsurge (Freeman 1984; Saltzman 1984, 1985; for a contrary view, see Goldfield 1987).

4. See "The Norris-La Guardia Anti-Injunction Act," 23 March 1932 (U.S. Congress Senate Committee on Labor and Public Welfare, 1979).

5. For divergent interpretations of this period, see I. Bernstein (1950), Preis (1964), Harris (1982a, 1982b), and Goldfield (1985a).

Relations (Wagner) Act of 5 July 1935. A primary stated purpose of the Wagner Act was to remove "certain recognized causes of industrial strife and unrest, by encouraging practices fundamental to the friendly adjustment of industrial disputes." The way to do this according to the NLRA was to redress the imbalance between employees and employers, that is, by aiding and abetting workers in the organization of unions. The NLRA established the NLRB to carry out this task. From 1935 to 1941, the NLRB took the task to heart, playing a highly partisan role (Gross 1974). From 1941 to 1947, the NLRB's contention that employers had no rights in the organizing process was challenged bit by bit through the Supreme Court.[6]

The passage of the Taft-Hartley Act in 1947 was a clear attempt to limit union rights, especially in new organizing. It took away many of their most effective tactics, and gave employers a variety of tools to participate (interfere) in the organizing process. The Labor-Management Reporting and Disclosure Act (Landrum-Griffin) of 14 September 1959 placed further limitations on unions. Together, these two acts had a number of adverse effects on new union organizing.

First, they outlawed or made more difficult certain militant tactics that could be used either by the unions themselves or by their supporters from other unions wishing to apply pressure in solidarity with those seeking recognition from their employers. They eliminated most forms of mass picketing, the type often used to intimidate those not striking (i.e., "scabs") or those attempting to move the employer's supplies and products; only "informational" picketing was allowed. Landrum-Griffin placed further limits on secondary boycotts and made "hot-cargo agreements" illegal,[7] two methods by which other workers and their unions could exert power to force union recognition. Taft-Hartley created a whole series of unfair labor practices that employers could file against unions. The teeth behind these new regulations were the new legal rights of employers to sue unions for damages and the strengthening of the injunctive powers of the courts and the executive.

6. For a detailed account of this see Gross (1981) and Harris (1982b). It is important to remember that the NLRB was not the only, or at times even the main, certification show in town. The War Labor Board also played this role from roughly 1942 until 1945.

7. Hot-cargo agreements were agreements between unions and employers in which the employer agreed not to handle another employer's products until the latter had settled with the union.

Second, Taft-Hartley made more difficult NLRB certification of a union by eliminating card checks and other more informal methods by which the NLRB might ascertain that a majority of workers desired a union. Thus elections (after a campaign period) became the only legal way that the NLRB could certify a union as the recognized bargaining agent.

Third, by granting employers "free speech" rights during the pre-election period, Taft-Hartley opened the way for the present-day large-scale intervention of employers in the process of employee organization and decision making. As opposed to the potential penalties that could be faced by a union, the penalties on employers for overstepping their "rights" were quite minimal. The 1970s have seen a vast enlargement of the acceptable areas of employer free speech by both the NLRB and the courts. Many statements that were formerly sufficient to overrule an election as prejudicial are now regarded as quite acceptable by the board.[8]

Fourth, Taft-Hartley made it legal for states to pass laws banning the union shop.[9] These so-called right-to-work laws have been politically quite controversial. Proponents and opponents alike have made their passage a matter of great principle; unions used to make a stand on the elimination of 14b of Taft-Hartley (the right-to-work section) as the litmus test for an elected official.

There has been much controversy among scholars over the effects of right-to-work laws. Most studies have argued that the passage by individual states of right-to-work legislation has little or no effect on organizing, even when other factors are controlled

8. In 1973, the NLRB held that citing a history of store closings for "economic reasons" was protected by "free speech" (J.J. Newbury Co., 1973 CCH NLRB Par. 25, 117; see Freeman and Medoff 1976). In 1977, the Supreme Court made the pro-employer *Shopping Cart Ford Market* decision. After that time, its positions wavered. Then in 1982, the 1977 decision was again asserted strongly in the *Midlife Insurance Company* case. See the *Chicago Sun-Times*, 10 August 1982, for a discussion of *Midlife Insurance*. A detailed discussion of the legal cases and many of the issues may be found in Klare 1978, Lachman 1982, and Weiler 1983. Discussions of the increasingly pro-employer bent of the NLRB beginning in 1983 may be found in Gould 1985, Kane 1985, Klare 1985, and Levy 1985.

9. A union shop is a shop where all workers who are hired must become members of the union within a short, definite period after they have started working for the employer. The union must accept as members all who are hired. This is distinguished from the closed shop, where workers must have membership in the union before gaining employment, or the open shop where workers need never join a union.

for in their models.[10] Many researchers have concluded that the laws are controversial more for their symbolic significance than for the actual effects they have on unionization.

Right-to-work legislation does not appear to have a significant effect on victory rates in NLRB certification elections. However, according to one recent publication, it does appear to have a dramatic effect on the extent of organizing activity. An extremely careful study by Ellwood and Fine proves conclusively that right-to-work laws do sharply depress the number of workers organized through NLRB union certification elections, particularly in the first five–ten years after passage by the state. They argue that the passage of such legislation, even after controlling for other variables, reduces on the average organizing activity nearly 50 percent during the first five years after passage and by half that amount in the second five years (Ellwood and Fine 1983, p. 32). This means that union membership is reduced from 5–10 percent as a result of passage of the act.

The reasons for the effects of right-to-work legislation may be manifold. Ellwood and Fine suggest one that pinpoints the importance of the political struggle between class forces on the organizing process.

A major part of the law's impact may be through the psychological/symbolic effect passage of a RTW (right-to-work) law may have on workers. Successful organization requires that a few workers inside a plant take a highly visible and activist role. The costs to these activists can be enormous, ranging from harassment to loss of their jobs. Even those who are not activists must take the highly visible step of signing an authorization card. And in considering whether or not to vote for a union, workers often fear they will lose their jobs or suffer other costs if their company is hostile. Thus the perceived strength of the union may be critical to the willingness of activists and others to become involved in an organizing drive. A highly visible defeat such as the passage of RTW law (or the crushing of PATCO) may severely damage the union's credibility and appeal to workers. There is at least some evidence that the psychological impact may be important. In Missouri, for example, after a RTW law was defeated, new organizing jumped dramatically. (Ellwood and Fine 1983, p. 32)

10. See Meyers (1955), Lumsden and Petersen (1975), Miller (1976), Wessells (1981). Hunt and White (1983) argue that right-to-work states have more recently had more organizing activity and more "pro-union outcomes" in NLRB union certification elections. See Moore and Newman (1985) for a partial literature review.

Their argument and analysis are convincing.[11] If nothing else, a right-to-work campaign is another public opportunity for those opposed to worker organization to engage in acceptable political agitation against unions.

Right-to-work legislation and activities on its behalf are one barometer of the balance of class forces. The failure of unions to force repeal of section 14b of Taft-Hartley at the national level is an enduring reminder of their political weakness. The passage of right-to-work legislation in twenty states (many in the South) and the continuing campaigns in others are a further indicator of severe working-class weakness in many parts of the country. Most important, however, the growing strength and activity of right-to-work advocates is a further sign that the balance of class forces is shifting away from workers and their unions toward employers.

SHIFTS IN PUBLIC POLICY

To what degree can one attribute the change in public policy toward labor unions, especially toward new union organizing, as being at least the partial cause of trade union decline? To answer this question, it is instructive to look at several other cases where it is arguable that differences or changes in public policy have had a strong effect on union organizing.

1. The rapid rise of the Foreman's Association of America (FAA) during the 1940s and its rapid demise after the passage of the Taft-Hartley Act in 1947 is a particularly poignant example. Charles Larrowe (1961) refers to the FAA as a "meteor on the industrial relations horizon." He argues that the rises and falls in FAA membership during the 1940s were closely correlated with the shifting positions of the NLRB on whether foremen had a legal right to organize and be recognized by their employers. The prospects for FAA growth appeared excellent after the favorable Packard decision of December 1945. Yet the exclusion of foremen from NLRB coverage by the Taft-Hartley Act, in the opinion of many, sealed the fate of the FAA.[12]

11. See Moore and Newman (1985) for a contrary view. They do not, however, refer to the Ellwood and Fine article, much less deal with their argument.

12. Besides Larrowe, Shister (1953) presents a similar view on the importance of the public policy changes in the demise of the FAA. For a different view of the demise of the FAA, see Harris (1982b, pp. 78–85, 147–48). Harris traces the decline to a combination of factors, including the weakened economy after peacetime reconversion began, the lack of full union solidarity with the FAA

2. During the same period that one witnessed the decline in new organizing success rates in the private sector (the 1960s and 1970s), there was a tremendous outburst of organizing activity among public employees. Various studies of this recent union organizing emphasize public policy changes toward public employee unions (according them the right to organize) as a major factor in stimulating their growth. Further, public employers, with some notable exceptions, have not generally fought union organization as have employers in the private sector.

3. Freeman and Medoff present an illuminating comparison of the U.S. and Canadian situation:

An interesting perspective on the potential impact of differing legal systems on union success is given by Canada, a country with many of the same unions and employers but a different mode for workers to obtain union recognition. In contrast to the U.S., Canada does not rely on secret ballot elections; instead, employers are obligated to recognize unions when the union has 55% of workers signed up. Only in cases where the union has 45–55% of workers signed are elections held. The fundamental difference between the U.S. and Canada is that the Canadian process of unionization does not, in general, permit the same level of employer involvement as do U.S. election procedures. The different institutional structure appears, moreover, to have led to a very different outcome in Canada than in the U.S. Whereas in 1957 unions had a larger share of workers in the U.S. than in Canada (33% vs. 29%), in 1978 the pattern was reversed (24% vs. 29%) due to the declining percentage unionized of the U.S. While not all of the differences in trend may be attributed to the difference in laws, few would dispute the statement that the Canadian system, by limiting the ability of management to fight unions, has contributed to the comparative stability of Canadian private sector unionism. (Freeman and Medoff 1984a, pp. 20–21; see also Canada Department of Labor 1970).

4. Kochan argues that the instability of the United Farm Workers Union (UFW) before the passage of legislation in California guaranteeing the rights of farmworkers to organize was a result of unfavorable public policy (Kochan 1980, p. 137).

5. The stability of U.S. labor union membership has been much greater, despite its cyclical rises and falls, since the passage of the NLRA in 1935. As noted by many earlier scholars, including Commons (1958, p. 19) and Ullman (1955, p. 134),

---

critical to leverage of foremen's organizations, and the vehemence with which employers opposed the organization of their lower level managerial representatives.

trade unions often disappeared during unfavorable economic times, only to rebloom when economic conditions became more favorable.

It is certainly possible that changes in public policy toward labor unions have at times had a strong effect on the success of new union organizing. As indicated in chapter 6, more than a few commentators have taken this position. It is clear, however, that much of the correlation of public policy shifts with union difficulties may be merely a reflection of changes in the relative strength of the working class and the employing class on the state and national level.[13] Most of the unfavorable policies stem from the passage of the Taft-Hartley Act in 1947. What is most significant is the degree to which employers have been able to make use of provisions and loopholes in these long-standing laws to undermine union growth and stability; in response, unions have been unable to force the government to tighten the loopholes and provisions (viz., the defeat of the highly limited 1978 Labor Law Reform Act) or to devise tactics to undermine employers' use of them. While the independent effects of labor law and public policy may indeed be real, they may also be largely a reflection of the interrelations between unions and capitalists to which we shall now turn.

The Capitalist Offensive

Since 1981, there has been an increase in attempts to weaken and to break unions. The late 1960s and the whole of the 1970s were also accompanied by a tremendous rise in employer opposition to unions, particularly to new union organizing. The story, however, must go back further.

Throughout each of the past several decades, various observers have discovered the beginning of a "new" capitalist offensive. The more perceptive commentators have found, at various junctures, the emergence of new tactics and forms of resistance to unions. In one sense, they have all been right. Their failures, however, have been in their identification of each new tactic as a new wave of opposition to unions by capitalists in general. Rather, I would argue, there has been a continuous, growing capitalist anti-union offensive, widening in both its forms of

13. See Griffin, Wallace, and Rubin (1986) for an insightful discussion of this question for the 1920s.

resistance and its sectoral importance, since at least the mid-1950s.

In contrast to their counterparts in other developed capitalist countries, most U.S. capitalists have never fully accepted the legitimacy of unions. After the passage of the Taft-Hartley Act in 1947, the purging of the left from the AFL and the CIO, and the establishment of more regularized relations between major employers and the CIO unions, resistance to unions began to increase. This resistance is reflected in part in the rise of discharges and employer unfair labor practices, beginning in the middle 1950s.

This opposition is also registered in the increase of national industrial opposition to unions; the establishment, growing strength, and renewed concentration of trade associations emphasizing union busting; the burgeoning anti-union management consulting industry; the large-scale climb in active employer oppositions to NLRB union certification, which is partially reflected in the growing numbers of political firings and other illegal employer tactics; and the rise of decertification election attempts and successes.

Not all these tactics began at once. Some did not blossom until the 1960s or 1970s. Others only began in the 1980s. Some tactics have existed for a long period of time but have only become important in the more recent period. As each new tactic has emerged, it has been incorporated into the arsenal of the growing opposition movement to unions.

This section begins with some broad descriptions that will provide the context both for dating the emergence of new tactics and for interpreting the more narrow quantitative material that will follow.

ANTI-UNION INDUSTRY TRADE ASSOCIATIONS

Trade associations that have developed vigorous anti-union programs include the National Association of Manufacturers (NAM), the American Hospital Association, the Associated Builders and Contractors (ABC), the Associated General Contractors (AGC), the National Retail Merchants Association, the National Public Employee Relations Association, and the Master Printers Association (MPA).[14]

14. Much of the descriptive material that follows is taken from the comprehensive statement of Robert Georgine, President of the Building and Construction Trades Department of the AFL-CIO, before the Subcommittee on Labor-

The activity of the MPA exemplifies the current attempt to break the power and degree of employee control exerted by the traditionally conservative skilled craft unions. The MPA, an inconsequential anti-union association after World War II, since then has come to represent two-thirds of the printing industry. It holds seminars on breaking and preventing unions, gives information and support in strike breaking, provides strike insurance, aids in decertification attempts, and maintains information on potentially available nonunion printing tradesmen.

The Council on a Union-Free Environment (CUE), on the other hand, was only recently established (1977). CUE, formed as a tax-free educational and research arm of NAM has as its goal the elimination of unions, as its name implies. One of its co-chairman is Arthur Prine of R. R. Donnelly, the largest non-union printing company in the world. CUE coordinates leaflets, questionnaires, legal services, and other "aid." It does research, often through universities, having associated scholars on the editorial boards of reputable academic journals including the *Journal of Labor Research*, thus providing an aura of respectability to what is quite often a very sordid business.[15]

The most successful attempts at union busting so far have been in the construction industry. The spearhead of this attack has come, not from the two major construction employer associations (ABC and AGC), although they have been integrally involved, but from an association consisting of the largest industrial companies in the country, the biggest nongovernmental users of unionized construction labor. This association is the Business Roundtable.[16]

Management Relations of the House of Representatives Committee on Education and Labor, 17 October 1979 (Georgine 1979). For obvious reasons, most of the publicly available material on union busting comes from clearly biased sources, the labor unions themselves. Georgine's account, however, contains much documentation and generally coincides with material often appearing in more probusiness publications, including the *Wall Street Journal, Forbes*, and *Business Week*.

15. Professors James T. Bennett and Manuel H. Johnson, editors of the *Journal of Labor Relations*, for example, are the authors of a CUE pamphlet entitled "Pushbutton Unionism."

16. Much of the information on the Business Roundtable has been supplied by the Building Construction Trades Department of the AFL-CIO. Two especially informative documents include a special issue of *The Builders* (undated) on the Business Roundtable, and a statement by J. C. Turner, General President, International Union of Operating Engineers, AFL-CIO, May 1979, entitled "The Business Roundtable and American Labor." Additional information may be gleaned from a series of Roundtable pamphlets, which began publication in

Since the foundation of the Business Roundtable in 1969, originally chaired by Roger Blough, former chairman of U.S. Steel, union coverage in the construction industry has plummetted.[17] Union density in construction is estimated to have been well over 50 percent for the 1960s. Accurate Current Population Survey estimates are not available until the late 1970s. For 1977, according to CPS estimates, union density had fallen to 37.9 percent, by 1980 to 31.6 percent, to 27.5 percent by 1983, and by 1984 to 23.5 percent.[18]

The Business Roundtable began with a comprehensive program including the enlargement of the nonunion sector (in which they have greatly succeeded), the support of litigation challenging protections currently enjoyed by construction workers, the repeal of the Davis-Bacon Act (which guarantees prevailing union wages on government contracts), and the undermining of what they consider expensive collective bargaining agreements in previously stable unionized areas. It has developed legal ways for contractors to engage in "double breasting," a method, formally illegal, in which contractors set up parallel nonunion operations, often to compete with their own union companies, in order to avoid paying union wages and benefits. The Business Roundtable consults and provides aid in "bargaining to impasse," strike breaking, decertification elections, arranging dual gates (making on-site picketing difficult), and obtaining nonunion labor from common pools.

Other traditional anti-union groups, including the National Right-to-Work Committee, have flourished in this fertile envi-

---

1974, called "Coming to Grips with Some Major Problems in the Construction Industry." One interesting thing about the Business Roundtable is their method of punishing contractors who have been satisfied with their union shops and refuse to double breast. According to construction union sources, they have actively diverted business away from them toward nonunion contractors.

17. In 1969, this organization was called the Construction Users Anti-Inflation Roundtable; this organization was formed from an earlier group, founded in 1965, called the Labor Law Study Group. For additional information on the Business Roundtable, see also Domhoff (1979, pp. 79–81) and Burch (1981).

18. See BLS 1981e for 1980 figure, BLS 1979e for 1977 figure, and BLS 1985a (p. 209) for the 1983 and 1984 figures. Freeman and Medoff (1979a) calculate estimates of labor-management coverage (which register slightly higher than membership figures) for certain earlier years; their calculations for 1969–72 from their analysis of EEC (Expenditures for Employee Compensation) data, administered by the BLS survey, show figures of well over 50 percent for those SIC codes associated with the construction industry.

ronment. But perhaps the largest growth has been among the antilabor consulting firms.

ANTI-UNION MANAGEMENT CONSULTING FIRMS

In Chapter Two we will show you how to screw your employees (before they screw you)—how to keep them smiling on low pay—how to maneuver them into low-pay jobs they are afraid to walk away from—how to hire and fire so you always make money.[19]

Anti-union labor relations consultants became fairly active in the 1950s; they were important enough to be the subject of congressional investigations in 1958 and 1959. By the 1970s, however, they came to represent a quantitatively and qualitatively different phenomenon. From being atypical in the late 1950s, they became the usual occurrence in the 1970s; their activities continue unabated today. As Robert Georgine of the AFL-CIO testifies:

Our records show that out of 6,000 organizing campaigns of 10 or more workers, two-thirds involve some form of outside anti-union expertise. By some estimates there are more than 1,000 firms directly and indirectly involved in union-busting activities with more than 1,500 individual practitioners engaged in the full-time activity of preventing unionization efforts. Union-busting is now a major American Industry with annual sales well over $1/2 billion. (Georgine 1979, p. 7)

Informal 1982 estimates by the AFL-CIO Department of Organization state that the figure had reached $2 billion. Thus it would seem that the involvement of the consulting firms in two-thirds of the certification elections in units of over ten workers is today an understatement.

The anti-union consulting firms are involved in three basic situations: (1) If a union does not yet exist, they provide programs of preventive unionization, which range all the way from so-called positive industrial relations (getting supervisors to "act nice" and providing union wages and benefits) to blacklists, spies, discharges and, harassment of potential union sympathizers.[20] (2) They aid in getting rid of established unions through creating bargaining impasses, strike breaking, and decertifica-

19. From the description of a book by Financial Management Associates, *Why Sons of Bitches Succeed and Nice Guys Fail in a Small Business* (quoted in Everling 1981, p. 13).
20. See various issues of the AFL-CIO *Report on Union Busters* and McConville (1975, 1980).

tions. (3) Their main field of activity, however, is probably their involvement in defeating union organizing drives.

The typical strategy for defeating an organizing drive involves the following general steps. First, they attempt to create a psychological profile of every member of the work force. If there is time, they require workers to complete an often innocuous-looking attitudinal survey. A number of the questions on these surveys are those that past attitudinal studies have correlated with either pro-union or anti-union attitudes. Although billed as confidential, the questions about type of work, department, and so on, are sufficiently detailed to identify virtually any worker. One questionnaire I have seen, for example, given to Northern Indiana Public Service Company (NIPSCO) workers, analyzed by the Human Resources Center of the University of Chicago (1981), purports to give the worker a chance to "offer suggestions on how to make the company more effective and productive."[21] In addition, supervisors are questioned in depth about the company loyalty of each and every employee.

The consulting firms themselves generally have little contact with the workers. Rather, they spend great amounts of time with the supervisors, coaching, preparing, and often intimidating them into becoming the "foot-soldiers in the anti-union campaign" (Georgine 1979, p. 2). The supervisor army, often referred to as "terrorists" in congressional testimony by individual workers, usually begins, at the instruction of the consultants, a campaign of harassment, discharge, rumor mongering, selective promotions, and occasional transfers of union activists to isolated situations.

Simultaneously, a series of legal maneuvers are utilized. Unfair labor practices are committed and dilatory motions are filed to delay the NLRB election. While ultimately the company may be found guilty by the NLRB, the benefits of delay outweigh the costs. (Georgine 1979, p. 3)

Though many may find the union accounts extremely biased, their general correctness seems to be confirmed, not merely in NLRB hearings, but in the advertisements and private seminars of the labor relations firms themselves. The largest firm, Modern Management Methods (now Modern Management, Inc.), whose slogan is "We Never Lose," supposedly once had a 98 percent

21. I am indebted to the Division of Labor Studies at Indiana University, Northwest, for a copy of the NIPSCO questionnaire.

success record in defeating unions in certification elections.[22] Despite the sophistication of psychological testing and intricate legal maneuvers, however, Georgine argues that "while different tactics have been used through the years, the strategy of union-busting remains timeless—divide workers from one another to prevent them from organizing" (1979, p. 4).

THE RESULTS OF THE ANTI-UNION OFFENSIVE

What has just been described, though based on large amounts of documented evidence, is ultimately impressionistic. Most of the work of anti-union consulting firms is done in secret; many of them evade the law, failing to file their financial reports as required under the 1959 McClelland Labor-Management Reporting Act. The results, however, of the capitalist offensive against U.S. labor unions are clearly apparent in a variety of statistics.

Much of the resistance to new union organizing since the early 1950s has been through means that are today considered legal. These include active campaigning against a union by a company through verbal and written communication, holding meetings of "captive" employees on company time, making various predictions about the deleterious effects of a union election victory (including strikes, conflict, and even potential job loss). In addition, employers fight to include or exclude various groups of workers from the potential bargaining unit in the hopes that they will get the unit least likely to vote union. Employers attempt to delay through legal tactics the holding of elections, knowing that the longer they are put off, the less likely the chance of union victory.

Other tactics of employers, rising sharply since the 1950s and increasingly popular, however, are illegal. Certain of these are reflected in NLRB statistics. As shown in table 32, there has been a geometric increase in unfair labor practice charges against employers, rising sevenfold between 1955 and 1980 (charges against employers are the 8-a-1 charges). There has been a sixfold increase in 8-a-3 charges against employers (usually for discharges for union activity) since 1955, a doubling in the period from 1970 to 1980. Despite the increasingly clever means of firing pro-union workers devised by consultants and

22. According to information from the AFL-CIO's *Report on Union Busting* 51 (Nov.–Dec. 1985), Modern Management has fallen on hard times, losing business, cutting salaries, with at least one top director being pursued by the IRS.

TABLE 32   Employer Opposition to Unions as Reflected in Unfair Labor Practice Cases, 1950–1980

Year	Section 8(a)(1)	Section 8(a)(3)	Reinstates	Number of Backpay Cases	Backpay Amount (in thousands)
1950	4,472	3,213	2,111	2,259	$ 1,078
1955	4,362	3,089	1,275	1,836	785
1960	7,723	6,024	1,885	3,110	1,041
1965	10,931	7,367	1,875	4,530	2,699
1970	13,601	9,290	3,779	6,706	2,639
1974	17,978	11,620	4,778	6,800	8,156
1975	20,301	13,426	3,816	7,405	11,286
1976	23,496	15,090	4,442	7,238	11,636
1976q	6,223	3,982	(the transitional quarter)		
1977	26,105	16,697	4,458	7,552	17,373
1978	27,056	17,125	5,533	8,623	13,439
1979	29,026	17,220	5,837	14,627	16,538
1980	31,281	18,317	10,033	15,566	32,136

Source: Annual reports of the NLRB, 1950–80.

Note: This table is an expanded and updated version of one used by Freeman and Medoff (1976).

industrial relations departments (not to say the more conservative nature of the NLRB, which rules in these cases), reinstatements of workers to their jobs has increased tenfold from 1955 to 1980. The number and percentage of workers receiving backpay for 8-a-3 violations has likewise risen dramatically. Finally, the amount of backpay has risen even more sharply, indicating that employers have been increasingly successful in keeping illegally disciplined union supporters off the job longer. It should be noted that the backpay awards greatly underestimate the amount of time lost by workers. A common tactic of a company is to offer a settlement to a worker far less than his or her full due; workers accept these offers in order to get back to work and to avoid waiting months and years longer for the NLRB procedures and court appeals to be exhausted.

Of course, there are other illegal tactics that do not have their own separate statistical categories, but are apparent from reading the AFL-CIO *RUB* sheets and accounts of various labor-management consultants. A large and growing body of research indicates that all these tactics, legal and illegal, of management opposition to new union organizing through the NLRB do have their impact on union success.

One quite graphic study is that presented to the House Special Subcommittee on Labor in 1967 by William Kircher, then director of organization for the AFL-CIO (see Kircher 1968). In a study of 495 NLRB elections held between 1966 and 1967, the AFL-CIO found that the union won over 95 percent of those where there was no campaign by the employer.[23] Three-quarters of these elections were won by at least two-to-one margins; the majority were won by six to one margins. Unions won, however, only 70 percent where captive audience speeches were given, barely 50 percent when these speeches were given within seventy-two hours of the election. There was only a 43 percent victory rate when the elections were held subsequent to firings, layoffs, or demotions of union activists; there was only a 43 percent victory rate when surveillance took place, and a 37 percent victory rate when a wage increase was put into effect by the company during the campaign.

The findings of this study are paralleled by those in one sponsored by the National Industrial Conference Board (Curtin 1970). The results of the NICB research, based on 140 organizing drives, show that where there was merely written communication from the employer to the workers (or none at all), the union won 85 percent of all elections among white-collar workers. Where there were, instead of written communication, individual and group meetings, unions won barely over 50 percent. In those campaigns where employers engaged in written communication and individual or group meetings (or both), unions were only successful in 34 percent of the elections. Both these studies seem to lead to the same conclusion: the more opposition from employers, the less chance there is for a union victory.

Two other studies highlight the importance of illegal campaign activities by the employer. Les Aspin's study (1966) of seventy-two NLRB elections held in New England between 1962 and 1964 where reinstatements of fired workers were ordered shows the following results. The average success rate in the region during the period under study was 62 percent. When there were 8-a-3 violations, this rate dropped to 48 percent. If the election was held before the worker returned to work or if the worker refused to return, the rate dipped still further to 41

23. The exact figure is twenty-eight out of twenty-nine, with a "no decision" for the remaining one. See Kircher (1968).

percent. If, however, the election were held after the worker returned to work, the success rate was 67 percent.

Later studies by William Dickens (1980, 1983) come to even more far-reaching conclusions. Dickens studied attitudinal data from 966 workers participating in thirty-one elections from 1972 to 1973. Using a simulation model, Dickens concluded that with no (or a light) campaign against the union by the employer, there was a 53–67 percent likelihood of unions winning a certification election. With an intense campaign against the union, there was a 22–34 percent chance of unions winning the election. When there were violations of the law, unions were likely to win only 4–10 percent of the elections. Drastic conclusions indeed.

David Ellwood and Glen Fine in their study of the effects of right-to-work laws have modeled the effects of employer unfair labor practices by state. They use as their dependent variable the number of employees in bargaining units where unions have won NLRB certification elections divided by the nonagricultural labor force in the state. They tested the number of unfair labor practice charges against employers by state and found that a level of one standard deviation higher actually lowered their dependent variables by 10 percent (Ellwood and Fine 1983, p. 18). If we accept this finding, then the dramatic rise in unfair labor practice charges indicated in table 32 would have a significant impact on organizing successes.[24]

There is at least one study, however, that argues against the view propounded above. Getman, Goldberg, and Herman did an in-depth analysis of thirty-one NLRB certification elections between February 1972 and September 1973. They were able to interview 1,239 of the 1,300 employees involved in these elections, both before the start of the campaign and after the election had taken place. In twenty-eight of the elections vigorous employer campaigning took place; in twenty-two of them unlawful acts were committed. In all campaigns, there was a dropoff of initial union supporters from the beginning to the end of the campaign. In general, Getman, Goldberg, and Herman conclude, there were "no characteristics that served to distinguish the successful employer campaigns from those less successful"

24. They also tested a variable called COPE, which measured the prolabor rating of the congressional delegation of each state. They found that this variable had very little impact on the degree of success unions had in organizing new members in a particular state.

(1976, p. 101). Of special importance for our concerns here, they conclude:

The data do not, however, support the Board's assumption that unlawful campaign practices affect the voting behavior of union sympathizers. The unions did not lose significantly more support in unlawful elections than in clean elections. (1976, p. 128)

The Getman study has been widely acclaimed in probusiness quarters, yet also criticized by a number of scholars. Dickens (1983) argues that it adheres to too strict a criterion of statistical significance and that it fails to take into account the degree to which NLRB outcomes hinge on small numbers of votes. I find this latter point partially substantiated in the study itself, where it is reported that in nine of the thirty-one elections, changes among the undecideds and voters who switched preferences would have changed the outcomes.

The conclusions of the Getman study also seem to hinge on a number of very narrow assumptions. Although there was a high correlation between employee vote and attendance at a union or company meeting, the investigators did not feel able to assign causal significance to this factor because they did not feel they could separate it from other factors, in particular, employee predispositions. But they failed to make a crucial distinction. While attending a union meeting may bear a significant relation to a worker's precampaign preferences, attending an employer meeting, particularly a "captive audience" meeting, may not be so clearly related. Perhaps, looking at captive meetings by the employers separately would have eliminated the predispositions of the employees as a variable affecting attendance at the meetings. Another problem with the Getman approach is the investigators' attempt to isolate the legal campaign period from the whole process of organizing a union (a large amount of which takes place before the union even files for a bargaining election). It is both possible and likely that employer opposition has already worked its effect before the filing has taken place. Getman, Goldberg, and Herman virtually concede as much:

The apparent failure of unlawful campaign tactics to affect vote does not mean that some employees are not deterred from supporting union representation for fear of the employer's reaction. The data suggest, rather, that most employees susceptible to coercion have been weeded out before the pre-election campaign takes place. (1976, p. 129)

Thus illegal tactics by the employer may not change employee preferences during the campaign period because they fit into the longer term anti-union tactics (also often illegal) that have been used by employers and their advisors over a broader time frame. Yet strict prohibition of illegal tactics might lift the veil of intimidation from the heads of employees of militantly nonunion employers. Reanalysis and reevaluation of the Getman data by William Dickens (1983) and others may even alter the conclusions of this study on its own terms.

Other tactics by employers, often legal, are sometimes seen as the cause of union failures in certification elections. This is the position argued quite articulately by Richard Prosten, director of research of the Industrial Union Department of the AFL-CIO. Prosten reports on an aggregate study of 130,000 union representation elections held between 1962 and 1977. He concludes that "pre-election time-delays are the most likely source of labor's problems" (Prosten 1978, p. 240). The trend to longer time delays has been reinforced, according to Prosten, by the virtual disappearance of consent elections, which were until 1965 the most common form of NLRB certification procedure.[25] And, he argues,

Although the rules and regulations governing representation elections have changed only modestly in recent years, it is clear that one side has managed a *de facto* gutting of the guarantees promised workers by the National Labor Relations Act. (1978, p. 240)

He adds:

In essence, the strategy is to do whatever is necessary to generate as much delay as possible. Delayed hearings, delayed meetings, delayed elections, appeals, appeals of appeals, stalled negotiations, and the like are not news. (Ibid., p. 243)

Nonconsent elections take much longer than consent elections. Examination of NLRB annual reports reveals that in 1962, 46.1 percent of all NLRB elections were consent elections. In 1977, only 8.6 percent were consent elections. Stipulated elections, on the other hand, were less than 27 percent of the total in 1962, but accounting for over 73 percent in 1977. According to Prosten, most of the changes in delays occurred during the 1960s. As was noted in chapter 6, there is a decided dropoff of

25. This figure is not exactly accurate, as can be seen from Prosten's own figures discussed below.

union victory rate for each month of additional delay up to six months.

Prosten reports further on other stalling tactics by the employers even after union victories in certification elections. In 1970, the AFL-CIO received responses from unions, accounting for 2,656 NLRB election victories in that year. They found that 22.35 percent of the units (13.64 percent of the workers) were never brought under contract; 13.2 percent of the units (10.4 percent of the workers) were brought under contract for a short time, but were no longer under contract five years later.[26] Though some of the employers "succumbed to natural disasters," the majority involved employers who managed to exploit, "the weakness of the National Labor Relations Act to frustrate the results of the election. Typically, the employer had dragged the process out long enough to decimate the union's majority" (Prosten 1978, p. 247). These later failures are heavily correlated with pre-election time delays.

On the bases of these and other studies, Freeman and Medoff argue that between one-half and two-thirds of the "declining union success in certification representation elections is due to rising employer opposition—that is to say, unions would be winning roughly 60–65 percent rather than 48 percent of NLRB elections today if employer opposition were at the 1950s levels." (Freeman and Medoff 1984a, p. 18). In another study, they conclude,

The increase in employer opposition, as indicated by unfair labor practices, delays, changes in types of elections, workers reinstated for illegal firing and the like is so large that even modest impact on electoral results goes a long way in explaining the downward trend in union success in NLRB elections. (Freeman and Medoff 1983, p. 19)

My research for the period of 1972–84 confirms certain of the above statements and qualifies several others. The decline in win rates associated with greater pre-election delay is definitely reflected in the NLRB data for 1972–84; the quantities are somewhat different than Prosten found for the 1962–77 period. Below is a reporting of NLRB victory rates for each month delay (I have also used the time period between the filing for an election and the closing of the case subsequent to the election, that is, when there are no longer any appeals and the board

26. Another study by Cooke (1985) indicates even more drastic results.

finalizes the result, and achieved results similar to those in table 33 below).

TABLE 33   Percentage of Union Victories per Months' Delay

Average Rate	Delay Time
53.9%	0 (same month)
53.0	1 month
47.5	2 months
46.3	3 months
45.4	4 months
43.1	5 months
42.9	6 months
42.5	7 months
39.9	8 months

Likewise, the period showed a dramatic decrease in the number of certification elections closed during the same month of filing and within one month of filing. While 3.24 percent were closed during the same month in 1972, the figure steadily declined to 1.2 percent by 1984. Those closed after one month in 1972 constituted 40.51 percent of all certification elections, and the figure had dropped to 27.36 percent by 1981. The mean delay by year, however, does not indicate such a consistent trend. The average wait for the whole period under consideration was 2.18 months. There was a peak of 2.34 months for 1975 and 2.24 months for 1976, a decline, then a sharp rise in 1980 (2.26 months) and 1981 (2.41 months).

When this variable is examined in various regression models, however, the results are mixed. Examined by cross section, the average delay is a highly significant and important variable. When placed in our pooled cross-section time-series model, the variable is almost never significant, no matter how the pooling is accomplished. This leads one to conclude that growing delays have not been as significant a factor for union decline in the middle and late 1970s and early 1980s as they were in the 1960s and early 1970s. It is, however, the unevenness of the growth in delays during the 1970s that makes the variable statistically unimportant as a factor in the time series model.

Disaggregation of the delays by state, NLRB region, union, industry, occupational unit, and size produced varied results, none giving a clear pattern. For example, it was found that many regions with high success rates (e.g., New York City and Brooklyn) or reputedly pro-union regional offices (e.g., Detroit) had lengthy delays, while certain areas with low success rates and less reputedly pro-union sentiment had very short delays (e.g., Atlanta and Alburquerque).

An even sharper picture emerges when one looks at changes in the type of election held by the NLRB. From 1972 to 1984, consent elections decreased from 15.9 percent of all elections to only 2.5 percent of all elections; stipulated elections increased from 63.4 percent to 82.3 percent. These results are summarized in table 34. The trend is a continuation of the results described

TABLE 34   Election Type by Year, 1972–1984

Year	Consent		Stipulated	
	Number	Percentage	Number	Percentage
1972	744	15.9%	2,975	63.4%
1973	1,312	14.8	5,897	66.4
1974	1,045	11.9	6,149	69.7
1975	805	10.0	5,487	68.0
1976	870	9.6	6,355	70.4
1977	897	8.1	8,032	72.7
1978	488	7.1	5,169	75.2
1979	350	5.1	5,297	77.6
1980	380	4.5	6,543	76.6
1981	190	3.1	4,687	76.6
1982	97	2.8	2,675	76.9
1983	96	3.0	2,539	78.5
1984	87	2.5	2,878	82.3

by Prosten (1978). It is quite significant since the victory rates by unions by election types have remained fairly constant for the period 1972–84 (see table 35).

Thus a major portion of the decrease in union victory rates may be accounted for in the change of election types from one indicating employer acceptance of the legitimacy of the union to one suggesting employer resistance. In the cross-sectional analysis, consent elections are highly significant. The consent variable has coefficients of .51 for Mississippi, .29 for Virginia, .16 for California, and .11 for New York (all with significant t-statistics). The differences in these coefficients by state suggest the relative importance of employer cooperation or, conversely, the lesser

TABLE 35   Union Victories by Election Type by Year, 1972–1984

Year	All Elections		Consent Elections		Stipulated Elections	
	Number	Percentage	Number	Percentage	Number	Percentage
1972–84	89,641	49.1%	7,398	62.7%	55,725	47.8%
1972	4,714	52.0	746	61.5	2,989	50.1
1973	8,909	51.4	1,313	64.0	5,917	49.3
1974	8,848	50.3	1,046	63.9	6,166	48.3
1975	8,108	50.6	807	64.9	5,512	49.5
1976	9,073	49.1	872	62.9	6,380	47.2
1977	11,083	48.1	898	58.7	8,056	47.2
1978	6,954	49.0	491	62.3	5,230	47.7
1979	6,844	48.2	350	65.7	5,310	46.6
1980	8,552	48.5	381	60.6	6,550	48.3
1981	6,118	46.2	190	56.3	4,687	44.6
1982	3,477	47.2	97	59.8	2,675	46.7
1983	3,236	48.9	96	63.5	2,539	48.6
1984	3,498	48.1	87	73.6	2,878	48.0

likelihood of union success with employer resistance in Mississippi and the lesser effectiveness of employer resistance in New York (the most highly unionized state). In the time-series model, consent elections are also a highly important explanatory variable, suggesting that the decreases in consent elections, even when other factors are taken into account, are important in explaining the increasing union failures in new organizing.

One interesting question is why election type appears to behave so much more strongly than election delays as an explanatory variable, especially in the time series model. It is possible that delays capture more than just employer resistance. The 1972–84 data show that the amount of delay rises quickly in larger units, which might have to do with greater employer resistance, but may also be the result of longer administrative delays. On the other hand, the delay tactics may have been perfected during the 1960s (the period in which Prosten's study begins) and have been operating on a relatively constant level throughout the 1970s and early 1980s. Election type, however, is probably a slightly better indicator of the willingness of the employer to accept the unionization of his work force without more than token opposition.

The accumulation of evidence is strong. The increased employer resistance over the past three or so decades, as displayed in the increases in illegal tactics, the increases in delays, the diminishing of consent elections, and a large number of other indicators, has been a major cause for the decline in union success in new organizing through the NLRB.

THE UNIONS

Given the attitudes and current propensities of workers to join unions, the current economic situation, public policy, and the capitalist offensive against unions, to what degree do unions bear responsibility for the current decline?[27] An initial response is to ask whether unions are making the effort that they could be making or that they need to make to be successful in new union organizing. There is a large amount of descriptive and anecdotal material that suggests that they are not. I shall begin, however, with more quantitative data.

UNION ORGANIZING PROGRAMS

As has been previously indicated, there was large-scale self-organization of workers during the CIO period of 1935–39. Today, successful union organizing may require knowledge of NLRB procedures, the ability to produce frequent, timely printed material, legal information, and the resources to obtain appropriate legal services. A readiness to do battle with management and anti-union consultants is also often needed. Thus even when workers begin the process of new organizing themselves, they generally seek the services of a union and its professional organizing staff.

Paula Voos has done the only careful study of union organizing programs. She asks two connected questions: How do these programs influence or affect the process of new union organizing through the NLRB? To what degree may the decline in new union organizing successes (and in union density) be traced to declines in new union organizing programs. She finds,

not that organizing expenditures are the sole determinant of organizing success, but that the extent of union organizing programs does increase the number of new union members brought into unions by representation elections relative to the number who could be potentially orga-

---

27. This is not the only way, or even necessarily the most reasonable way, to frame the question, given the interactions and historical responsibility of unions for these factors that the reader is now asked to hold constant.

nized, given the overall economic, social, political, and industrial context. (1982, p. 184)

Voos concludes that there is (1) a one-to-three year lag between expenditures and results and (2) an average expenditure on organizing programs per person won of anywhere from $500 to $1,000, depending on the method of calculation. She argues that there has been a slight to moderate increase in organizing per union in her study of the expenditures of the twenty largest unions. When one looks at the real expenditures per nonunion member (deflated by the wage rate),[28] however, a significant drop is indicated. In 1953, unions spent $1.033 per each non-union member, in 1964 $.866, and in 1974, $.711. This is a substantial decline, certainly indicating a decrease of expenditures on union organizing programs.

Yet it is arguable whether this criterion is "better" than one that looks at aggregate budget expenditures as suggested by Voos. These figures and even those that show unions spending as much in recent years as they did in the past must be put into context. It is doubtful that one gets the same amount of organizing for the deflated buck as one did in the early and middle 1950s. At that time, there were many more volunteer organizers, stemming back from the days when virtually all organizing was low-paid and unstable. Today, the organizing staffs of large unions are no different from other union functionaries. They work nine to five, make much more than their average constitutents, have expense accounts, are usually white males, and in general are older than those they desire to organize.[29] Qualitative evidence suggests that there has been a rise in organizing costs unassociated with more productive results.

Linear regressions by Voos suggest that greater effort (i.e., money) would give more results. The question arises whether we have a problem of diminishing returns. If new organizing takes place in the choicest spots, further organizing might take place in less choice areas. Voos concludes that "in no case, do diminishing returns seem to characterize the regressions predict-

28. This is the criterion that Freeman and Medoff (1984a) choose to use.
29. A number of union officials and organizers have told me that AFSCME is among the few exceptions. It is reputed that they hire relatively young organizers who throw themselves into their work for several years. If they succeed, then these organizers may move on to becoming officials of the units that they have organized. The high turnover prevents the accumulation of "burnt out" organizers remaining on the union organizing staff.

ing the proportion of possible new members for whom the union wins bargaining rights in any year." She cites as evidence "the analysis that unions with disproportionately more elections in the South (or in any region for that matter) do not necessarily have less overall organizing success than other unions" (1982, pp. 208, 232).

The question that the regression equations cannot deal with is that of a massive expansion of organizing. What would be the effects, for example, of concentrating a large amount of resources (money, organizers, attention, other union priorities) on one area (e.g., a city, a company). Voos argues that her discussions with organizers were inconclusive. All agreed that a doubling of organizing staffs would not lead to more organizing. Many stated, however, that concentration of many existing organizers in one place would have large beneficial results. She finds this evidence contradictory. I, on the other hand, do not. It is clear that the first question implied (a) an increase in inexperienced new organizers and (b) sharp criticisms of existing programs. The second hypothetical situation is, rather, a use of existing resources in a tactically different way, which a number of the organizers in Voos's discussion had already successfully tried. Thus, the second conclusion would appear to be the more valid one. This confirms my own experience and "institutional" information as well.

MULTI-UNION ELECTIONS

One striking phenomenon, occasionally noticed by other researchers but never discussed, is the higher rate of success of unions in multi-union certification elections. These elections made up 6 percent of those held from 1972 through 1984. The percentage diminished during this approximately thirteen-year period.

First, what is most interesting is how much higher the success rates are than those of other types of elections—76.4 percent, a win rate comparable to that of unions at the height of their organizing success, from 1937 to 1940 and after World War II. Further, the rate is actually higher for the period 1977–81—78.0 percent.

There are several possible explanations for this. One is that competition only takes place when it looks like the first union making the certification bid is almost sure to win, that is, competition takes place for the plums that are likely to go union.

But a careful analysis of detailed frequency tables shows neither a tendency toward more multi-union elections in those sectors where victory rates are especially high nor even significant variance by union. Thus the more likely conclusion is that unions are willing to exert a greater effort when competing with other unions. They are more afraid of losing out to another union than in being beaten by the company. Losing an organizing campaign to the company merely deprives the union of new members; another attempt may be made after the lapse of a year with a greater likelihood of success (Czarnecki 1969). If, however, the election is lost to another union, the constituency is for all practical purposes lost forever. Even more important, a jurisdictional competitor has gained strength, which might ultimately lead to the demise of the losing union itself. The implications of this latter explanation are, first, that even with their highly paid, institutionalized, more sedate organizing staffs, unions can put out the necessary effort to win when they have to; second, most of the time unions do not put out this sufficient effort.

A striking characteristic is the high degree of consistency that union victory rates in multi-union NLRB elections have across different variables (victory rates by union may be seen in table 36). Virtually all the very high and very low figures can be explained by special circumstances. In the electrical and electronics industries, several unions with large bases in these areas compete. When the United Electrical Workers (UE), a left-wing union, has major support, it almost always wins (97.1 percent). The International Brotherhood of Electrical Workers (IBEW) and the International Union of Electrical Workers (IUE) are renowned for their use of "dirty" tactics against the UE, including various kinds of red-baiting. Their low victory rates in multi-union elections suggest that some of the tactics through which they build their own support are not conducive to workers voting union at all. The two longshore unions, the International Longshoremen's Association (ILA) (57.7 percent) and the International Longshoremen's and Workingmen's Union (ILWU) (50 percent), dominate unionization on their respective coasts and are not fundamentally involved in competitive situations. No other unions have less than 60 percent victory rates in our sample.

One further indication of the beneficial effects of competition on union success rates may be found in analysis of public sector

TABLE 36   Victory Rates in Multi-Union Elections by Union, 1972–1984

Union	Average Rate
Service Employees (SEIU)	71.8%
Bakers (BCW)	86.1
Carpenters (CJA)	67.1
Clerks (RCIA)	76.1
Electrical Workers (IBEW)	64.4
Operating Engineers (IUOE)	69.0
Hotel and Restaurant Employees (HRUE)	69.0
Garment Workers (ILGW)	80.0
East Coast Longshoremen (ILA)	57.7
Machinists (IAM)	68.8
Meatcutters (MCBW)	78.6
Office Employees (OEIU)	67.7
Printers (IPGC)	89.9
Paperworkers (UPI)	62.7
State, County, Municipal Employees (AFSCME)	72.4
Teamsters (IBT)	72.3
Teachers (AFT)	78.9
Autoworkers (UAW)	71.3
Electrical Workers (IUE)	59.4
Miners (UMW)	87.5
Oil, Chemical Workers (OCAW)	78.4
Department Store Employees (RWDSU)	78.6
Steelworkers (USA)	71.1
Textile Workers (TWMA)	82.4
Communications Workers (CWA)	67.4
Electricians (UE)	97.1
Longshoremen (ILWU)	50.0
Coopers (CIU)	96.9

union organizing. Many commentators suggest that it is the intense competition among large numbers of unions that is a major factor in the rapid growth of many public sector unions. As Jack Steiber argues:

Competition among organizations for members and exclusive representation of public employees is more widespread and more intense than at any time since . . . 1955. AFL-CIO unions compete with one another and with independents, as well as with associations and professional organizations. . . . Competition often results in more workers being organized. (1974, p. 830)

This point is echoed by Bakke, who argues that competition

between unions makes the leaderships more militant in order "to demonstrate . . . to prospective members that they have most to gain by expressing their preference for the union that will really stand up to management" (1970, p. 28). Alice Cook (1970, p. 251) also suggests that competition between several rival unions spurred on the organization of clerical workers in New York City.

Multi-union elections are significant in both the cross-section and time-series models. The disaggregated results would lead us to expect that in the cross-sectional analysis, multi-union elections would be highly positively related to union victories. Their declining number throughout the 1970s and early 1980s is one factor associated with the declining success rates of unions in NLRB certification elections.

If multi-union elections possess higher union victory rates largely due to their taking place in the most pro-union units, we would expect to see more of them (and higher rates) in those areas where union victory rates are highest or where unions were growing quite rapidly. Yet this is not the case. Disaggregating multi-union elections by union, industry, unit size, occupational unit, state and NLRB region shows little significant variation in amount of elections or in victory rates. An extreme case, for example, is the health services industry, which is rapidly unionizing and has a high victory rate. There the percentage of multi-union elections (8.8 percent) is slightly above the average (8.8 percent is 487 out of 5,526), but the multi-union election victory rate is below the average (66 percent). It is also important to note that in the health services industry, a number of unions all have legitimate competing claims.

This conclusion is in striking contrast to the general claim about private sector union organizing that competition among unions invariably hurts organizing. I take the high victory rates in multi-union certification elections as another piece of evidence that the decline in new union organizing is in good part due to the lack of aggressiveness and allocation of resources by U.S. trade unions themselves.

VICTORY RATES BY UNION

An examination of the cross-classifications by union is revealing. Particularly interesting is the International Brotherhood of Teamsters (IBT). The IBT accounts for between one-fourth and one-third of all NLRB certification elections each year. It participated in 26,837 of the 88,980 elections in our data set. Its decline was more sharp than that of all other unions together (see table 37). In 1973 it won 52.4 percent of certification elections,

TABLE 37   Union Victories by Year for IBT, 1972–1984

Year	Number	Average Rate
1972–84	26,837	46.6%
1972	1,471	51.3
1973	2,720	52.4
1974	2,649	50.5
1975	2,220	48.4
1976	2,764	44.9
1977	3,345	45.1
1978	2,140	46.2
1979	2,182	46.6
1980	2,584	44.5
1981	1,817	40.7
1982	985	42.8
1983	917	44.0
1984	1,032	43.0

yet by 1981 the victory rate had declined to 40.7 percent. Its average during the period of consideration is almost three percentage points lower than that of other unions. Virtually all of this is accountable to its low percentages from 1975 to the present. The elimination of the IBT from consideration greatly lowers the rate of union certification election decline, showing a more gentle slope than the unadjusted figures previous to 1972.[30]

The low victory rate for the IBT is especially surprising since its elections take place in smaller average unit sizes (thirty-nine employees compared to sixty-five for all other unions) and it has smaller average pre-election delays than other unions (1.9 months compared to 2.1 months). Thus, as one might suspect, the IBT is important in the cross-section and time-series regression models. By cross-section, with other things being held constant, if the union is the IBT, it accounts for a 4–7 percent drop.

The IBT had a strong depressing effect on the time-series trend of declining victory rates in NLRB certification elections. Its coefficients, as may be seen from Appendix C, range from .08 to .14 (which may be interpreted in percentage terms since the

30. These conclusions are in sharp contrast to the assertions in Warren 1982 and BNA 1985 that the IBT does particularly well.

IBT is represented by a dummy variable) in the pooled cross-section and time-series model. Thus we are led to the conclusion that the weakening performance of the IBT has had a substantial responsibility for the overall decline in union victory rates in NLRB certification elections.

Of less significance (because they represent a much smaller percentage of certification elections), but certainly of interest, is the drastic decline of the percentage of union victories by craft unions. In the 1960s, craft unions seem to have won an unusually high percentage of these elections. Rose (1972) reports that in 1966, craft unions won 94.4 percent of NLRB certification elections in which they participated. He attributes this to the acceptance of craft unions in the construction industry by the employers. Yet in the period examined here, craft unions have decreased to a stable average of 56.4 percent victories.

The decline in victory rates, as well as the relatively low rates for the period of many of the old AFL craft unions, is particularly marked in the construction and printing trades. This general trend is significant since the construction and printing trade unions have formed the backbone of the political conservatism of the official trade union structure. (Table 38 summarizes the results for major craft unions; see table 39 for white-collar unions.)

TABLE 38   NLRB Victories of Major Craft Unions, 1972–1984

Union	Number	Average	Trend
All	88,980	49.0%	Down
Plumbers (PPF)	431	56.6	Stable
Electricians (IBEW)	3,080	51.2	Declining
Carpenters (CJA)	1,896	44.2	Declining
Laborers (LIU)	1,421	48.8	Stable
Ironworkers (BSOIW)	564	43.6	Declining
Typographers (ITU)	444	54.4	Stable
Graphic Artists (GAIU)	791	50.2	Varying
Bakers (BCW)	841	49.6	Varying
Boilermakers (BBF)	437	41.6	Varying
Operating Engineers (IUOE)	1,900	50.6	Stable
Graphic Communication (IPGC)	764	49.9	Varying

Major industrial unions also show interesting trends. Only two unions, neither of which is large or has been central to the history of the labor movements, have made significant increases

TABLE 39   NLRB Victories of White-collar Unions, 1972–1984

Union	Number	Average	Trend
Retail Clerks (RCIA)[1]	2,757	52.3%	Declining
Department Store (RWDSU)	1,761	56.4	Stable
Service Employees (SEIU)	3,491	58.9	Rising
State, County (AFSCME)	406	53.2	Stable
Teachers (AFT)	207	63.8	Stable
Hotel and Restaurant (HREU)	2,204	41.9	Stable
Insurance (IWIU)	521	50.3	Stable
Office Employees (OEIU)	886	48.8	Stable

[1]Merged into United Food and Commercial Workers in 1979.

in their victory rates. These are the furniture workers (UFW) and the textile workers (TWUA), both of which have taken on aggressive new organizing in the South. The furniture workers are most active in the Deep South. The textile workers, who during most of the period covered by this data met with continued failure at J. P. Stevens, are operating in an industry with an extremely low union success rate. A combination of their general aggressiveness and their image from having continued a long battle with Stevens may be partly responsible for their increasing rate of success in general.

It is important to see whether high and low success rates are correlated with any particular characteristics of industrial unions. Does the political orientation of a union have anything to do with its success rate? Do the liberal positions and militant rhetoric of its leadership help or hinder its success rate? What about a reputation for aggressive organizing activity? Is the history of the union an important factor in the present? Although it is impossible to answer these questions definitively from the data examined here, there are many suggestive associations.

A number of major industrial unions seem to have held their own during the period of decline of union victory rates among industrial units (table 40). These include the Autoworkers, Meatcutters, and Communication unions. The UAW has had, perhaps, the most militant and volatile work force since the 1930s. It had extensive Communist influence during its periods of rapid growth and maintains (at least in contrast to many other large unions) progressive social stands against racial discrimination and discrimination against women, and in favor of much broad-ranging social legislation. Of course, similar remarks

TABLE 40   NLRB Victories of Major Industrial Unions, 1972–1984

Union	Number	Average	Trend
Communications Workers (CWA)	1,568	52.7%	Rising
Steelworkers (USA)	3,092	48.0	Declining
Rubber Workers (URW)	611	37.6	Declining
Garment Workers (ILGU)	500	37.6	Declining
Machinists (IAM)	4,098	45.5	Declining
Meatcutters (MCBW)[1]	1,690	52.4	Stable
Paperworkers (UPI)	938	41.0	Declining
Autoworkers (UAW)	3,323	48.2	Stable
Furniture Workers (UFW)	307	52.4	Varying
Miners (UMW)	294	48.0	Varying
Oil, Chemical, Atomic Workers (OCAW)	825	44.6	Declining
Food and Commercial Workers (UFCW)[1] (1979–84)	2,212	47.1	Varying

[1]The Meatcutters, along with several other unions, joined in 1979 to form the United Food and Commercial Workers.

might be made about the United Mine Workers, perhaps the most extreme case of declining union strength in the 1980s. Whether coal market volatility, severe factionalism in the union, or some other factor is responsible must await a thorough analysis. The CWA is the union that represents most telephone workers, with the exception of several trades and operators. Its history over the past two decades has been characterized by widespread rank-and-file militancy. The case of the Meatcutters is more complicated. Originally, it was more conservative and less militant than other industrial unions, although not as conservative as many of its brethren within the AFL. Slightly over a decade ago, it merged with the Packinghouse Workers, a historically militant, left-led union with a large percentage black membership. Although never fully shedding its former attire, the Meatcutters began to adopt a more militant stance within AFL-CIO councils (even calling for a general strike against the Nixon wage-price freeze in 1973).[31]

Militant rhetoric and liberal (or even socialist) posturing is, of course, not sufficient to achieve higher rates of union victories in NLRB certification elections. The International Association of Machinists (IAM), whose president William Winpisinger is out-

31. The union has since merged again, forming the United Food and Commercial Workers.

spoken, an avowed socialist, a verbal defender of workers' rights, and a sometime supporter of the Citizens' Party in the 1980 presidential election, had a low and decreasing rate. The machinists have one of the largest of U.S. unions. The militant rhetoric of their leadership is unmatched by an increase in job and bargaining militancy or aggressive new organizing. The Oil, Chemical, and Atomic Workers (OCAW) likewise puts on a liberal stance (e.g., they opposed the war in Vietnam long before the UAW or other major unions). Yet their rate of success in bargaining elections is low and dropping.

Those unions with neither militant rhetoric nor aggressive actions fare even worse. The Ladies Garment Workers (ILGWU) was never known for its democracy, militancy, or progressiveness. These traditions continue to this day. The Rubber Workers (URW) has been faced by a partially organized work force, an industry hit hard by foreign competition, and the destruction of their major union center in Akron, Ohio. Despite occasionally militant rhetoric, the union has generally conveyed the appearance of weakness (this is said without judging whether or not their leadership has been more or less adequate than more successful unions).

In the technical, clerical, service, and government unions, results are much the same. Four unions that have aggressively organized new constituencies in the last decade or more have achieved dramatic rates of success in certification elections. Two more traditional unions have not. These results may be seen from the comparisons in table 41 below.

LEFT UNIONS

Although the majority of the major CIO unions had Communist leadership or significant Communist influence, Communist par-

TABLE 41   Victories of Service, Governmental, and Clerical Unions, 1972–1984

Union	Number	Average	Trend
Service Employees (SEIU)	3,491	58.9%	Stable
Government Employees (AFSCME)	400	56.3	Varying
Teachers (AFT)	207	63.8	Varying
Department Store (RWDSU)	1,761	56.4	Stable
Retail Clerks (RCIA)	2,757 (1972–79)	52.3	Declining
Hotel and Restaurant (HREU)	2,204	41.9	Varying

ticipation was largely destroyed (as well as that of other militant groupings) during the late 1940s and early 1950s. Two left unions, the UE (electrical workers) and the West Coast longshore union (ILWU) retained their leadership groups intact, as well as maintaining some influence in their respective industries. Neither remains politically or even from the standpoint of trade union militancy what they once were; times have, of course, changed. Yet both offer a reputation for honesty, lower salaries for officials, and occasional militancy and progressive stances on social issues that serve to distance them from other former CIO unions. Thus it is instructive to compare their victory rates with those of the more conservative unions formed to displace them. Both of the more liberal unions have better success rates than their counterparts, the IUE and the ILA, respectively. These results are further borne out when the unions are tested in our cross-sectional regression model (described in Appendix B). When other factors are controlled for, it is found that the union's being the ILWU adds 8.4 percent to 9.4 percent greater likelihood of victory. When the union is the UE, the greater likelihood of victory ranges from 11.7 percent to 12.9 percent. Information on comparative victory rates for the left and non-left unions appears in table 42 below.

TABLE 42   Comparison of Victories of Left and Non-Left Unions, 1972–1984

Union	Number	Average	Trend
ILA	310	51.9%	Varying
ILWU	462	59.7	Stable
IUE	763	43.1	Varying
UE	217	60.4	Stable

In reviewing the above results by union, it should be noted that individual unions sometimes vary greatly from year to year. This is, of course, more generally true when the frequency of elections is relatively small. But this is sometimes the case when the frequency is greater, thus suggesting further analysis is needed. For example, the IBT seems to do much better in years when it participates in smaller numbers of elections, indicating that it may at times overextend itself considerably. The United Mine Workers, on the other hand, does more poorly when it participates in smaller numbers of elections than when it participates in larger numbers. Its more extensive participation may also be related to the periods when widespread strike activity has taken place, suggesting that coal organizing successes may be tied to the militancy of the miners' movements. Likewise, the UAW success rate seems to increase slightly around contract time and after periods of considerable wildcat strike activity.

CONCLUSION

From the analysis in this chapter, we may conclude the following:

1. The workers themselves do not seem to be a major impediment to the formation of new unions. Many workers, sympathetic to unions, are there as potentially organizable new members.

2. Public policy toward labor unions in this country, particularly in the private sector, poses more difficulties for union organizing than in other economically developed capitalist countries. Still, the unfavorable government policies are largely a reflection of the relative strengths of organized labor and employers.

3. The resistance of employers to the organization of their employees into labor unions is a major cause of declines in organizing successes by unions. The employer offensive of the past three decades has made a significant contribution to the overall decline of union strength in this country.

4. The unions themselves do not seem to have risen to this new challenge. They have neither devoted the resources nor put sufficient effort into new union organizing to counter the employer offensive.

A number of questions might still be asked. How did this situation come about? Why is the relation of class forces in this country so much more unfavorable to unions than in other economically developed capitalist countries? Are there anomalies in the data presented here, unevenness and irregularities that might provide us any clues? What are the prospects for a resurgence on the part of U.S. labor unions (i.e., can the empire strike back)? It is these questions that I will attempt to address in the final chapters.

Part 4
Conclusion

10

Summary

A good deal of evidence has been presented to document the decline in union strength over the last three decades and to chart its general trends. Our analysis shows that, contrary to accepted wisdom, there exists little evidence that labor union problems may be traced primarily to events or changes that have taken place either during the 1970s or the 1980s. Those who have argued that there has been a recent accelerating decline are surely mistaken. Rather, union decline appears to have been relatively steady since the mid-1950s. A many-decades-long growing capitalist offensive and an inadequate union response have helped change the relation of class forces in the United States. Many standard and widely accepted explanations for labor union weakness and decline, although they possess superficial plausibility, upon examination prove unconvincing.

CHANGES IN THE STRUCTURE AND COMPOSITION OF LABOR FORCE

COMPOSITIONAL CHARACTERISTICS

Contrary to the generally accepted view, all compositional changes in the character of the work force seem to be either potentially favorable to unions (e.g., race, sex, and age) or not very significant (e.g., education). There seem to be no grounds for blaming union decline on such changes.

GEOGRAPHIC CHARACTERISTICS

The evidence presented in this study also calls into question the belief that the movement of industry to the Sunbelt is a major reason for declining union successes in new organizing. As I have argued, it is important to disaggregate data about the South; my hope is that this is one contribution of the ongoing research presented in this book.

The South and the Southwest do not represent an area of the country of uniformly high, successful resistance to union organizing. This conclusion is contrary to that in the literature cited earlier, and also to generally accepted wisdom. Different areas in "the South" must be separated; analysis of data about the South must take into account very different organizing rates. The Southwest, indeed, is the only region of the country where union success rates are rising, and it is in general an area of high union success. This high rate in the Southwest is in good part attributed to the better success of unions there in winning elections in industrial units.

Those who attempt to explain supposed failures in the South and Southwest are caught in a contradiction. Southern culture and the reportedly more vigorous employer offensive in the South and Southwest do not seem to be insurmountable barriers to union success. Much documentation has been provided by a variety of commentators that there is an employer offensive that has intensified during the 1970s; there is convincing argument that it is especially strong in the South and Southwest. Certain of the data presented in chapter 9 indicate that employer resistance is relatively successful in the South. Yet while it may have contributed to union setbacks in many places, its precise effect on the organized and unorganized labor movements must be examined more carefully. Those theories that rely on seeing a "new worker" or anti-unionism in Southern culture are not argued with great precision. If they are to be taken at all seriously, they must be more rigorously presented. This is particularly true since they have been brought forth to explain phenomena (including supposedly uniformly low union success rates across the South) that turn out not to have occurred.

Nevertheless, given the increase of economic growth in these parts of the country, it is clear that neither the quantity nor the percentage of union victories is sufficient to change drastically the industrial and geographic patterns of unionization largely established by the organizing of the 1930s. Although union success rates in the Southwest and parts of the South are comparable to victory rates in the North and Midwest now, they are not comparable to the success rates in these latter areas during the 1930s and 1940s, which created the current unionization patterns. While my analysis has demonstrated the incorrectness of the claims about low organizing rates throughout the Sunbelt, it would also be wrong to overplay the significance of these rates even in the Southwest. Thus the next successful union organizing upsurge (which the analysis in chapter 4 suggests is likely to happen sooner or later) must inevitably have a major thrust in the South and Southwest, the areas of lowest unionization. The analysis of NLRB elections finds little that would preclude such a movement from developing there.

OCCUPATIONAL CHANGES

Those who attribute the decline of new organizing successes to the changing occupational structure of the work force are also in error, since the declines seem to be most sharp in traditional areas of union strength, rather than in the more rapidly growing service, professional, clerical, and technical segments of the work force. This conclusion must be qualified with respect to clerical workers since they represent such a disproportionately low percentage of certification elections. Still, the opposite conclusion is unsupportable from the data.

INDUSTRIAL CHANGES

The changing employment structure by industry has certainly weakened unions in many of the areas of their traditional strength. Prospects for new union organizing in more rapidly growing industrial sectors do not now look gloomier, however, than those in the traditional sectors. Rather, attitudinal data, recent union successes, and average and above average NLRB union success rates in these more rapidly growing sectors suggest that the industrial changes have not closed the door on extensive new union organizing. This assessment is strengthened when one views the successes in other economically developed capitalist countries in expanding union membership into these newer, rapidly growing sectors. We may conclude that these changes cannot be taken to be the major cause of the declines in union density and in new union organizing successes in the private sector.

CYCLICAL VARIABLES

THE ECONOMIC CYCLE

The slow increases in unemployment in the postwar period and the more rapid increases in output per man hour seem to correlate in part with the general trend of declining NLRB successes. In addition, several other economic variables help to explain a large amount of the cyclical variation in NLRB union victory rates. The variables likely to be influential include changes in unemployment, productivity, and to a lesser extent, final sales. The variables play only a minor role, however, in explaining the long-term decline.

POLITICAL VARIABLES

It was found that certain of the political variables played a significant role in determining the long-range trend. The upholding of the NLRA by the Supreme Court in 1937 probably boosted union success rates, and the passage of Taft-Hartley in 1947 likely helped to depress them.[1] These, of course, were one-time interventions. The growing number of Republicans in the White House in the postwar period undoubtedly has played a small role in lowering the victory rates, although the change of administrations seems to be far more significant in explaining the cyclical variations.

MILITANCY AND SOLIDARITY OF THE WORK FORCE

The theories that claimed there would be a sharp decline in class conflict in this country and that this would prove the undoing of U.S. unions were wrong in important respects. Likewise, those who claim that union gains will be reflected in lower levels of conflict are mistaken, at least in the application of their theories to this country. First, strike activity on the part of U.S. workers does not seem to have diminished from the mid-1950s to 1980. Second, increases in strike activity seem to correlate well with

1. It is arguable that 1937 reflected the growing strength of a massive labor insurgency, while 1947 reflected the institutionalization of a tamed, housebroken movement, unwilling to fight to defend its rights (Goldfield 1985a; Lichtenstein 1982).

cyclical increases in the success rates of unions in NLRB certification elections. Comparing U.S. strike rates to those of other countries does not show a high variance of conflict in this country. The variance that exists is not sufficient to play a major role in explaining the long-range trends in union membership decline or in increased failures at new organizing.

THE RELATION OF CLASS FORCES

WORKERS' ATTITUDES

None of the data examined here suggest that the attitudes of unorganized workers toward unions represent a major impediment to their organization. Rather, workers in unorganized sectors of the population have indicated stronger preferences in favor of joining unions than have workers in many organized sectors of the population. Public opinion data reported in chapter 3 indicate high approval of unions, but low ratings for current leaders. Such attitudes should definitely not be confused with anti-unionism. Thus the argument that a major explanation of union failures may be found in the development of strong anti-union feelings among unorganized workers is unconvincing.

THE DEVELOPMENT OF U.S. PUBLIC LABOR POLICY

National labor public policy has become increasingly unfavorable to labor unions, especially as it applies to new union organizing in the private sector. The period from 1937 to 1941, from the upholding of the NLRA until after the Smith Committee hearings in the House of Representatives, may be regarded as a highly favorable one for new union organizing. Changes in public policy during the period from 1941 until 1945 were mixed, allowing for easy union growth under the War Labor Board but more stringent interpretations of labor law under the NLRB. The passage of Taft-Hartley in 1947 marked the beginning of a more unfavorable legal period, punctuated again in 1959 with the passage of Landrum-Griffin.

The unfavorable legal situation has provided the context in which employers can more and more exploit the law to their advantage in resisting the organization of unions. The development of national labor law and the growing conservatism of national labor public policy have added to the difficulties of union organizing over the last several decades. National labor public policy must be regarded as one piece of the explanation, even if not the dominant one, for the decline of labor unions in this country.

INCREASED EFFECTIVENESS OF EMPLOYER RESISTANCE

What one does find, however, is the increased effectiveness of employer resistance to unions in this country over the last thirty or more years. A major capitalist offensive has been, in the main, successful in steadily eroding union strength and in lowering the probabilities of union successes in new organizing. While the traditional weapons of the blacklist and blackmail, of spies and thugs, have not disappeared, new weapons have risen to prominence. These include the use of antilabor consulting firms, the large-scale growth of anti-union employer organizations, the rise in numerous illegal tactics, the engagement in lengthy election delays, and the lessening of the ready acceptance of union rights and prerogatives, even in traditionally unionized sectors. These manifold tactics, and their concerted, widespread application, have proven to be a major reason for union decline in this country.

THE UNIONS

Unions themselves seem to have become less aggressive and, in general, less committed to new organizing campaigns in the private sector. This is so despite much of the verbiage by many large labor organizations about the importance of increasing their efforts in this area. This assessment is made on the basis of certain hard data and by comparing union organizing in general to the new organizing of those unions that are doing well. First, there seem to have been declines in new union organizing expenditures by major private sector unions; there also would appear to be less organizing for the dollar. Several rapidly growing unions (e.g., AFSCME and SEIU), in contrast, have higher organizing expenses. AFSCME, according to at least one report, does not seem to have suffered the declines in organizing energies due to the growing inertia of high-tenured organizing staffs. Second, the high success rates of unions engaged in multi-union elections is one indicator that unions can do better than they do, when they place a higher priority on putting forth more effort.

Unions that are more aggressive and militant, or that are at least perceived as such, seem to have more success than those that are not. Traditional industrial unions like the UAW that have both a history of struggle and militant work forces seem to do better than traditional industrial unions that have a more staid history and conservative stance.

Unions that have shown recent aggressiveness in their approach to new organizing appear to do well. The textile workers (TWUA) have a high and rising victory rate in an industry that as a whole has an extremely low rate. AFSCME and the AFT, two aggressive unions organizing public employees, have high success rates; RWSU and SEIU, both organizing service workers, have also done well recently.

Former left unions, especially the UE, because of its competitive position in the electrical and electronics industry, must by the nature of their situation keep up a militant posture. Though their rivals have had large-scale financial and organizational support from the AFL-CIO, aid and sympathy from the press and employers, the UE and ILWU have higher victory rates than their rivals the IUE and ILU.

OTHER FACTORS

The above conclusions should not be accepted without certain qualifications. Several potentially important factors have not been taken into consideration: the saturation effect, employer acceptance of unions, racial and national composition, and the city of New York.

SATURATION

Saturation occurs when a union (or unions) has organized a high percentage of its potential constituency; its losses begin to reflect, not its failure rate, but the large amount of success it has already had. There is, of course, a difficulty in the initial organizing in a new sector or area (e.g., Southern textile or computer manufacturing). Saturation occurs at the other end of the spectrum. We would not want to count, for example, the low percentage of victory rates by the UAW in auto manufacturing in the Detroit area as a sign of UAW failure, when in fact they have been successful in organizing the vast majority of places. Their failures might merely be continued attempts to organize the last few resistant places. Thus a union that had been extremely successful in a certain area and industry and was aggressively trying and failing to organize the few remaining unorganized places might appear to be unsuccessful if saturation were not taken into account.

Saturation data are available and easily calculated at the aggregate national level. Investigators who have used such data in their models, including Adams and Krislov (1974), have never found it to be statistically significant. Detailed disaggregated data are not available, particularly as time-series data, at least before the inclusion of extensive questions about unions in the 1977 CPS surveys. I do not think that the acquisition of such information and the creation of saturation variables at this level would greatly change the results presented in this essay. I base this assessment, in part, on the declining union densities and percentages of labor-management agreement coverage in the traditionally union geographic areas and economic sectors. This opinion, however, should be recognized as a conjecture. The successes in organizing teachers and hospital workers, for example, have been both widespread as well as with a high percentage of victory. Some of the areas of the highest successes have been in places most near saturation (e.g., New York City). Still, the possibility of saturation effects gives us reason to qualify the degree to which the Southwest is ahead of the Midwest in victory rates, and the degree to which professional, technical, and service workers are currently more organizable than industrial workers.

EMPLOYER ACCEPTANCE

It is also important to note that companies are sometimes more tolerant of the organizing efforts of moderate unions, particularly when there is a threat of a more militant union getting in, but sometimes even when this is not the case. This may have been the case with the previously mentioned high success rates of construction workers in the 1960s. In the late 1940s, the IBEW and the IUE were actually courted by companies in many cases, when companies desired to dislodge the UE or keep it from getting in. Though there are many stark examples such as these, the difficult problem is deciding to what degree the success of moderate, openly collaborationist unions like the ILGWU, IUE, and IBEW makes their percentage of victory higher than if they had been perceived as more militant. This question, though important, is not one of the most likely to be quantified, although there are obviously some quantitative measures that provide indirect bearing on the issue.

Certain other factors do seem to correlate with higher union success rates in the current period.

RACIAL AND NATIONAL COMPOSITION

New union organizing data, as presently collected, are in general especially unsuited for a detailed analysis by race (and, even more so, by sex). Nevertheless, a number of things tend to confirm in practice the attitudinal studies reported by Kochan (1979) that nonwhite workers are more likely to vote for union representation than white workers. It should be noted that the main data set taken from surveys during and after NLRB elections also confirms this result.

The NLRB regional offices that have relatively high success rates and have suffered no decline are New York City, averaging 56.5 percent; Hato Rey, Puerto Rico, averaging 55.4 percent; Brooklyn, averaging 54.6 percent; San Francisco, averaging 55.6 percent; and Honolulu, averaging 55.1 percent. Of the other regional offices in the Northeast, Midwest, and West, there are two categories, those whose percentage of union victories have been stable over the 1972–1984 period and those that have declined significantly. There is no obvious reason for the difference. The areas that have remained stable, however (e.g., Newark, Detroit, Chicago, Baltimore, Cleveland, and Pittsburg), all have substantial black populations. Those that have declined (e.g., Cincinnati, Minneapolis, Seattle, Indianapolis, Milwaukee, Portland, Los Angeles) tend to have a smaller percentage of blacks in their regions. This situation seems to reinforce the argument that nonwhite workers tend to be substantially more pro-union than any other category, which may also be reflected in the high victory rates for Puerto Rico and Hawaii.[2] Thus the percentage of whites and nonwhites in the work force may be seen as one important factor influencing the likelihood of union success.

NEW YORK CITY

The case of New York is especially interesting. Until the late 1970s, it was a region with a declining economy and population, and with a tight municipal budget in its major metropolitan area. Nevertheless, New York contains a combination of all the other factors associated with high union success rates, some of them in more abundance than other areas. It is worth noting them.

2. It should also be mentioned that in Puerto Rico unions are more political than in this country, tending to follow more closely Western European patterns.

First, New York during the 1930s and 1940s was the center of left-wing trade union activities. The Communist Party led and dominated much of this activity with especially great influence in maritime and the needle trades.[3]

Second, in the recent period New York City has been both the pacesetter and the most militant arena for the organizing of hospital workers, teachers, and municipal workers in general. New York area postal and telephone workers have been among the most aggressive in the country, both at different times rejecting national leadership and, during the 1970s, striking for more far-reaching concessions from their employers.

Third, the New York area has an especially high percentage of nonwhites, including by far the largest concentration of Puerto Ricans in the country.

The evidence presented so far gives us much information about the immediate causes of trade union decline in this country. In the next chapter, I try to place these causes in a broader historical context.

3. The majority of U.S. Communist Party membership was in New York state, with almost 40 percent in New York City alone during this period. For extensive references about membership figures for the Communist Party and its influence in the CIO, see Goldfield 1980a.

11

Some Speculations

In previous chapters, I have identified labor unions' problems as primarily due to these aspects of the changing relation of class forces:

1. A growing offensive of U.S. capitalists that has been meeting with increased success in defeating attempts at new union organizing.

2. Changes in public policy tending to favor more and more the employers.

3. An inability, and even an unwillingness, of labor unions in this country to devote the energies and resources necessary to combat effectively declines in the number of their members or in their general influence.

In trying to gain a broader perspective on these indications of the changes in class forces, certain general conclusions may be extracted. First, there has been no sudden, stark, or "spectacular" decline in either new union organizing or in union growth since 1937, 1948, or even 1954 (the year of the highest percentage of union penetration into the labor force). Second, the steady if undramatic quantitative declines are not only the result of, but have reinforced and accelerated, a qualitatively different relation of class forces than existed in 1937, 1948, or 1954.

If we accept these general assessments, a number of questions come forth, cup in hand, begging for answers. One wants to know why the capitalist offensive has been so much more effective in this country, particularly in the late 1960s and throughout the 1970s, than in Western Europe and other economically developed capitalist societies. Or alternatively, why have unions here been so vulnerable to such tactics; why have they been so unwilling or unable to mount a successful counteroffensive. Finally, what would be the necessary requirements for a resurgence of new union organizing or a change in the relation of class forces.

HISTORICAL ANSWERS

The quantitative and descriptive material presented in this book gives the general contours of trade union decline in the United States. It also presents us with some of the immediate factors most closely correlated with the plight of unions. This material by itself, however, cannot provide us with a full answer. To understand fully the *why* of trade union decline, one must probe deeper into historical factors. To have engaged in this investigation before establishing the nature of the decline and its most immediate causes, however, would have been precipitous, if not foolhardy. Here a sketch of what I believe to be the deeper historical reasons will be given, following the framework presented in chapter 4.

There is a general answer to the question about the deeper reasons for trade union decline given by a number of conservative pluralist writers. They argue variously that there was an "end of ideology" in the West, that the rise of "industrial society" brought with it a lessening of class conflict and the disappearance of class identifications by workers. The most popular formulations were those by Bell (1960), Lipset (1960), Ross and Hartman (1960), and Kerr, Dunlop, Harbison, and Myers (1960). These writers viewed unions, class conflict, and broad class struggle as characteristic of preindustrial society, not stable industrial or "postindustrial" society. Their analyses, though not without some merit, were highly discordant with reality. Not even in the United States are unions disappearing; in other developed capitalist societies, their density has grown in the past few decades. The United States, as the most economically developed society, was supposed to be the forerunner of the "end of ideology." Thus it has been somewhat ironic (and

completely contrary to the theories of these conservative pluralists) that among the developed nations the United States has had
one of the highest degrees of strike activity.[1] In retrospect, it is
easy to see, as many Marxists argued at the time, that these
theorists, in the wake of the Cold War, had substituted their own
moral predispositions for clear rigorous analysis.[2]

There have, of course, been many accounts of U.S. history that
attempt to locate the weaknesses of class organization among its
workers in the "exceptional" character of its society rather than
in its "advanced" industrial state. Frederick Jackson Turner, for
example, placed great emphasis on the existence of the frontier
as a safety valve for those wanting to escape the rigors of urban
factory life. Others have attempted to play up unique opportunities for social mobility, often strengthened by the continued
replenishment of a new underclass by waves of newly arrived
immigrants. One of the most coherent and challenging arguments for American exceptionalism is that of Louis Hartz (1955).
Hartz argues that the lack of a feudal class in this country is in
large part responsible for the failure of a collective class spirit or
culture to have sunk strong roots among workers. This culture
and cohesiveness supposedly developed in many other countries
as a consequence of the long struggle against feudalism. In the
United States, on the other hand, it was a liberal or Lockean
individualism that gained cultural dominance. Thus the American culture or general psyche did not provide the fertile soil for
the collectivist and socialist ideologies which at times gained
majority influence in the European and other working classes.

A different type of explanation concerning the exceptional
characteristics of U.S. society has been offered in various of his
works by Ernest Mandel. In one of these works (Mandel 1969),

1. As discussed in chapter 3, Hibbs (1976) and Martin and Kassalow (1980)
find U.S. strike activity to be among the highest in the developed nations. The
United States not only ranks high in overall strike activity, but in the percentages
of unauthorized wildcat stoppages.

2. See Korpi (1978); Goldthorpe, Lockwood, Bechhofer, and Platt (1969);
and Gordon (1981). Despite the fact that the Cold War wishful thinking of the
conservative pluralists is so easy to criticize in retrospect, I do not wish to argue
that none of what they saw was true. Certainly earlier Marxists had difficulty
focusing on precisely those aspects of reality that certain of the pluralists
emphasized. Marxists underestimated the difficulties in displacing the conservative leadership of the trade unions. They assumed a more rapid radicalization of
the masses of U.S. workers. Early U.S. socialists like Debs and De Leon assumed
that the success of industrial unionism would be the precursor for revolutionary
struggle. This view was also held by many Marxists during the CIO organizing in
the 1930s.

he argues that the decades of postwar prosperity in this country created conditions of affluence among U.S. workers that mitigated their desires for broad class struggle. This affluence also found them ready to tolerate a less militant, more class-collaborationist type of union leadership, which ultimately was not prepared to defend its membership from the increased attacks of the late 1960s. Mandel predicted in his article that the loss of world economic dominance by U.S. businesses would not only lead to declining affluence of U.S. workers, but to a resurgence of union activity and class struggle. Neither this automatic result, which has, of course, not yet come to pass, nor the causal analysis upon which its prediction was based, is totally convincing.

Though each of the above attempts to answer the general questions about the weaknesses of U.S. labor have elements of truth, and contain important perceptions, all fail to provide a major explanation for the current relation of class forces, so unfavorable to unions. It is not my purpose to provide even partial critiques of these various views.[3] Let it merely be noted that I find them to be both incomplete theories of U.S. history and unsatisfactory as full or even major explanations of the problems at hand.

LARGE-SCALE GROWTH IN UNIONISM

The questions that we have been addressing in this book in the main have concerned the decline in the strength of unions in the last several decades. This period, at least up until the advent of the Reagan presidency, has been one of general stability, a "steady-state" period, so to speak. Yet there is much to suggest that large-scale growth in unions does not take place as a direct result of incremental factors. Rather, as I. Bernstein (1954a) and Dunlop (1948) argue, it is tied to major social upheavals and major social movements, as accompanied the development of the CIO in this country. This is also true of earlier periods of major union growth, including the extensive movement leading up to the eight-hour strikes of 1 May 1886; the attempts to unionize the rail industry leading to the establishment of the American Railroad Union in 1894, led by Eugene Debs; and the attempts to organize the packinghouse and steel industries in 1919. The

3. Such critiques may be found among other places in Allen 1969, Korpi 1978, and Katznelson 1981.

CIO drive was accompanied by massive strike activity, beginning in some sense with the pre-CIO Briggs auto strikes in 1932 and 1933, the upheavals in coal from 1931 to 1933, the 1934 Toledo Autolite and Minneapolis Teamsters strikes, and the 1934 San Francisco general strike. The strike movement culminated with the 1936–37 plant seizures (or sitdown strikes), which inflicted a strategic defeat upon the major U.S. corporations. These unionization drives, preaching racial solidarity and support for workers in faraway places such as Spain and China, allied themselves with the movement for black equality and the mass organizations of the unemployed. No unionization attempts since this time, with the possible exception of the beginning organizing in the early 1960s by farmworkers, have approached this character. There were, of course, large strike waves after World War II, yet they were unconnected with any widespread social movement.

It is my belief that the decline of organized labor, a phenomenon directly traceable to the changing relation of class forces, can only be fully understood in a longer historical perspective. The present decline of organized labor may ultimately be traced to major (although not necessarily easily identifiable) defeats suffered by the working class and the left-wing within it from the mid-1930s to the mid-1950s (viz., the period just before the beginning of the steady decline). In short, the present weakness of U.S. unions and the present relation of class forces (increasingly unfavorable to unions) have their roots in the weaknesses of labor in the last period of major trade union upsurge.

My view in skeleton form is as follows. I would argue, first, that U.S. labor is politically weak in comparison to the labor movements in other economically developed capitalist countries because unionization in the United States exists mainly as a regional phenomenon. In the Northeast, the Midwest, and along the West Coast, labor unions have had until recently a density quite favorable in comparison to those in other countries, particularly in manufacturing, construction, mining, transportation, and government employment. Nationally, however, their lack of political influence is a reflection of their negligible presence in much of the South, Southwest, and West. This regional isolation is readily traceable to events of the 1930s and 1940s. Second, the stifling of rank-and-file democracy in the late 1930s, the bureaucratization of major unions during World War II, the elimination of radical oppositions and unions from 1946 to 1955, and the political subordination of U.S. unions to the Democratic Party have all worked to undermine the ability of labor unions to extend themselves nationally and to redress the unfavorable balance of class forces. Third, these limitations have been the result both of defeats suffered by the labor movement and of choices made by its leadership. These choices, which helped determine the present situation, include ones made by the left wing of the labor movement during the time of the last major upsurges.

This is the skeleton of my analysis. In the remainder of this chapter, I will attempt to place some flesh on its bones and, in so doing, to convince the reader of its plausibility.

BUREAUCRATIZATION AND DEMOCRACY

As Mike Davis notes,

The original Committee for Industrial Organization (CIO) was an alliance of dissident trade union bureaucrats, with important financial resources and friends in high places, created for the purpose of capturing an already existing mass movement of industrial shop committees and rebel locals—a movement with dangerous embryonic proclivities toward an anti-Gompersian model of class struggle unionism. (1980b, p. 47)

The early CIO upsurge was remarkable, both for its dramatic character and for its mass rank-and-file initiatives. The 1932 and 1933 Briggs auto strikes, the 1934 San Francisco general strike, the Minneapolis Teamster strike, and the Toledo Autolite strike were all characterized by aggressive mass tactics and democratic decision-making. The 1936–37 sitdown strikes at General Motors had similar features, being led by Communist Party activists in a united front with Socialists. Yet only a year or two later, in contrast to the militant organizing of 1936 and 1937, many of the union successes had the appearance of sweetheart deals between more conservative CIO officials and various capitalists.

Davis convincingly argues that "the intervention of the Lewis-Hillman wing of the AFL bureaucracy, supported by Roosevelt and Secretary of Labor Perkins, was ultimately a Greek gift to the rank and file movements involved" (1980a, p. 47).

However, not all of the fault for the ascendancy of the new CIO bureaucrats may be laid at their door. In many of the struggles during the 1935–37 period, the Communists (with the vast majority of union activists in workplaces around the country) had allied with the Socialists in a united front, stimulating and encouraging rank-and-file activity and providing the tactical leadership that often outflanked Lewis and the top CIO officials. By 1938, however, the Communists and Socialists were no longer allied. The Communists saw their main tactics as involving support for and subordination to the Lewis-Hillman forces, building their center-left coalition as part of a broad popular front (Cochran 1977; Goldfield 1980a, 1985b). Their distance from rank-and-file struggles was accentuated during the war, when they became the most vehement enforcers of the no-strike pledge.

The extent of mass participation and control in the organizing during the thirties has left an indelible stamp on many unions today. An example of how this is true may be seen in comparing the differences between the way Big Steel and the automobile industry were organized. The UAW was organized directly by militant strikes and sitdowns, many often initiated by local leaders not directly under the control of the national leadership. The union itself had a large left-wing and was quite democratic at both the national and local levels. Big Steel, on the other hand, was unionized in the aftermath of the UAW sit-down strikes. U.S. Steel and the top CIO leadership agreed to avoid the militant organizing of the auto industry. U.S. Steel accepted the union without a struggle. John L. Lewis's assistant in the United Mine Workers, Philip Murray, was installed as the United Steel Workers (USA) president; a relatively undemocratic local and national union structure was created.

Partly as a consequence, the UAW today remains one of the more democratic of the established unions, the USA, particularly in Big Steel, one of the least democratic. In the latter case, workers have no chance to ratify contracts, few local rights to strike, and a history of little democracy. The national union was the first major union to negotiate away the right to strike on a national level. In contrast, most UAW locals are relatively democratic, occasionally defying national leadership, even to the point of engaging in wildcat strikes to settle their local grievances. The national leadership not only receives low salaries compared to officials of most major unions, but is occasionally rebuffed at the local level (as happened in the late 1970s, when large numbers of UAW locals refused to allow the terms of office of local officials to be extended from two to three years). These differing histories are also reflected in the high and stable success rates of the UAW in NLRB elections (during the period covered by our data), and the declining victory rates in steel. Both unions bear heavily the history from which they were formed.

The strong rank-and-file impulses, worker militancy, and even union successes in NLRB certification elections may still be seen in those areas where the former Communist influence lingers on. I have discussed the high victory rates of the UE and the ILWA in chapter 9. In chapter 10, the former Communist concentration was seen as one factor keeping success in new organizing particularly high in New York City. The old tradition of the Farm Equipment Workers (dissolved into the UAW in 1955) at International Harvester (now Navistar) still maintains a faint glow in the form of more democratic shop-steward systems, wildcat strikes, and stronger contract provisions.

Overall, however, the bureaucratization of U.S. unions begun in the late thirties stifled opposition, dissent, and much rank-and-file initiative. Thus, unlike in Western Europe, where the struggles of the 1960s and early 1970s brought forth a whole new layer of more radical and militant secondary union leaders—who have provided the cadre and manpower for extensions in new union organizing—in the United States, similar groups and individuals were defeated, and occasionally absorbed. With some minor exceptions, the League of Revolutionary Black Workers, the more radical black union caucus movements, the oppositions in mining, the national network of groups fighting for a "democratic" contract in steel, the hundreds (possibly thousands) of mass local struggles led by radicals and self-proclaimed Marxists during the 1970s made little permanent impact on the unions and workplaces they had so electrified for short periods. Only the Teamsters for a Democratic Union, perhaps the exception that proves the rule, still remains with any organizational coherency.

OPERATION DIXIE

The central cause of the political weakness of U.S. labor unions, and the underlying reason for their generally defensive stance, is the failure to organize the South immediately after World War II. The failure to organize the South left both a political and economic bastion of reaction (represented by the control of the Senate and House committees by openly racist Southern Dixiecrats) and helped to stabilize a section of the country that represented both a source of cheap labor and an area of lower-than-union wages. It is worth reviewing certain of this history, to gain some understanding of the multifaceted reasons for this failure, so disastrous to the fortunes of U.S. labor.

All segments of the U.S. labor movement during the 1930s and 1940s regarded the organization of unions throughout the South as the key to long-run union successes. The CIO had planned to attempt organizing the South after Northern industry was unionized. This great task was postponed until after World War II. After the war, Operation Dixie, the plan for mobilizing the whole labor movement to aid in unionizing the South, was announced with great fanfare. Even the more conservative CIO leaders, like Philip Murray, viewed Operation Dixie as of paramount importance.

The organization of the South seemed overripe. Not only had it been a prewar goal, but the war itself had brought rapid industrial development. A large percentage of the rural population, particularly among blacks, had moved to industrial jobs in the cities. Further, the initial failures had been countered by new successes. Dramatic textile struggles—Gastonia in 1929, a national textile strike in 1933—had been defeated; yet, in steel, particularly in the Birmingham mills, unions had established a secure beachhead. The UMW, in 1941, under the threat of a national strike, had extended its own organization, forcing the government defense contractors to accept a union shop and the abolition of the Southern wage differential.

There was, of course, great resistance by Southern Dixiecrats, large cotton landlords, and many capitalists to the unionization of the South. But given the financial resources of the labor unions, the thousands of hardened organizers, the combativeness of the unionized workers, and the militance of the millions of returning veterans, it is perhaps more important to focus on why Operation Dixie was a complete failure.

Davis (1980b) locates the cause in the fratricide taking place between the left and right wings of the CIO. He cites the preoccupation of the Philip Murray–led CIO steelworkers union with destroying the Communist-led Mine, Mill, and Smelter Union in Alabama, rather than with obtaining new recruits. The conservative CIO officials were more interested in purging their organizing staffs of radicals than in mobilizing the most organizing talent and energy as had been done during the 1930s. The scenario in steel was repeated in the key Southern textile and tobacco industries.

It is indeed true that the fear of the conservative CIO leaders that Operation Dixie would provide an opening for the left put a brake on its success. The struggle between the CIO and the AFL also took its toll heavily in the South. Yet there are more overriding reasons, which not only undermined the energies of the conservative CIO leadership, but kept the left, particularly the Communist Party, from launching or participating in any independent initiatives. There are, in my opinion, two interrelated reasons that helped doom Operation Dixie. These reasons placed Operation Dixie itself, or at least the means that would be needed for it to be a success, in opposition to the main orientation of the CIO.

First, there was the unwillingness of the CIO, including the left, to confront the black question fully, to demand equality for blacks, a prerequisite for unity within the labor movement, especially in the South. From the late 1920s to the mid-1930s, the Communist Party placed a major priority on fighting against racial discrimination and on organizing black people in the South. The Scottsboro defense and the Alabama Sharecroppers Association were perhaps symbolic of this thrust. After 1935, the Communists drew back from this work, partly in the hopes of engaging in broader, less controversial coalitions. They even went so far as to dissolve most of the independent work among blacks in the South (Goldfield 1980a, 1985b).

Second, a good part of this unwillingness of both the right and left CIO leaders to pull out all the stops in the South was based on the disruptive effects such a confrontation, and the drive itself, would have had on the Roosevelt coalition, based as it was, not only on the labor movement, Northern liberals, Western farmers, and major capitalists, but on Southern Dixiecrats. Thus the attachment of the CIO leaders in the Roosevelt wing of the Democratic Party was a roadblock to securing their long-term, yet most immediate, interests.

With the failure of Operation Dixie, other defeats were soon to come. The passage of Taft-Hartley in 1947 was the culmination of these setbacks and marked a decisive legal and political defeat for organized labor. Even here, it is not clear that it was too late to reverse the trap into which labor had fallen. The Communist-led UE and the UMW, led by John L. Lewis, proposed that the whole labor movement act in noncompliance with Taft-Hartley;

this noncompliance was to have included mass mobilizations, a possible general strike, and abandonment of the legal procedures of the NLRB. The CIO balked. The fact that certain unions were already benefiting from several of the Taft-Hartley anticommunist provisions surely did not encourage them to oppose the act with militant actions. The UAW under Walter Reuther was already raiding the Farm Equipment Workers and the United Electrical Workers. The consequences of acceptance of Taft-Hartley followed quickly. On one day in Chicago, five hundred UE officials were fired. These discharges were, of course, upheld by the NLRB (and thus do not appear in NLRB unfair labor practice statistics).

The final defeat that set the trade union movement on its present course was the expulsion of the left from the trade unions, a process ranging from 1946 to the middle 1950s (e.g., the Farm Equipment Workers, a Communist-led union, was not finally dismantled until 1955), which robbed the unions of the majority of their most militant and innovative leadership and activists.

Cochran (1977) presents a great deal of evidence to support his thesis that the Communists bore major responsibility for their own vulnerability to these expulsions. Going even further, I would argue that the general defeats of the labor movement described above were in good part the result of political errors by the left itself. This conclusion is not meant to minimize the difficulties faced by radicals and militants, among which were (1) the conservatism of the working class (including the racial prejudices of many of the whites and their general political attitudes, ranging from strong patriotic support for Roosevelt above that for the CIO to influence by such open reactionaries as Father Coughlin, who had a large following among Flint autoworkers, even at the height of the sit-down strikes); (2) the development of the Cold War and the anti-communism and patriotism that accompanied it; and (3) the intensive government repression of the left, which became so widespread that even many liberals were persecuted along with large numbers of leftists.

The seeds of today's situation in the trade union movement were planted during the 1930s and 1940s. The history of that time weighs heavy on the present; in a sense there is very little new history being created now. The massive struggles of the past have indelibly stamped the present and will continue to do so until large-scale workers' movements are again the order of the day.

THE PRESENT SITUATION

From the high points of struggle and union organizing (coincident with very high rates of union victories in NLRB certification elections) up to the present, a steady condition has existed. This steady state has, in general, been one of decline. The dramatic reversal of this trend will undoubtedly require bold new initiatives both from new groupings in the labor movement and from within the established union structures; this, of course, is what happened in the 1930s. Some have argued that appropriate strategies are emerging from the present AFL-CIO leadership. In particular, the much-publicized report "The Changing Situation of Workers and Their Unions" released in 1985 by the AFL-CIO is often mentioned in this context. The main emphasis of this document, however, is for more labor-management cooperation, better public relations by unions, and for less belligerent tactics in organizing certain new groups of employees. In particular, it argues to the employers who are defeating unions that "confrontation and conflict are wasteful." It suggests that many workers do not like this "adversarial relationship" and would join benefit organizations that hark back to the pre–craft union sickness-and-burial societies. Rather than urging or leading workers in their struggle against bolder employer attacks at the workplace, the AFL-CIO authors cite the need for more corporate campaigns and better use of the electronic media. In order to reverse the disaffection of present members, the report proposes conferences and more opportunities for leadership and local unionists to interact. In addition, it urges better orientation programs for new members and more careful selection and training of new organizers.

As corporations and their political allies are successfully weakening or breaking one union effort after another, the lack of realism of the new AFL-CIO program is perhaps best indicated by the two quotes with which the report ends. The first is from George Meany, former AFL-CIO president, who bragged at one time that he had never been on strike in his life. The second is from Eugene V. Debs in 1894 about the inevitable triumph of the historic mission of the working class. Unmentioned is that this historic mission for Debs, as for Marx, was the revolutionary organization of workers for the overthrow of the capitalists and the establishment of socialism. Needless to say, attempting to draw guidance simultaneously from Meany and Debs is like trying to square a circle or deciding to get rich as a small farmer.

Massive employer offensives against workers' organizations and standards of living have historically been met and defeated by massive working-class counteroffensives and insurgencies. Such movements require more than aggressive and militant postures by established union leaders, although this will probably be a tell-tale sign. It is most likely that union gains and large-scale growth in union membership will only be won in the foreseeable future on the basis of broad class struggle and innovative disruptions of production (as happened during the 1930s). The defeat of PATCO, Phelps-Dodge, and Hormel were not due to a lack of corporate campaigns and innovative tactics. All these struggles lost because they did not receive timely solidarity from workers and unions around the country. Worker participation and attendance at meetings, often to provide a rubber stamp for decisions already made by leaders, are rarely problems in the midst of struggle. Meetings during strikes, during wildcats, when safety and firings are being protested or when workers are trying to oust leadership they feel is inadequate, rarely lack for attendance. The problems at Hormel were hardly those of lack of enthusiasm, participation, or of a too confrontational approach. According to news reports, all the workers there were prepared to do battle with the company. What they lacked was support from their international union, other unions, and the broader labor movement.

For innovative tactics, the AFL-CIO might have supported, rather than undermined, those West Coast longshoremen who in 1985 refused to unload South African ships. For publicity they might gain greater media attention for their highly laudable refusal to talk with Jonas Savimbi, the CIA and South African-supported leader of Angolan counterinsurgency.

There are, of course, differences between the situation today and the early 1930s. In the 1930s, workers in the United States had tremendous leverage based on their employment in relatively technologically advanced and highly profitable islands in the world economy. Today, the international mobility of capital has diffused high-technology production, not merely to Europe and Japan, but even to the underdeveloped parts of the world (as the AFL-CIO report rightly notes). It is indicative that the most advanced techniques of steel production are today employed in

South Korea. Within the United States, much low-paid production work today, in contrast to the 1930s, employs large percentages of nonwhite workers, whether they are black and Latin
women textile workers in the South and Southwest, Asian
sweatshop workers in New York City, or minority workers in
small, highly oppressive shops in many urban areas.

Hence the questions of broad international coordination, of
multinational and multiracial solidarity, must of practical necessity be an even more central feature of current trade union
practice than was true of certain of the struggles that built the
CIO.[4] Yet unions cannot organize such a broad struggle by
themselves. As many Marxists have understood, at least since
Lenin and Gramsci, unions in capitalist societies are primarily
defensive organizations. Thus, if broad class struggles are required, appealing to and coordinating the struggles of all whom
capitalism oppresses, broader forms of organization are required
along with transformed unions. It is perhaps also true that union
gains will only be solidified with the independent reorganization of the U.S. working class, the formation of its own class
party, and the definitive break with both procapitalist parties.

How likely is such a development to occur? The question is
hard to answer. In the wake of the recent recession, unions have
been even more weakened. The possibilities for large-scale
growth seem, on the surface, quite slim. Yet one must bear in
mind that much of the political conservatism of organized labor
has not been unrelated to the job security, large benefit pack-
ages, and liveable wages enjoyed by many organized workers.
These standards of living, particularly for industrial workers,
may be a thing of the past. The politically conservative construction trades—who in 1969 organized tens of thousands of workers
in patriotic "hard-hat" demonstrations in support of Nixon's
Vietnam policy—have been ravaged by their supposed benefac-
tors. Unemployment in the construction trades is much higher
than in other industries. Living standards and wage rates have

4. Of course, there were many variations in the 1930s, with the maritime
workers especially being noted for their antidiscriminatory practices. On the
other hand, white autoworkers, despite the strong union stance against racial
discrimination, occasionally had militant (unauthorized) antiblack job actions.
The Communist-led transit workers in New York City only reluctantly began to
attack discrimination, for fear of antagonizing its majority white base. Today,
such activities would not only be counterproductive in the long run, but would
destroy elementary union solidarity in the bud.

plummeted, while union strength has been continually under attack.

It is hard to know the degree to which this new situation provides the tinder for an explosion in union growth, or fertile ground for the early rebirth of a militant, independent labor movement. Those who are sure that it does not, however, might take pause at the assessments made by two eminent economists in late 1932, just before "all hell broke loose" and union growth skyrocketed.

Lyle Cooper, writing in the *American Economic Review* in December of 1932 in an article entitled "The American Labor Movement in Prosperity and Depression," voiced something of a consensus:

Little reason appears to exist for the expectation that a weak labor movement will be replaced soon by one which is strong. (Cooper 1932, p. 641)

This consensus was expressed even more forcefully in the Presidential address to the the American Economic Association by George E. Barnett on 29 December 1932:

The past ten years have seen changes of amazing magnitude in the organization of American economic society. It is one of these fundamental alterations that I wish to speak this evening. . . . The change to which I refer is the lessening importance of trade unionism in American economic organization. (Barnett 1933, p. 1)

With these sage assessments to temper its prospects, the largest explosion in union growth in this country's history began to take place.

Appendixes

A

The Data

The large data set consists of summary records from all of the almost ninety-thousand NLRB certification elections held from the beginning of fiscal year 1973 (i.e., July 1972) to the end of calendar year 1984. Among the variables in this data set are the following:

1. Region
2. Industry code
3. Union code
4. State
5. Unit type
6. Size
7. Date of election (month, year)
8. Type of election
9. Number eligible
10. Winning vote
11. Losing vote
12. Ruling

A number of other variables have been created from these and other variables. The raw data contain three data sets, all with different record structures. These data sets have been sorted, cleaned, and merged, after making the variables compatible (for example, the size category had to be recreated so that it was uniform for each data set).

My basic strategy in examining this data was to create useful summary statistics for setting up informative cross-classification tables. For this purpose, a number of variables were created. First, each record was checked for its closing date and assigned a fiscal year. The data were initially analyzed by both fiscal and calendar year. Then two additional variables were assigned. A variable VICT was assigned a value of "1" if a union won the election and a value "0" if a union did not win the election. A variable UNION1 was given the value for the winning union, if a union won the election. If the decision was for no union, then UNION1 was assigned the value of the primary losing union (the one that received the most votes). For analytic purposes, it was useful to regard each certification election as either a win or a loss for the union involved. The overwhelming majority of elections did, in fact, involve only one union. Even in those cases where more than one union was involved, the additional unions were not always serious participants. Finally, it seemed unreasonable to regard the certification of a union in a bargaining election as a loss for one union and a victory for another (giving unions in general a 50 percent success rate) when in fact a union was certified. Likewise, it seemed unreasonable to give unions in general two failures in losing one election. Thus the decision was made to give the primary (and, in general, only) participant the win or the loss for each particular election.

These new variables allowed me to find a further variable—likelihood of a union victory (or percentage of union victories)—for any particular grouping by fiscal year. The likelihood (or mean) for the variable VICT could be calculated for each particular category.

Thus we would have the probability of victory,

$$\text{MEANVICT} = \frac{N_{(\text{VICT} = 1)}}{N_{(\text{VICT} = 1)} + N_{(\text{VICT} = 0)}}.$$

The results of these two-way and three-way cross-classifications are summarized in the text.

It could quite plausibly be argued that I should have calculated logits, rather than likelihoods and percentages for each category. For the initial and general examination of the data set here, however, it is useful to view a broad sweep of the results by looking at likelihoods and percentages. A further step might be to plot the logits by month rather than by year, creating a time-series model to probe the data more intensely. The logit could be constructed as follows:

$$N = A + B,$$

where N = the number of elections, A = wins, and B = losses.

$$L = \text{Log} \left[(A + 1/2)/ (B + 1/2) \right],$$

where L is the logit.

$$S = \left[(A + B)/ (AB) \right]^{1/2},$$

where S is the standard error of estimate.

As more complex technologies for modeling become widespread among social scientists, there is a tendency to downplay the importance of simple frequency tables. In the examination of victory rates in NLRB union certification elections, cross-tabulations play a useful, informative, supplementary role, although they provide no method for controlling for the different weights of particular variables. They do, however, have the advantage of providing more detailed information than can often be gained from more sophisticated models. (An example is the high variance in victory rates among states in the South, usually missed by investigators who use more sophisticated models for which they supply merely the regional variable representing the South.)

In order to understand more fully various subtleties, union victory rates were cross-tabulated into frequency tables at the smallest possible useful level. For geography, this meant by state and by NLRB region. For industry, this was done by two-digit SIC codes; while for occupation, the breakdowns are limited by the nine NLRB election-unit classifications. To gain a view of employer resistance, disaggregation was done by election delays and by consent and nonconsent elections (usually stipulated by the board or regional director). As a further check, union victory rates were grouped by each of the hundreds of unions, both for single union elections and for multi-union elections. Where appropriate, this frequency information is reported to supplement the analysis.

B

The Cross-sectional Models

Cross-tabulation of frequency distributions as described in Appendix A is useful since it allows one to view detailed characteristics often hidden by more aggregated figures. These simple tabulations, however, do not allow one to ascertain the independent contribution of a particular variable while all others are controlled for.

In order to assess the independent contribution of each variable to union success rates, a simple cross-sectional multiple regression model was estimated. This model allows estimation of the effect of a particular variable while controlling for the effects of others. As we saw in chapter 7, the basic model is

$$Y = \beta_0 + \beta_1 \text{ REG} + \beta_2 \text{ TRAD} + \beta_3 \text{ BLUE} + \beta_4 \text{ TEAM} + \beta_5 \text{ ELIG} + \beta_6 \text{ DELAY} + \beta_7 \text{ MULT} + U,$$

where Y is the dependent variable, likelihood of a union victory (EW), or percentage of union votes (UV); β_0 is the intercept; REG is the state or region of the country; TRAD is the traditionally unionized industries; BLUE is for blue-collar occupations; TEAM is if the union is the Teamsters; ELIG is the number of workers eligible to vote in the election unit; DELAY is the number of

TABLE B.1   Cross-section Regression Models

Model	1	2	3	4	5	6
			Variable			
DEP	UV	UV	UV	UV	UV	UV
INTERCEPT	.55	.54	.63	.58	.63	.60
	(14.5)	(14.2)	(13.6)	(8.3)	(56.7)	(57.1)
TRAD	−.0014	.0014	.0077	−.045	−.04	−.04
	(−.039)	(.039)	(.204)	(−.70)	(−2.7)	(−2.8)
BLUE	−.06	−.06	−.06	−.007	−.13	−.13
	(−1.67)	(−1.65)	(−1.63)	(−.12)	(−9.12)	(−9.37)
TEAM	−.03	−.04	−.03	.03	−.07	−.06
	(−.72)	(−.87)	(−.74)	(.61)	(−4.1)	(−4.1)
ELIG	−.00002	−.00002	−.00002	−.0004	−.0002	−.0002
	(−.76)	(−.74)	(−.73)	(−3.1)	(−4.5)	(−4.4)
MULT	.37	.38	.36	.08	.37	.36
	(4.5)	(4.6)	(4.4)	(.87)	(15.8)	(15.7)
DELAY	−.0007				−.0067	
	(−.42)				(−3.0)	
CONSENT		.285		.49		.10
		(2.95)		(1.98)		(6.02)
STIP			−.11			
			(2.82)			
Durbin-Watson	1.50	1.51	1.50	1.56	1.48	1.50
Subset	VA	VA	VA	MS	NY	NY

Note: t-statistics are in parentheses.

months' pre-election delay; MULT is for multi-union elections; and U is the disturbance (or error) term. All independent variables with the exception of ELIG and DELAY are dichotomous (Boolean or dummy) variables. The coefficients of these two variables (as well as the others) are measured in their simple unstandardized forms. The unit of analysis, represented by the dependent variable, is one union representation election.

In certain versions of the model DELAY is changed to a dummy variable registering CONSENT (a consent election) or STIP (a stipulated election), giving several alternative measures of employer resistance. In various versions REG is Southwest, South, Mississippi, Virginia, etc. In some cases, TEAM was replaced by one or another union. The model is estimated across different populations (region and time periods in years). This provides a check on whether the independent effects are conditional on the particular population or not. Various tests were also made to check for interaction; none of significance was found.

TABLE B.2   Cross-section Regression Models Continued

Model	7	8	9
		Variable	
DEP	*UV*	*UV*	*UV*
INTERCEPT	.63	.61	.61
	(19.2)	(53.4)	(54.0)
TRAD	.06	−.03	−.03
	(1.77)	(−2.8)	(−2.7)
BLUE	−.12	−.10	−.10
	(−.38)	(−9.0)	(−9.0)
TEAM	−.14	−.06	−.06
	(−4.3)	(−4.8)	(−4.8)
ELIG	−.0002	−.0004	−.0004
	(−1.86)	(−11.0)	(−11.0)
MULT	.32	.35	.34
	(4.3)	(12.8)	(12.8)
DELAY	−.009	−.0007	−.007
	(−1.78)	(−3.7)	(−3.8)
REG-VAR		SOUTHWEST	DEEP SOUTH
		.05	−.006
		(2.3)	(−.21)
Durbin-Watson	1.14	1.52	1.52
Subset	CA-1980	1980	1980

Note: *t*-statistics are in parentheses.

In Tables B.1 and B.2, national results are presented first as a benchmark. The state populations presented here represent the range of effectiveness (by state) of employer resistance; they also illustrate the general stability of most other coefficients of the model across populations.

C

Pooling of Cross-section and Time-series Data Models

Viewing cross-sectional data in a regression model can inform us of the impact of each independent variable on the value of the dependent variable. Thus tables B.1 and B.2 indicate that delays only have a modest effect on the percentage of union victories, while type of election (consent election or multi-union election) has a very large impact. What the cross-section models do not show, however, is the influence of each particular factor over time on the decline of union successes in NLRB certification elections. To do this, one must, of course, use a time-series model.

A model that pools cross-section and time-series data utilizes the richness of the 1972–84 data set employed here to a far greater degree than would a simple time-series model.

Essentially, the pooled models allow one to examine together a multitude of time series across various concurrent sections, for example, in the present case by state, industry, occupation, and so on. (See, e.g., Kuh 1959; Balestra and Nerlove 1966; Maddala 1971; Nerlove 1971; Henderson 1971; Kmenta 1971; Hannan and Young 1977; Judge et al. 1982; Zuk and Thompson 1982.) Thus, they are better able to take account of the complexity and variations within a large-scale data set than would be the case with a model that depended on more aggregated units.

As is noted in much of the literature, the statistical problems concern the development of estimators that take account simultaneously of two different types of disturbances. The behavior of the disturbances across concurrent cases (e.g., many states) is very likely to be different from the disturbances of a particular cross-section unit (e.g., one state) over time. It is the choice of estimators and the techniques for calculating estimators that control for both types of disturbances that has been the focus of much of the econometrics literature.

There are various assumptions that may be made about the relation of the observations themselves and their disturbance terms. First, as in all time-series models, one must assume an invariant causal structure over the period being modeled. With respect to the error terms, the most reasonable assumption here would seem to be a cross-sectionally correlated and time-series autoregressive model. This is because disturbances between cross-sectional units are almost always likely to be heteroskedastic when the units themselves vary disproportionately. It is thus reasonable in our case to assume that highly unionized states, industries, and occupational groups will not all vary proportionately to less unionized ones. On the other hand, we should expect correlations between many of the cross-sectional units since we are dealing with states in the same country and industries in the same economy. It is highly questionable whether they can be regarded as mutually independent (i.e., uncorrelated). Finally, autocorrelation is the usual type of disturbance for time-series data; it seems reasonable to assume it here.

The estimation method employed here is one developed by Parks (1967). The model used has N cross-section points over T periods of time with X variables. There are thus $N \times T$ observations in the new dataset. T in this case is always thirteen, N depends on the particular variable (e.g., state or industry) by which one aggregates the cross-sectional data, and X will be the same seven variables used in the cross-section regression models. The form of the model is

$$Y_t = b_{1i} + \sum_{k=2}^{N} b_{ki} x_{kit} + e_{it},$$

where $i = 1, 2, \ldots, N$ refers to the cross-sectional unit, t is a given

TABLE C.1   Pooled Cross-section and Time-series Models

Model	1	2	3	4
		Variable		
DEP	UV	UV	UV	UV
INTERCEPT	.62	.65	.66	.52
	(25.9)	(28.9)	(25.7)	(33.0)
TRAD	.012	.019	−.04	.08
	(.43)	(.74)	(−1.37)	(4.30)
BLUE	−.14	−.11	−.13	−.10
	(−5.04)	(−4.28)	(−4.72)	(−5.18)
TEAM	−.17	−.19	−.14	−.14
	(−4.07)	(−5.23)	(−4.68)	(−4.00)
ELIG	−.0001	−.0002	−.0004	−.0006
	(−.75)	(−2.02)	(−4.01)	(−9.68)
MULT	.22	.39	.48	.36
	(2.54)	(4.48)	(4.98)	(12.47)
DELAY		−.001	.00006	
		(−.39)	(.018)	
CONSENT	.20			.18
	(4.83)			(4.95)
REG-VAR	SOUTH	SOUTH	SOUTHWEST	SOUTH
REG	−.03	−.04	.03	−.19
	(−2.67)	(−4.05)	(3.86)	(−6.30)
POOL-VAR	STATE	STATE	STATE	WAIT
N	53	53	53	15

Note: t-statistics are in parentheses.

point in time, x_{kit} is an observation on the kth explanatory variable for the ith individual (i.e., cross-sectional unit), and the tth time period; e_{it} is the error term for the ith individual and the tth time period. According to our assumptions, we expect

$$E(e^2_{it}) = s_{ii} \qquad \text{heteroskedasticity}$$

$$E(e_{it}e_{kt}) = s_{it} \qquad \text{mutual correlation}$$

$$e_{it} = c_i e_{i,\,t-1} + u_{it} \qquad \text{autoregression}$$

where c is a coefficient and u is a disturbance term.

From these assumptions, a variance-covariance (OMEGA) matrix is constructed and estimated with a two-stage procedure. This matrix is analogous to, but different from, the standard OMEGA used with the usual GLS estimation procedure. Parks's method allows substitution of the new OMEGA matrix in the well-known GLS procedure. GLS estimation then proceeds in the usual manner. One important feature of Parks's method is that no observations are lost, thus leaving one with "true," rather than approximate, regression coefficients.

The results of several regressions from this model may be found in table C.1.

D

The Yearly Aggregate Data

In this appendix, the sources for all the yearly aggregate data used in various models, charts, or other calculations are given. Many of the particular items were used either in the actual or the preliminary models presented in chapter 8.

Yearly figures for NLRB certification and decertification elections and for unfair labor practices are taken from the NLRB *Annual Report* for fiscal years beginning in the middle of 1935 and ending in the fall of 1981. Figures for later years are calculated, as indicated in the notes to various tables, from NLRB raw data tapes.

Information for the years 1929–81 about the size of the civilian labor force, the number of unemployed, and the percentage of the labor force unemployed was obtained from the Historical Household Data of the Current Population Survey (CPS) taken by the Bureau of Labor Statistics (BLS). This information is published in the March 1982 issue of *Employment and Earnings*. Similar information for later years was obtained from CPS data published in the February 1985 issue of *Employment and Earnings*.

Yearly strike and work stoppage data, including information on the number of work stoppages per year, the number of workers involved, and the percentage of the labor force on strike in any particular year are taken from the BLS publication *Analysis of Work Stoppages, 1980.* Later data were obtained in unpublished form directly from the BLS.

Gross National Product (GNP) and Gross Private Domestic Investment (GPDI) data series are taken from two sources. For the years 1977–81, they are obtained from the February 1982 *Economic Report of the President* (table B.2, p. 234). For the years 1929–76, the information was taken from the *National Income and Product Accounts, Statistical Tables,* published by the Bureau of Economic Analysis of the Department of Commerce. These figures are all converted to 1972 dollars.

The series on corporate profits (after taxes), 1948–81, also in 1972 dollars, was obtained from the April 1981 *Business Conditions Digest* (p. 98), published by the Department of Commerce. The series for final sales of business, 1947–81, used in several places in chapter 8 as a surrogate for corporate profits (also in 1972 dollars) was obtained from the above-mentioned 1982 *Economic Report of the President.*

A wide variety of productivity variables were used at preliminary stages of the development of the econometric model presented in chapter 8. Many of these were obtained on computer printout sheets, dated 1 March 1982, from the Productivity Department of the BLS. Among these variables are output per hour of all employed persons (with 1977 = 100), change in output per hour per year compounded quarterly, output per person, change in the latter by year, real wages, and change in real wages per year. These variables were available to me for 1947–81. In addition, another productivity variable, output per hour in manufacturing, was obtained for the period 1929–80 from the 1981 BLS publication *Productivity and the Economy: A Chartbook.*

The party in control of the White House for the years 1935 to 1981 may be found in Wilson 1982 (p. 645).

Bibliography

Aaron, B.; Grodin, J.; and Stern, J. 1979. *Public Sector Bargaining.* Washington, D.C.: Bureau of National Affairs.

Adams, A. V., and Krislov, J. 1974. New Union Organizing: A Test of the Ashenfelter-Pencavel Model of Trade Union Growth. *Quarterly Journal of Economics* 88:304–11.

Adams, L. T. 1985. Changing Employment Patterns of Organized Workers. *Monthly Labor Review* 108(2):25–31.

Addison, J. T. 1982. Are Unions Good for Productivity? *Journal of Labor Research* 3:126–51.

Alford, R. 1963. *Parity and Society: The Anglo-American Democracies.* Chicago: Rand McNally.

Allen, T. 1969. *Can White Workers (Radicals) be Radicalized?* Detroit: Radical Education Project.

Alinsky, S. D. 1949. *John L. Lewis: An Unauthorized Biography.* New York: Putnam.

American Federation of Labor and Congress of Industrial Organizations (AFL-CIO). 1979–85. *Report on Union Busters (RUB).* Issues 1–50.

———. 1980. *Statistical and Tactical Information Report.* Issue No. 1. (November). Washington, D.C.

———. 1982. *Statistical and Tactical Information Report.* Issue No. 10. (October). Washington, D.C.

———. 1985. *The Changing Situation of Workers and Their Unions.* Publication No. 165. Washington, D.C.

American Nurses' Association. 1982. Medicare to Pay for Anti-Union Activities. *American Nurse* 14:1.

American Union Busting. 1979. *Economist,* 17 November.

Andersen, K. 1979. *The Creation of a Democratic Majority, 1928–1936.* Chicago: University of Chicago Press.

Anderson, J. C.; Busman, G.; and O'Reilly, C. A. 1979. What Factors Influence the Outcome of Decertification Elections? *Monthly Labor Review* 102(11):32–35.

———. 1980. Union Decertification in the U.S., 1947–1977. *Industrial Relations* 19:100–07.

———. 1982. The Decertification Process: Evidence from California. *Industrial Relations* 21:178–95.

Antos, J.; Chandler, M.; and Mellow, W. 1980. Sex Differences in Union Membership. *Industrial and Labor Relations Review* 33:162–69.

Aronowitz, S. 1973. *False Promises: The Shaping of American Working Class Consciousness*. New York: McGraw-Hill.

———. 1983. Remaking the American Left. Part One: Currents in American Radicalism. *Socialist Review* 13:9–51.

Arrighi, G., and Silver, B. J. 1984. Labor Movements and Capital Migration: The United States and Western Europe in World-Historical Perspective. In *Labor in the Capitalist World-Economy*, edited by C. Bergquist. Beverly Hills: Sage.

Ashenfelter, O., and Pencavel, J. H. 1969. American Trade Union Growth, 1900–1960. *Quarterly Journal of Economics* 83:434–48.

Aspin, L. 1966. A Study of Reinstatement under the National Labor Relations Act. Ph.D. dissertation, M.I.T.

Bachrach, P., and Baratz, M. S. 1973. *Power and Poverty: Theory and Practice*. New York: Oxford University Press.

Bagli, C. 1980. Labor Unrest in the P.O.: Postal Worker—Do Not Mutilate. *Nation*, 7 June, pp. 690–92.

Bain, G. S., and Elsheikh, F. 1976. *Union Growth and the Business Cycle*. Oxford: Basil Blackwell.

Bain, G. S., and Price, R. P. 1976. Union Growth Revisited: 1948–1974 in Perspective. *British Journal of Industrial Relations* 14:339–55.

———. 1980. *Profiles of Union Growth: A Comparative Statistical Report of Eight Countries*. Oxford: Basil Blackwell.

Balestra, P., and Nerlove, M. 1966. Pooling Cross-Section and Time-Series Data in the Estimation of a Dynamic Model: The Demand for Natural Gas. *Econometrica* 34:585–612.

Baker, G. 1977. *Repeal Section 14(b) of the Taft-Hartley Act*. Chicago: Workers Press.

Bakke, E. W. 1945. Why Workers Join Unions. *Personnel* 22:37–47.

———. 1970. Reflections on the Future of Bargaining in the Public Sector. *Monthly Labor Review* 92(7):21–25.

Barbash, J. 1964. The Elements of Industrial Relations. *British Journal of Industrial Relations* 2:66–78.

———. 1965. The Labor Movement in the Changing Industrial Order. *Labor-Management Relations: The Forensic Quarterly* 39:97–112.

Barkin, S. 1961. *The Decline of the Labor Movement*. Santa Barbara, Cal.: Center for the Study of Democratic Institutions.

———, ed. 1975. *Worker Militancy and Its Consequences, 1965–1975*. New York: Praeger.

Barkin, S.; Dymond, W.; Kassalow, E. M.; Meyers, F.; and Myers, C. A., eds. 1967. *International Labor*. New York: Harper and Row.

Barnett, G. E. 1933. American Trade Unionism and Social Insurance. *American Economic Review* 23:1–8.

Baugh, W. H., and Stone, J. A. 1982. Teachers, Unions, and Wages in the 1970s: Unionism Now Pays. *Industrial and Labor Relations Review* 35:368–76.

Bedell, B. 1980. Labor Organizing Losing Ground. *Guardian,* 20 August 1980.

Bell, D. 1953. The Next American Labor Movement. *Fortune,* April, pp. 120–206.

———. 1954. Comments on Bernstein, Union Growth and Structural Cycles. In *Proceedings of the Seventh Annual Meeting of the Industrial Relations Research Association.* Madison, Wisconsin.

———. 1960. *The End of Ideology.* New York: Free Press.

Belous, R. S. 1984. Wage "Moderation" in the 1980s. *Congressional Research Service Review* 5 (July-August):8–10.

Bennett, J. T. 1981. *Private-Sector Unions in the Political Arena.* Washington, D.C.: Council on a Union-Free Environment.

Bennett, J. T., and Johnson, M. H. 1980. *Pushbutton Unionism.* Washington, D.C.: Council on a Union-Free Environment.

Bernstein, I. 1950. *The New Deal Collective Bargaining Policy.* Berkeley: University of California Press.

———. 1954a. The Growth of American Unions. *American Economic Review* 44:301–18.

———. 1954b. Union Growth and Structural Cycles. In *Proceedings of the Seventh Annual Meeting of the Industrial Relations Research Association.* Madison, Wisconsin.

———. 1961. The Growth of American Unions, 1945–1960. *Labor History* 2:131–57.

———. 1966. *The Lean Years: A History of the American Worker, 1920–1933.* Baltimore: Penguin.

———. 1971. *The Turbulent Years: A History of the American Worker, 1933–1941.* Boston: Houghton-Mifflin.

Bernstein, J. 1980. *Union-Busting and the Law: From Benign Neglect to Malignant Growth.* Washington, D.C.: Center to Protect Workers' Rights.

Beyme, K. 1980. *Challenge to Power: Trade Unions and Industrial Relations in Capitalist Countries.* London: Sage.

Block, F. 1985. Postindustrial Development and the Obsolescence of Economic Categories. *Politics and Society* 14:71–104.

Block, F., and Burns, G. A. 1985. Productivity as a Social Problem: The Uses and Misuses of Social Science Indicators. Manuscript.

Block, R. N., and Saks, D. H. 1979. Union Decision-Making and the Supply of Union Representation: A Preliminary Analysis. In *Proceedings of the Thirty-second Annual Meeting of the Industrial Relations Research Association.* Madison, Wisconsin.

Bluestone, B., and Harrison, B. 1980. *Capital and Communities: The Causes and Consequences of Private Disinvestment.* Washington, D.C.: Progressive Alliance.

———. 1982. *The Deindustrialization of America.* New York: Basic Books.

Blumberg, P. 1980. *Inequality in an Age of Decline.* New York: Oxford University Press.

Bok, D., and Dunlop, J. 1970. *Labor and the American Community.* New York: Simon and Schuster.

Box, G. E. P., and Jenkins, G. M. 1976. *Time-Series Analysis: Forecasting and Control.* San Francisco: Holden-Day.

Boyer, R. O., and Morais, H. M. 1970. *Labor's Untold Story.* New York: United Electrical Workers.

Browning, R. X. 1985. Presidents, Congress, and Policy Outcomes: U.S. Social Welfare Expenditures, 1949–1977. *American Journal of Political Science* 29:197–216.

Burawoy, M. 1979. *Manufacturing Consent.* Chicago: University of Chicago Press.

Burch, P. H. 1981. The Business Roundtable: Its Make-up and External Ties. *Research in Political Economy* 4:101–28.

Bureau of National Affairs (BNA). 1982. *Directory of U.S. Labor Organizations, 1982–83 Edition.* Washington, D.C.

———. 1984. *Directory of U.S. Labor Organizations, 1985 Edition.* Washington, D.C.

———. 1985. *Unions Today: New Tactics to Tackle Tough Times.* Washington, D.C.

Burke, D. R., and Rubin, L. 1973. Is Contract Rejection A Major Collective Bargaining Problem? *Industrial and Labor Relations Review* 26:820–33.

Burton, J. F. 1979. The Extent of Collective Bargaining in the Public Sector. In Aaron, Grodin, and Stern 1979.

Campen, J. T. 1976. Public Expenditure Analysis: A Critical Analysis of Current Theory and Practice, Together with Some Contributions Toward a Participatory Alternative. Ph.D. dissertation, Harvard University.

Canada Department of Labour. 1970. *Union Growth in Canada, 1921–1967.* Ottawa: Information Canada.

Cappelli, P. 1982. Concession Bargaining and the National Economy. In *Proceedings of the Thirty-fifth Annual Meeting of the Industrial Relations Research Association.* Madison, Wisconsin.

———. 1983. Union Gains under Concession Bargaining. In *Proceedings of the Thirty-sixth Annual Meeting of the Industrial Relations Research Association.* Madison, Wisconsin.

Center to Protect Workers' Rights. 1979. *From Brass Knuckles to Briefcases: The Changing Art of Union-Busting in America.* Washington, D.C.

Chacko, T. I., and Greer, C. R. 1982. Perceptions of Union Power, Service, and Confidence in Labor Leaders: A Study of Member and Nonmember Differences. *Journal of Labor Research* 3:211–21.

Chaison, G. N. 1973. Unit Size and Union Success in Representation Elections. *Monthly Labor Review* 96:51–52.

————. 1981. Union Growth and Union Mergers. *Industrial Relations* 20:98–108.

Chamberlain, N.; Pierson, F. C.; and Wolfson, T., eds. 1958. *A Decade of Industrial Relations Research, 1946–1956*. New York: Harper.

Chamberlain, N. W.; Cullen, D. E.; and Lewin, D. 1980. *The Labor Sector*. New York: McGraw-Hill.

Clegg, H. 1976. *Trade Unionism under Collective Bargaining*. Oxford: Basil Blackwell.

Cochran, B. 1977. *Labor and Communism*. Princeton: Princeton University Press.

————, ed. 1959. *American Labor in Midpassage*. New York: Monthly Review Press.

Coleman, J. S. 1964. *Introduction to Mathematical Sociology*. London: Free Press.

Commons, J.; Saposs, D.; Sumner, H.; Mittelman, E. B.; Hoagland, H. E.; Andreas, J. B.; and Perlman, S. 1918. *History of Labor in the United States*. Volumes 1–4. New York: Macmillan.

Commons, J.; Phillips, U. B.; Gilmore, E. A.; Sumner, H. L.; and Andrews, J. B., eds. 1958. *A Documentary History of American Industrial Society*. Vol. 5. New York: Russell and Russell.

Cook, A. H. 1970. Public Sector Bargaining in New York City. *Industrial Relations* 9:249–67.

Cooke, W. N. 1985. The Failure to Negotiate First Contracts. *Industrial and Labor Relations Review* 38:163–78.

Cooper, L. W. 1932. The American Labor Movement in Prosperity and Depression. *American Economic Review* 22:641–59.

Crouch, C. 1980. Varieties of Trade Union Weakness: Organized Labour and Capital Formation in Britain, Federal Germany, and Sweden. *West European Politics* 3:87–106.

Crouch, C., and Pizzorno, A., eds. 1978. *The Resurgence of Class Conflict in Western Europe since 1968*. London: Macmillan.

Cupper, L., and Hearn, J. 1981. Unions and the Environment: Recent Australian Experience. Industrial Relations 20:221–31.

Curtin, E. R. 1970. *White-Collar Unionization*. New York: National Industrial Conference Board.

Czarnecki, E. R. 1969. Unions' Record in Repeat Elections. *Labor Law Journal* 20:703–15.

Dahl, R. 1983. Response to Manley 1983. *American Journal of Political Science* 77:386–89.

Dalton, A. H. 1982. A Theory of the Organization of State and Local Government Employees. *Journal of Labor Research* 3:163–77.

Davis, M. 1980a. Why the U.S. Working Class Is Different. *New Left Review* 123:3–44.

————. 1980b. The Barren Marriage of American Labour and the Democratic Party. *New Left Review* 124:43–84.

Debs, E. V. 1921. *Industrial Unionism*. New York: New York Labor News Company.

Delaney, J. T. 1981. Union Success in Hospital Representation Elections. *Industrial Relations* 20:149–61.

De Leon, D. 1921. *Industrial Unionism*. New York: New York Labor News Company.

Dennis, B. D., ed. 1978. *Proceedings of the Thirty-first Annual Meeting of the Industrial Relations Research Association*. Chicago.

Derber, M., and Young, E. 1957. *Labor and the New Deal*. Madison: University of Wisconsin Press.

Dickens, W. T. 1980. Union Representation Elections: Campaign and Vote. Ph.D. dissertation, M.I.T.

———. 1983. The Effect of Company Campaigns on Certification Elections. *Industrial and Labor Relations Review* 36:560–75.

Do Representation Elections Need the NLRB? 1977. *Business Week*, 21 March.

Dobb, M. 1963. *Studies in the Development of Capitalism*. New York: International Publishers.

Domhoff, G. W. 1979. *The Powers That Be*. New York: Random House.

Douty, H. M. 1968. Wage Differentials: Forces and Counterforces. *Monthly Labor Review* 91(3):74–81.

Draper, N., and Smith, N. 1981. *Applied Regression Analysis*. New York: Wiley.

Dubofsky, M. 1969. *We Shall Be All*. New York: Quadrangle.

Dubois, P.; Durand, C.; and Erbes-Seguin, S. 1978. The Contradictions of French Trade Unionism. In Crouch and Pizzorno 1978.

Dunlop, J. T. 1948. The Development of Labor Organization: A Theoretical Framework. In Lester and Shister 1948.

———. 1958a. The American Industrial Relations System in 1975. In *U.S. Industrial Relations: The Next Twenty Years*, ed. Jack Steiber, pp. 7–54. East Lansing: Michigan State University Press.

———. 1958b. *Industrial Relations Systems*. New York: Henry Holt.

———. 1980. The Changing Character of Labor Markets. In Feldstein 1980.

———. 1982. Interview in *Fortune*, 20 Sept., pp. 98–108.

Dworkin, J. B., and Extejt, M. M. 1979a. The Union-Shop Deauthorization Poll: A New Look after Twenty Years. *Monthly Labor Review* 102(11):36–40.

———. 1979b. Recent Trends in Union Decertification/Deauthorization Elections. In *Proceedings of the Thirty-second Annual Meeting of the Industrial Relations Research Association*. Atlanta.

Drotning, J. E. 1965. An Unused Research Source: A Description of NLRB Election Case Files. *American Behavioral Scientist* 9:23–25.

Edwards, R. 1979. *Contested Terrain: The Transformation of the Workplace in the Twentieth Century*. New York: Basic Books.

Ehrenberg, R. G., and Smith, R. S. 1985. *Modern Labor Economics*. Glenview, Ill.: Scott, Foresman.

Elliot, R. D., and Hawkins, B. M. 1982. Do Union Organizing Activities Affect Decertification? *Journal of Labor Research* 3:153–61.

Ellwood, D. T., and Fine, G. A. 1983. The Impact of Right-to-Work Laws on Union Organizing. Working Paper No. 1116. Cambridge, Mass.: National Bureau of Economic Research.

Engels, Friedrich. [1845] 1968. *The Condition of the Working Class in England*. Stanford: Stanford University Press.

Esping-Anderson, G., and Korpi, W. 1983. The Social Democratization of Postwar Capitalism. Manuscript.

———. 1984. Patterns of Power and Distribution in Postwar Welfare States. Manuscript.

Estreicher, S. 1984. Unjust Dismissal Laws in Other Countries: Some Cautionary Notes. *Employee Relations Law Journal* 10:286–302.

Everling, C., ed. 1982. *Union Busting: What It Is and How to Beat It*. Gary: Division of Labor Studies, Indiana University Northwest.

Farber, H. S., and Saks, D. H. 1980. Why Workers Want Unions: The Role of Relative Wages and Job Characteristics. *Journal of Political Economy* 88:349–69.

Feldstein, M., ed. 1980. *The American Economy in Transition*. Chicago: University of Chicago Press.

Ferguson, T., and Rogers, J. 1979a. Labor Law Reform and Its Enemies. *Nation*, 6–13 Jan., pp. 1–20.

———. 1979b. The State of the Unions. *Nation*, 28 April, pp. 462–65.

———, ed. 1981. *The Hidden Election*. New York: Pantheon.

Ferro, L. 1982. The National Labor Relations Board: Help or Handicap to Labor? *Labor Update* 2:3–14.

Feuille, P., and Anderson, J. C. 1980. Public Sector Bargaining: Policy and Practice. *Industrial Relations* 19:309–24.

Feinberg, S. E. 1977. *The Analysis of Cross Classified Data*. Cambridge, Mass.: M.I.T. Press.

Fiorito, J. 1982. American Trade Union Growth: An Alternative Model. *Industrial Relations* 21:123–27.

Fiorito, J., and Greer, C. R. 1982. Determinants of U.S. Unionism: Past Research and Future Needs. *Industrial Relations* 20:1–32.

Flanagan, R. J. 1984. *Wage Concessions and Long-term Union Wage Flexibility*. Brookings Papers on Economic Activity. Washington, D.C.

Flora, P., and Heidenheimer, A. J., eds. 1981. *The Development of Welfare States in Europe and North America*. New Brunswick, N.J.: Transaction Books.

Foner, P. 1947–82. *History of the Labor Movement in the United States*. 6 vols. New York: International Publishers.

———. 1950. *The Fur and Leather Workers Union*. Newark, N.J.: Nordan Press.

Foster, W. Z. 1922. *The Bankruptcy of the American Labor Movement.* Chicago: Trade Union Education League.

Fox, A., and Flanders, A. 1969. The Reform of Collective Bargaining: From Donovan to Durkheim. *British Journal of Industrial Relations* 7:151–80.

Freedman, A. 1982. A Fundamental Change in Wage Bargaining. *Challenge* 25:14–17.

―――. 1985. Major Changes in Employee Relations. Manuscript.

Freedman, A., and Fulmer, W. E. 1982. Last Rites for Pattern Bargaining. *Harvard Business Review* 60:30–48.

Freeman, R. B. 1977. *Labor Economics.* Englewood Cliffs, N.J.: Prentice-Hall.

―――. 1980. The Evolution of the American Labor Market, 1948–80. In Feldstein 1980.

―――. 1984. *Unionism Comes to the Public Sector.* Working Paper No. 1452. Cambridge, Mass.: National Bureau of Economic Research.

Freeman, R. B., and Medoff, J. L. 1976. Where Have All the Members Gone? Manuscript.

―――. 1979a. New Estimates of Private Sector Unionism in the United States. *Industrial and Labor Relations Review* 32:143–74.

―――. 1979b. The Two Faces of Unionism. *Public Interest* 57:69–93.

―――. 1981. The Impact of Collective Bargaining: Illusion or Reality? In *U.S. Industrial Relations, 1950–1980: A Critical Assessment,* ed. J. Steiber et al. Madison, Wis.: Industrial Relations Research Association.

―――. 1983. The Impact of Collective Bargaining. In *New Approaches to Labor Unions.* Greenwich, Conn.: JAI Press.

―――. 1984a. The Slow Strangulation of Private Sector Unions. Manuscript.

―――. 1984b. *What Do Unions Do?* New York: Basic Books.

Friedman, M. 1962. *Capitalism and Freedom.* Chicago: University of Chicago Press.

Gaillie, D. 1980. Trade Union Ideology and Workers' Conceptions of Class Inequality in France. *West European Politics* 3:10–32.

Gall, G. J. 1982. Heber Blankenhorn, the LaFollette Committee, and the Irony of Industrial Repression. *Labor History* 23:246–53.

Gallup, G. H., ed. 1976. *The Gallup International Public Opinion Polls, France 1939, 1944–1975.* New York: Random House.

―――. 1981a. *The Gallup International Public Opinion Polls, Great Britain 1937–1975.* New York: Random House.

―――. 1981b. *The International Gallup Polls: Public Opinion 1979.* London: George Prior Associated Publishers.

Georgakas, D., and Surkin, M. 1975. *Detroit: I Do Mind Dying.* New York: St. Martin's Press.

Georgine, R. A. 1979. Statement before the Subcommittee on Labor-

Management Relations of the Committee on Education and Labor of the U.S. House of Representatives, 17 October.

Geschwender, J. A. 1977. *Class, Race, and Worker Insurgency.* Cambridge: Cambridge University Press.

Getman, J. G.; Goldberg, S. B.; and Herman, J. B. 1976. *Union Representation Elections: Law and Reality.* New York: Russell Sage Foundation.

Gintis, H. 1972. A Radical Analysis of Welfare Economics and Individual Development. *Quarterly Journal of Economics* 86:572–99.

Glaberman, M. 1952. *Punching Out.* Detroit: Our Times Publications.

Goldberg, J. P.; Ahern, E.; Haber, W.; and Oswald, R. A., eds. 1976. *Federal Policies and Worker Status since the Thirties.* Madison, Wis.: Industrial Relations Research Association.

Goldberger, A. S. 1964. *Econometric Theory.* New York: Wiley.

Goldfield, M. 1980a. The Decline of the Communist Party and the Black Question in the U.S.: Harry Haywood's *Black Bolshevik. Review of Radical Political Economics* 12:44–63.

———. 1980b. Harvester Strike Ends in Victory. *Guardian,* 7 May.

———. 1982. The Decline of Organized Labor: NLRB Union Certification Election Results. *Politics and Society* 11:167–210.

———. 1985a. Labor's Subordination to the New Deal. Paper presented to the American Political Science Association Annual Meeting in New Orleans, Louisiana.

———. 1985b. Recent Historiography of the Communist Party USA. In *The Year Left,* edited by M. Davis, F. Pfeil, and M. Sprinker. London: Verso.

———. 1987. Public Sector Union Growth in the Early 1960s: Reasons for Takeoff. Manuscript.

Goldstein, R. J. 1978. *Political Repression in Modern America.* Cambridge, Mass.: Schenkman.

Goldthorpe, J. H.; Lockwood, D.; Beckhofer, F.; and Platt, J. 1969. *The Affluent Worker in the Class Structure.* Cambridge: Cambridge University Press.

———. 1971. *The Affluent Worker: Political Attitudes and Behaviour.* Cambridge: Cambridge University Press.

———. 1974. Industrial Relations in Great Britain: A Critique of Reformism. *Politics and Society* 4:419–52.

Gompers, S. 1920. *Labor and the Employer.* New York: E. P. Dutton.

Gordon, D. M. 1980. The Best Defense is a Good Defense: Toward a Marxian Theory of Labor Union Structure and Behavior. In *New Directions in Labor Economics and Industrial Relations,* edited by M. J. Carter and W. H. Leahy. London: University of Notre Dame Press.

Gordon, M. E., and Long, L. N. 1981. Demographic and Attitudinal Correlates of Union Joining. *Industrial Relations* 20:306–11.

Gorz, A. 1967. *Strategy for Labor.* Boston: Beacon Press.

————. 1982. *Farewell to the Working Class*. Boston: South End Press.

Gould, W. B. 1980. Labor Pains. *Nation,* 23 Feb., pp. 196–97.

————. 1985. Statement to the House Subcommittee on Labor-Management Relations. In U.S. Congress 1985.

Gramsci, A. 1968. Soviets in Italy. *New Left Review* 51:28–58.

Greenstone, J. D. 1977. *Labor in American Politics.* 2d ed. Chicago: University of Chicago Press.

Gregory, C. O., and Katz, H. A. 1979. *Labor and the Law.* 3d ed. New York: Norton.

Griffin, L. J.; Wallace, M.; and Rubin, B. 1986. Capitalist Resistance to the Organization of Labor before the New Deal. Manuscript.

Gross, J. A. 1974. *The Making of the National Labor Relations Board.* Albany: State University of New York Press.

————. 1981. *The Reshaping of the National Labor Relations Board.* Albany: State University of New York Press.

Haberman, S. J. 1978. *Analysis of Qualitative Data.* Vol. 1: *Introductory Topics.* New York: Academic Press.

Hamilton, R. F. 1972. *Class and Politics in the U.S.* New York: Wiley.

Hannan, M., and Young, A. 1977. Estimation in Panel Models: Results on Pooling Cross-Sections and Time Series. In *Sociological Methodology—1977.* Edited by David Heise. San Francisco: Jossey-Bass.

Hanushek, E. A., and Jackson, J. E. 1977. *Statistical Methods for Social Scientists.* New York: Academic Press.

Hard Times for U.S. Unions. 1980. *Personnel Management* 12:26–29.

Harris, Herbert. 1940. *Labor's Civil War.* New York: Knopf.

Harris, Howell. 1982a. Responsible Unionism and the Road to Taft-Hartley: The Development of Federal Labor Relations Policy, ca. 1932–1947. Paper from a colloquium at Kings College, Cambridge, Sept. 1982.

————. 1982b. *The Right to Manage.* Madison: University of Wisconsin Press.

Hartz, L. 1955. *The Liberal Tradition in America.* New York: Harcourt, Brace and World.

Hastings, E. H., and Hastings, P. K., eds. 1984. *Index to International Public Opinion, 1982–1983.* Westport, Conn.: Greenwood Press.

Hayward, J. 1980. Trade Union Movements and Their Politico-Economic Environments: A Preliminary Framework. *West European Politics* 3:1–9.

Haywood, W. D. 1929. *Bill Haywood's Book: The Autobiography of William D. Haywood.* New York: International Publishers.

Hedges, J. N., and Taylor, D. E. 1980. Recent Trends in Worktime: Hours Edge Downward. *Monthly Labor Review* 103(3):3–11.

Henderson, C. 1971. Comment on "The Use of Error Components Models in Combining Cross-Section with Time-Series Data." *Econometrica* 39:397–402.

Heneman, H. G., and Sandver, M. H. 1983. Predicting the Outcome of

Union Certification Elections: A Review of the Literature. *Industrial and Labor Relations Review* 36:537–59.

Hibbs, D. A. 1974. Problems of Statistical Estimation and Causal Inference in Time-Series Regression Models. In *Sociological Methodology, 1973–1974*. San Francisco: Jossey-Bass.

———. 1976. Labor Strikes in Industrial Society. *American Political Science Review* 70:1033–58.

———. 1977a. On Analyzing the Effects of Policy Interventions: Box-Jenkins and Box-Tiao vs. Structural Equation Models. In *Sociological Methodology, 1976–1977*. San Francisco: Jossey-Bass.

———. 1977b. Trade Union Power, Labor Militancy, and Wage Inflation: A Comparative Analysis. Manuscript. Cambridge, Mass.: M.I.T.

———. 1978. "On the Political Economy of Long-Run Trends in Strike Activity." *British Journal of Political Science* 8:153–75.

Hicks, A., and Swank, D. 1984. On the Political Economy of Welfare Expansion. *Comparative Political Studies* 17:81–118.

Hicks, J. R. 1963. *The Theory of Wages*. New York: St. Martin's.

Hines, A. G. 1964. Trade Unions and Wage Inflation in the United Kingdom, 1893–1961. *Review of Economic Studies* 31:221–52.

Hirsch, B. 1980. The Determinants of Unionization: An Analysis of Interarea Differences. *Industrial and Labor Relations Review* 33:147–61.

———. 1982. The Interindustry Structure of Unionism, Earnings, and Earnings Dispersion. *Industrial and Labor Relations Review* 36:22–39.

Hobsbawm, E. 1967. *Labouring Men*. Garden City, N.Y.: Doubleday.

———. 1969. *Industry and Empire*. Baltimore: Penguin.

Hook, R. 1982. The Timetable of Delay: The Unfair Labor Practice Process. *Labor Update* 3:6–7.

Houseman, G. L. 1985. American Labor Unions: Dependent upon, but Not Fairly Protected by, the Law. Manuscript.

Howard, R. 1982. Union or Bust. *In These Times*, 3 Feb., pp. 8–9.

Howells, J. M., and Cathro, S. 1981. Union Growth and Concentration Revisited. *Journal of Industrial Relations* (New Zealand) 23:23–32.

Hoxie, R. [1915] 1966. *Trade Unionism in the United States*. New York: Russell and Russell.

Hoyles, A. 1969. The Occupation of Factories in France, 1968. In *Trade Union Register*. London: Institute for Workers' Control.

Hunt, J. C., and White, R. A. 1983. The Effects of Right-to-Work Legislation on Union Outcomes: Additional Evidence. *Journal of Labor Research* 4:47–75.

Hyclak, T. 1980. Unions and Income Inequality—Some Cross-State Evidence. *Industrial Relations* 19:212–15.

Hyman, R. 1973. *Marxism and the Sociology of Trade Unions*. London: Pluto Press.

———. 1975. *Industrial Relations*. London: Macmillan.

———. 1978. *Strikes*. Glasgow: Fontana/Collins.

———. 1982. Contribution to the Review Symposium on Thomas Kochan's *Collective Bargaining and Industrial Relations* (1980). *Industrial Relations* 21:100–14.

Hyman, R., and Brough, I. 1975. *Social Values and Industrial Relations*. Oxford: Basil Blackwell.

Ingham, G. K. 1974. *Strikes and Industrial Conflict: Britain and Scandinavia*. London: Macmillan.

Irons, P. 1982. *The New Deal Lawyers*. Princeton: Princeton University Press.

Jackson, L.; Nordlund, J. V.; and Antone, C. C. 1982. The Antipathies of Organized Labor. *Labor Law Journal* 33:282–93.

Jacobs, P. 1963. *The State of the Unions*. New York: Antheneum.

James, C. L. R. 1958. *Facing Reality*. East Lansing, Mich.: Garvey Institute.

Jankowski, R. 1984. Conflict over Income Distribution: Implications for Class Struggle and Stagflation. Ph.D. dissertation, University of Chicago.

Jenson, J., and Ross, G. 1984. *The View from Inside: A French Communist Cell in Crisis*. Berkeley: University of California Press.

Johnson, J. 1972. *Econometric Methods*. New York: McGraw-Hill.

Judge, G. G.; Hill, R. C.; Griffiths, W.; Lütkepohl, H.; and Lee, J. 1982. *Introduction to the Theory and Practice of Econometrics*. New York: Wiley.

Juris, H.; Thompson, M.; and Daniels, W., eds. 1985. *Industrial Relations in a Decade of Economic Change*. Madison, Wis.: Industrial Relations Research Association.

Kahn, L. M. 1979. Unionism and Relative Wages: Direct and Indirect Effects. *Industrial and Labor Relations Review* 32:520–32.

Kane, J. Statement to the House Committee on Labor-Management Relations. In U.S. Congress 1985.

Kassalow, E. M. 1961. Organization of White-Collar Workers. *Monthly Labor Review* 84:234–38.

———. 1965. The Prospects for White-Collar Unionism. *Industrial Relations* 5:37–47.

Katz, H. C. 1984. Collective Bargaining in 1982: A Turning Point in Industrial Relations. *Compensation Review* 16:1:38–49.

Katznelson, I. 1981. *City Trenches*. New York: Pantheon.

Kau, J., and Rubin, P. 1981. The Impact of Labor Unions on the Passage of Economic Legislation. *Journal of Labor Research* 2:133–45.

Kaus, R. 1983. The Trouble with Unions. *Harper's*, June, pp. 23–35.

Kendrick, J. W. 1973. *Postwar Productivity Trends in the United States, 1948–1969*. New York: National Bureau of Economic Research.

Kenny, D. A. 1979. *Correlation and Causality*. New York: Wiley.

Kerr, C.; Dunlop, J. T.; Harbison, F.; and Myers, S. 1960. *Industrialism and Industrial Man*. Cambridge: Harvard University Press.

Kesselman, M. 1982. Prospects for Democratic Socialism in Advanced Capitalism: Class Struggle and Compromise in Sweden and France. *Politics and Society* 11:397–438.

Kircher, W. L. 1968. *Testimony before the Special Subcommittee on Labor of the Committee on Education and Labor of the U.S. House of Representatives, August 1967.* H.R. 11725. Washington, D.C.: Government Printing Office.

Kirchner, E. J. 1980. International Trade Union Collaboration and the Prospects for European Industrial Relations. *West European Politics* 3:124–38.

Kistler, A. 1977. Trends in Union Growth. *Labor Law Journal* 28:539–45.

Klare, K. E. 1978. Judicial Deradicalization of the Wagner Act and the Origins of Modern Legal Consciousness, 1937–1941. *Minnesota Law Review* 62:265–339.

———. 1985. The Application of the National Labor Relations Act during Union Organizing Drives. Statement to the House Subcommittee on Labor-Management Relations. In U.S. Congress 1985.

Klein, F. C. 1982. Some Firms Fight Ills of Bigness by Keeping Employee Units Small. *Wall Street Journal*, 5 Jan.

Kmenta, J. 1971. *Elements of Econometrics.* New York: Macmillan.

Knight, T. R. 1979. Procedure and Delay in NLRB Representation Elections: Is Remedial Legislation Justified. *Industrial and Labor Relations Forum* 13:3–43.

Kochan, T. A. 1979. How American Workers View Labor Unions. *Monthly Labor Review* 102(4):23–31.

———. 1980. *Collective Bargaining and Industrial Relations.* Homewood, Ill.: Richard D. Irwin.

Koeppel, B. 1978. The Coming Crunch for Labor. *Progressive* 42:16–20.

Kokkelenberg, E. C., and Sockell, D. R. 1985. Union Membership in the United States, 1973–1981. *Industrial and Labor Relations Review* 38:497–543.

Kornhauser, A. 1956. *When Labor Votes: A Study of Autoworkers.* New York: University Books.

Kornhauser, A.; Dobin, R.; and Ross, A., eds. 1954. *Industrial Conflict.* New York: McGraw-Hill.

Korpi, W. 1978. *The Working Class in Welfare Capitalism.* London: Routledge and Kegan Paul.

Korpi, W., and Shalev, M. 1979. Strikes, Industrial Relations, and Class Conflict in Capitalist Societies. *British Journal of Sociology* 30:164–87.

———. 1980. Strikes, Power, and Politics in the Western Nations, 1900–1976. In *Political Power and Social Theory*, vol. 1, edited by M. Zeitlin. Greenwich, Conn.: JAI Press.

Krislov, J. 1979. Decertification Elections Increase but Remain No Major Burden to Unions. *Monthly Labor Review* 102(11):30–31.

Kudrle, R. T., and Marmor, T. R. 1981. The Development of Welfare States in North America. In Flora and Heidenheimer 1981.

Kuh, E. 1959. The Validity of Cross-sectionally Estimated Behavior Equations in Time-Series Applications. *Econometrica* 27:197–214.

Lachman, J. A. 1982. Freedom of Speech in Union Representation Elections: Employer Campaigning and Employee Response. *American Bar Foundation Journal* 3:755–86.

Lange, P.; Ross, G.; and Vannicelli, M. 1982. *Unions, Change, and Crisis: French and Italian Union Strategy and the Political Economy, 1945–1980.* London: Allen and Unwin.

Larrowe, C. P. 1961. A Meteor on the Industrial Relations Horizon: The Foreman's Association of America. *Labor History* 2:259–94.

Lawler, J. J. 1984. The Influence of Management Consultants on the Outcome of Union Certification Elections. *Industrial and Labor Relations Review* 38:38–51.

Layard, R., ed. 1980. *Cost-Benefit Analysis.* New York: Penguin.

Ledwith, T. 1985. Union Artists Need Not Apply. *Allegro* 85:1.

Leggett, J. C. 1968. *Class, Race, and Labor: Working-Class Consciousness in Detroit.* New York: Oxford University Press.

Lenin, V. I. 1963. *Collected Works,* in 45 volumes. Moscow: Foreign Languages Publishing House.

Lens, S. 1949. *Left, Right, and Center: Conflicting Forces in American Labor.* Hinsdale, Ill.: Henry Regnery Company.

———. 1959. *The Crisis of American Labor.* New York: Sagamore Press.

Lester, R. A. 1958. *As Unions Mature: An Analysis of the Evolution of American Unionism.* Princeton: Princeton University Press.

Lester, R. A., and Shister, J. 1948. *Insights into Labor Issues.* New York: Macmillan.

Levine, G. N. 1963. *Workers Vote: The Political Behaviour of Men in the Print Trade.* Totawa, N.J.: Bedminster Press.

Levison, A. 1974. *The Working-Class Majority.* New York: Penguin.

Levy, P. A. 1985. Statement by the National Lawyers Guild to the House Subcommittee on Labor-Management Relations. In U.S. Congress 1985.

Lewin, D., and Goldenberg, S. B. 1980. Public Sector Unionism in the U.S. and Canada. *Industrial Relations* 19:239–56.

Lewin, D.; Feuille, P.; and Kochan, T. A., eds. 1977. *Public Sector Labor Relations.* New York: Thomas Horton.

Lewin, D.; Surck, R.; and Bleecher, C., eds. 1974. *The Urban Labor Market.* New York: Praeger.

Lewis, H. G. 1983. Union Relative Wage Effects: A Survey of Macro Estimates. *Journal of Labor Economics* 1:1–27.

Lichtenstein, N. 1980. The Communist Experience in American Trade Unions. *Industrial Relations* 19:119–30.

———. 1982. *Labor's War at Home.* Cambridge: Cambridge University Press.

Lillian, R. 1980. University Reinstates Victim. *Chicago Maroon*, 16 May.

Lindblom, C. E. 1983. Response to Manley 1983. *American Political Science Review* 77:384–86.

Lipset, S. M. 1960. *Political Man*. New York: Doubleday.

Lipset, S. M.; Trow, M.; and Coleman, J. 1956. *Union Democracy*. New York: Doubleday.

Lopez, A., and Bergmark, M. 1977. *Equality and Economic Justice: Why Section 14(b) Must Be Repealed*. Chicago: Equal Rights Congress.

Lozovsky, A. 1942. *Marx and the Trade Unions*. New York: International Publishers.

Louisville Workers Win Strike. 1978. *Guardian*, 31 May.

Lublin, J. S. 1982. Pugnacious Companies and Skeptical Workers Cost Unions Members. *Wall Street Journal*, 21 Oct.

Lumsden, K., and Petersen, C. 1975. The Effect of Right-to-Work Laws on Unionization in the United States. *Journal of Political Economy* 83:1237–48.

McCleary, R., and Hay, R. A. Jr. 1980. *Applied Time-Series Analysis*. Beverly Hills: Sage.

McConville, E. 1975. The NLRB Down South: How 7,041 Got Fired. *Nation*, 25 Oct., pp. 392–94.

————. 1980. Union Blacklists are Back: Dirty Tricks Down South. *Nation*, 9 Feb., pp. 142–45.

McCulloch, F. W., and Bornstein, T. 1974. *The National Labor Relations Board*. New York: Praeger.

McKersie, R. B., and Brown, M. 1963. Nonprofessional Hospital Workers and a Union Organizing Drive. *Quarterly Journal of Economics* 77:372–404.

MacPherson, C. B. 1962. *The Political Theory of Possessive Individualism, Hobbes to Locke*. Oxford: Oxford University Press.

MacShane, D.; Plant, M.; and Ward, D. 1984. *Power! Black Workers, Their Unions, and the Struggle for Freedom in South Africa*. Boston: South End Press.

Maddala, G. 1971. The Use of Variance Components Models in Pooling Cross-Section and Time-Series Data. *Econometrica* 39:341–58.

Magaziner, I., and Reich, R. 1982. *Minding America's Business: The Decline and Rise of the American Economy*. New York: Harcourt.

Magubane, B. M. 1979. *The Political Economy of Race and Class in South Africa*. New York: Monthly Review Press.

Mancke, R. B. 1971. American Trade Union Growth, 1900–1960: A Comment. *Quarterly Journal of Economics* 85:187–93.

Mandel, E. 1969. Where is America Going? *New Left Review* 54:3–15.

Manley, J. 1983. Neopluralism: A Class Analysis of Pluralism I and Pluralism II. *American Political Science Review* 77:368–83.

Markovits, A., and Allen, C. S. 1980. Power and Dissent: The Trade

Unions in the Federal Republic of Germany Re-examined. *West European Politics* 3:68–86.

Marshall, R. 1967. *Labor in the South*. Cambridge: Harvard University Press.

————. 1968. The Development of Organized Labor. *Monthly Labor Review* 91(3):65–73.

Marshall, R., and Rungeling, B. 1976. *The Role of Unions in the American Economy*. Washington, D.C.: Joint Council on Economic Education.

Martin, A., and Ross, G. 1980. European Trade Unions and the Economic Crisis: Perceptions and Strategies. *West European Politics* 3:33–67.

Martin, B., and Kassalow, E. M., eds. 1980. *Labor in Advanced Industrial Societies*. Washington, D.C.: Carnegie Endowment for International Peace.

Marx, K. [1857] 1970. *A Contribution to the Critique of Political Economy*. Moscow: Progress Publishers.

————. [1859] 1972a. *Zur Kritik der Politischen Ökonomie*. Berlin: Dietz Verlag.

————. [1848] 1972b. *Manifesto of the Communist Party*. Peking: Foreign Languages Press.

————. [1857–58] 1973. *Grundrisse*. Translated with a foreword by Martin Nicolaus. New York: Vintage.

————. [1864–83] 1974. *The First International and After*. Edited by David Fernbach. New York: Vintage.

————. [1867] 1977. *Capital*. New York: Vintage.

Marx, K., and Engels, F. 1968. *Selected Works*. New York: International Publishers.

Matles, J. J., and Higgins, J. 1974. *Them and Us*. Englewood Cliffs, N.J.: Prentice-Hall.

Maxey, C. 1980. Hospital Managers' Perception of the Impact of Unionization. *Monthly Labor Review* 103(6):36–38.

Mayo, E. 1960. *The Human Problems of an Industrial Civilization*. New York: Viking.

Medoff, J. 1984. The Public's Image of Labor and Labor's Response. Manuscript.

Meier, A., and Rudwick, E. 1979. *Black Detroit and the Rise of the UAW*. Oxford: Oxford University Press.

Meyers, F. 1955. Effects of 'Right-to-Work' Laws: A Study of the Texas Act. *Industrial and Labor Relations Review* 9:77–84.

Miller, R. L. 1976. Right-to-Work Laws and Compulsory Union Membership in the United States. *British Journal of Industrial Relations* 14:186–93.

Mills, C. W. 1948. *The New Men of Power*. New York: Harcourt.

Mitchell, D. J. B. 1980. *Unions, Wages, and Inflation*. Washington, D.C.: Brookings Institution.

————. 1981. A Note on Strike Propensities and Wage Developments. *Industrial Relations* 20:123–27.

————. 1982. *Recent Union Contract Concessions*. Brookings Papers on Economic Activity 1. Washington, D.C.

The Mixed Results of Labor-Law Reform. 1977. *Business Week*, 7 Nov.

Montgomery, D. 1979. *Workers' Control in America*. Cambridge: Cambridge University Press.

Moody, K. 1985. Concessions Alive and Well, Despite Recovery. *Labor Notes* 77:1.

Morand, M. J., and McPherson, D. S. 1980. Unionism's Effect on Faculty Pay: Handicapping the Available Data. *Monthly Labor Review* 103(6):34–36.

Mortimer, W. 1971. *Organize*. Boston: Beacon.

Moore, W. J., and Newman, R. J. 1975. On the Prospects for American Trade Union Growth: A Cross-Section Analysis. *Review of Economics and Statistics* 57:435–45.

————. 1985. The Effects of Right-to-Work Laws: A Review of the Literature. *Industrial and Labor Relations Review* 38:571–85.

Moore, W. J., and Raisian, J. 1982. Public-sector Union Wage Effects: A Time-Series Analysis. *Monthly Labor Review* 105(7):51–53.

————. 1983. The Level and Growth of Union/Nonunion Relative Wage Effects, 1967–1977. *Journal of Labor Research* 4:65–79.

Mounts, G. J. 1979. Labor and the Supreme Court: Significant Decisions of 1977–1978. *Monthly Labor Review* 102(1):51–57.

Mulvey, C., and Trevithick, J. A. 1973. Trade Unions and Wage Inflation. *Economic and Social Review* 4:209–29.

National Labor Relations Board. 1936–1981. *Annual Report of the National Labor Relations Board*. Washington, D.C.: Government Printing Office.

NLRB Vote Strikes Roots of Bargaining. 1982. *Chicago Sun-Times*, 10 August.

Nerlove, M. 1971. Further Evidence on the Estimation of Dynamic Economic Relations from a Time Series of Cross Sections. *Econometrica* 39:359–82.

New York State Assembly. Standing Committee on Labor. 1984. *A Report on the Plight of the Collective Bargaining System*. Albany.

Nie, N., and Verba, S. 1972. *Participation in America: Political Democracy and Social Equality*. New York: Harper and Row.

Nissen, B. 1981. U.S. Workers and the U.S. Labor Movement. *Monthly Review* 33(1):17–30.

Northrup, H. R. 1984. The Rise and Demise of PATCO. *Industrial and Labor Relations Review* 37:167–84.

No Welcome Mat for Unions in the Sunbelt. 1976. *Business Week*, 17 May.

Nyden, P. 1974. *Black Coal Miners in the United States*. Occasional Paper No. 15. New York: American Institute for Marxist Studies.

Offe, C. 1972. Advanced Capitalism and the Welfare State. *Politics and Society* 2:479–88.

––––––. 1984. *Contradictions of the Welfare State.* Cambridge, Mass.: M.I.T. Press.

Organization for Economic Co-operation and Development (OECD). 1979. *Collective Bargaining and Government Policies in Ten OECD Countries.* Paris.

––––––. 1984. *Employment Outlook.* Paris.

Ozanne, R. 1967. *A Century of Labor-Management Relations at Mc-Cormick and International Harvester.* Madison: University of Wisconsin Press.

Parks, R. 1967. Efficient Estimation of a System of Regression Equations When Disturbances Are Both Serially and Contemporaneously Correlated. *Journal of the American Statistical Association* 62:500–509.

Perlman, S. 1922. *A History of Trade Unionism in the United States.* New York: Macmillan.

––––––. 1949. *A Theory of the Labor Movement.* New York: Augustus M. Kelley.

Perlo, V. 1982. The False Claim of Declining Productivity and Its Political Uses. *Science and Society* 46:284–327.

Perry, J. L., and Angle, H. L. 1981. Bargaining Unit Structure and Organizational Outcomes. *Industrial Relations* 20:47–59.

Pestillo, P. J. 1979. Can the Unions Meet the Needs of a "New" Work Force? *Monthly Labor Review* 102(2):33–34.

Pfeffer, J., and Ross, J. 1980. Union-Nonunion Effects on Wage and Status Attainment. *Industrial Relations* 19:140–51.

––––––. 1981a. Unionization and Female Wage and Status Attainment. *Industrial Relations* 20:179–85.

––––––. 1981b. Unionization and Income Inequality. *Industrial Relations* 20:271–85.

Piven, F. F., and Cloward, R. A. 1971. *Regulating the Poor.* New York: Pantheon.

––––––. 1977. *Poor People's Movements.* New York: Pantheon.

Polsby, N. W. 1980. *Community Power and Political Theory.* 2d ed. New Haven: Yale University Press.

Pontusson, J. 1984. Behind and Beyond Social Democracy in Sweden. *New Left Review* 143:69–96.

Preis, A. 1964. *Labor's Giant Step.* New York: Pioneer Publishers.

Prosten, R. 1978. The Longest Season: Union Organizing in the Last Decade, aka How Come One Team Has to Play with its Shoelaces Tied Together? In Dennis 1978.

––––––. 1979. The Rise in NLRB Election Delays: Measuring Business' New Resistance. *Monthly Labor Review* 102(2):38–40.

Rahhe, B. 1980. Interview on Boston University Organizing Drive.

Unpublished material. Washington, D.C.: Center to Protect Workers' Rights.

Raiffa, H. 1982. *The Art and Science of Negotiation.* Cambridge: Harvard University Press.

Raskin, A. H. 1978. Management Comes Out Swinging. In Dennis 1978.

———. 1979. Management's Hard Line: "Class War" or Labor's Chance to Reform. *Monthly Labor Review* 102(2):34–36.

———. 1985. Labor's Grand Illusions. *New York Times Magazine,* 10 Feb.

Reid, J. D. Jr. 1982. Labor Unions in the American Economy: An Analytic Survey. *Journal of Labor Research* 3:275–94.

Rein, M., and Rainwater, L. 1981. *From Welfare State to Welfare Society: Some Unresolved Issues in Assessment.* Berlin: Institut für Vergleichende Gesellschaftsforschung.

Regini, M., and Esping-Anderson, G. 1980. Trade Union Strategies and Social Policy in Italy. *West European Politics* 3:107–23.

Reynaud, J. D. 1967. The Role of Trade Unions in National Political Economies (Developed Countries of Europe). In Barkin et al. 1967.

———. 1975. France: Elitist Society Inhibits Articulated Bargaining. In Barkin 1975.

Riche, M. F. 1981. The Future of Organized Labor. *American Demographics* 3(8):28–33.

Rones, P. L. 1980. Moving to the Sun: Regional Job Growth, 1968–1978. *Monthly Labor Review* 103(3):12–19.

Roomkin, M., and Juris, H. A. 1978. The Changing Character of Unions in the Traditional Sectors: The Mid-Life Passage of the Labor Movement. In Dennis 1978.

———. 1979. The Changing Character of Unionism in Traditionally Organized Sectors. *Monthly Labor Review* 102(2):36–38.

Rose, J. B. 1972. What Factors Influence Union Representation Elections? *Monthly Labor Review* 95:49–51.

Rosen, R. 1980. Identifying States and Areas Prone to High and Low Unemployment. *Monthly Labor Review* 103(3):20–24.

Ross, A. M., and Hartman, P. T. 1960. *Changing Patterns of Industrial Conflict.* New York: Wiley.

Ross, G. 1982. *Workers and Communists in France.* Berkeley: University of California Press.

Ross, G., and Martin, A. 1980. European Trade Unions and the Economic Crisis: Perceptions and Strategies. *West European Politics* 3:33–67.

Rothschild, E. 1973. *Paradise Lost: The Decline of the Auto-Industrial Age.* New York: Random House.

Rubin, B. A.; Griffin, L. J.; and Wallace, M. 1983. "Provided Only That Their Voice Was Strong"—Insurgency and Organization of American Labor From NRA to Taft-Hartley. *Work and Occupations* 10:325–47.

Ruse, R. S., and Pearlman, R. B. No date. *The Way to Win.* Patrick B. Gomer Associates.

Sabel, C. F. 1982. *Work and Politics.* Cambridge: Cambridge University Press.

Sadlowski, E. 1975. An Insurgent's View. *Nation,* 6 Sept., 173–75.

Sale, K. 1975. *Power Shift.* New York: Random House.

Saltzman, G. M. 1984. A Progressive Experiment: The Evolution of Wisconsin's Bargaining Legislation for Local Government Employees. Manuscript.

———. 1985. Bargaining Laws as Cause and Consequence of the Growth of Teachers' Unions. *Industrial and Labor Relations Review* 38:335–57.

Sandver, M. H. 1982. South-Nonsouth Differentials in National Labor Relations Board Certification Election Outcomes. *Journal of Labor Research* 3:30.

Sandver, M. H., and Heneman, H. G. 1981. Union Growth through the Election Process. *Industrial Relations* 20:109–16.

Schutt, R. K. 1982. Models of Militancy: Support for Strikes and Work Actions among Public Employees. *Industrial and Labor Relations Review* 35:406–22.

Seeber, R. L., and Cooke, W. N. 1983. The Decline in Union Success in NLRB Representation Elections. *Industrial Relations* 22:34–44.

Seidman, J. 1964. The Sources for Future Growth and Decline in American Trade Unions. In *Proceedings of the Seventeenth Annual Meeting of the Industrial Relations Research Association.* Chicago.

Seltzer, C. 1980. Death of Reform in the U.M.W. *Nation,* 31 May, pp. 641–60.

Seymour, J. 1976. The Many Faces and Long Waves of Ernest Mandel: A review of *Late Capitalism* by Ernest Mandel. *Workers Vanguard,* no. 121 (August):6–9.

Shalev, M. 1978a. Lies, Damned Lies, and Strike Statistics: The Measurement of Trends in Industrial Conflict. In Crouch and Pizzorno 1978.

———. 1978b. Strikers and the State. *British Journal of Political Science* 8:479–92.

———. 1979. The Politics and Economics of Industrial Conflict: Some Cross-National and Overtime Questions and Answers. Paper presented to the "State and Capitalism" seminar, Harvard University, 4 May 1979.

———. 1980. Trade Unionism and Economic Analysis: The Case of Industrial Conflict. *Journal of Labor Research* 1:133–73.

———. 1983. The Social Democratic Model and Beyond: Two Generations of Comparative Research on the Welfare State. In *Comparative Social Research,* vol. 6, edited by R. T. Tomasson.

Sheflin, N.; Troy, L.; and Koeller, C. T. 1981. Structural Stability in

Models of American Trade Union Growth. *Quarterly Journal of Economics* 95:77–88.

Shister, J. 1953. The Logic of Union Growth. *Journal of Political Economy* 61:413–33.

———. 1967. The Direction of Unionism, 1947–1967: Thrust or Drift. *Industrial and Labor Relations Review* 20:578–601.

Shulenburger, D. E.; McLean, R. A.; and Rasch, S. B. 1982. Union-Nonunion Wage Differentials: A Replication and Extension. *Industrial Relations* 21:248–55.

Skeels, J. 1961. The Background of UAW Factionalism. *Labor History* 2:158–81.

Skocpol, T., and Ikenberry, J. 1982. The Political Formation of the American Welfare State in Historical and Comparative Perspective. Paper presented at the annual meeting of the American Sociological Association, San Francisco, September 1982.

Skotzko, E. 1974. Significant Decisions in Labor Cases. *Monthly Labor Review* 97(12):64–78.

Smith, R. L., and Hopkins, A. H. 1979. Public Employee Attitudes Towards Unions. *Industrial and Labor Relations Review* 32:484–95.

Snedecor, G. W., and Cochran, W. G. 1980. *Statistical Methods.* Ames: Iowa State University Press.

Sorrentino, C. 1976. Unemployment Compensation in Eight Industrial Nations. *Monthly Labor Review* 99(7):18–24.

Stephens, J. 1979. *The Transition from Capitalism to Socialism.* London: Macmillan.

Stieber, J. 1974. The Future of Public Employee Unionism in the United States. *Industrial Relations/Relations Industrielles* 29:825–37.

Street, R. S. 1980. The Lettuce Strike Story. *Nation,* 19 Jan., pp. 45–49.

Swank, D. H. 1984. The Political Economy of State Domestic Spending in Eighteen Advanced Capitalist Democracies, 1960–1980. Paper delivered at the annual meeting of the American Political Science Association, Washington, D.C., Sept. 1984.

Tanner, L. D.; Weinstein, H. G.; and Ahmuty, A. L. 1980. Collective Bargaining in the Health Care Industry. *Monthly Labor Review* 103(2):49–52.

Theil, H. 1971. *Principles of Econometrics.* New York: Wiley.

———. 1978. *Introduction to Econometrics.* Englewood Cliffs, N.J.: Prentice-Hall.

Thieblot, A. J. Jr. 1978. *An Analysis of Data on Union Membership.* Working Paper 38. St. Louis: Washington University, Center for the Study of American Business.

———. 1979. *Recent Trends in Workforce Organization by Labor Unions.* Washington, D.C.: Council on a Union-Free Environment.

Thompson, E. P. 1963. *The Making of the English Working Class.* New York: Random House.

Tilly, L. A., and Tilly, C. 1981. *Class Conflict and Collective Action*. Beverly Hills: Sage.

Tronti, M. 1972. Workers and Capital. *Telos* 14:25–62.

Trost, C. 1984. AFL-CIO Chief Calls Labor Laws a "Dead Letter." *Wall Street Journal*, 16 Aug.

Trotsky, L. [1923–37] 1969. *The Trade Union Question*. New York: Pathfinder.

Troy, Leo. 1957. *Distribution of Union Membership among the States, 1939 and 1953*. Occasional Paper No. 56. New York: National Bureau of Economic Research.

———. 1965. *Trade Union Membership, 1897–1962*. New York: National Bureau of Economic Research.

Troy, L., and Sheflin, N. 1985. *Union Sourcebook*. West Orange, N.J.: Industrial Relations Data and Information Services.

Turner, J. C. 1979. *The Business Roundtable and American Labor*. Washington, D.C.: International Bureau of Operating Engineers, AFL-CIO.

Ullman, L. 1955. Marshall and Friedman on Union Strength. *Review of Economics and Statistics* 37:384–401.

Unfair Dismissal Law Changes Will "Undermine the Rights of Individuals," says Warwick IR Unit. *Personnel Management* 12(2):9.

U.S. Bureau of the Census. 1975. *Historical Statistics of the United States, Colonial Times to 1970*. Parts 1 and 2. Washington, D.C.: Government Printing Office.

———. 1979. *Statistical Abstract of the United States, 1979*. Washington, D.C.: Government Printing Office.

———. 1982. *Statistical Abstract of the United States, 1982–83*. Washington, D.C.: Government Printing Office.

———. *Census of Manufacturers* (published every five years). Vol. 1 (census year followed by publication date in parentheses): 1947 (1950); 1954 (1957); 1958 (1961); 1963 (1966); 1967 (1971); 1972 (1976); 1977 (1981); 1982 (1986). Washington, D.C.: Government Printing Office.

United States Congress. 1976. *Statutes at Large*. Vol. 49 (chap. 372, National Labor Relations Act, 3 July 1935). 74th Congress, 1st session. Washington, D.C.: Government Printing Office.

U.S. Congress. House. Committee on Education and Labor. Subcommittee on Labor-Management Relations. 1984. *The Failure of Labor Law: A Betrayal of American Workers*. Washington, D.C.: Government Printing Office.

———. 1985. Oversight Hearings on the Subject "Has Labor Law Failed." Part 1. Washington, D.C.: Government Printing Office.

U.S. Congress. Senate. Committee on Government Affairs. 1982. *Hearings on the Hotel Employees and Restaurant Employees International Union, June 22 and 23, 1982*. Washington, D.C.: Government Printing Office.

United States Congress. Senate. Committee on Labor and Public Welfare. Subcommittee on Labor. 1979. *Compilation of Selected Labor Laws Pertaining to Labor Relations.* Washington, D.C.: Government Printing Office.

U.S. Department of Commerce, Bureau of Economic Analysis. 1973. *Long-Term Economic Growth, 1860–1970.* Washington, D.C.: Government Printing Office.

————. 1981a. *The National Income and Product Accounts of the United States, 1929–76, Statistical Tables.* Washington, D.C.: Government Printing Office.

————. 1981b. *National Income and Product Accounts, 1976–79, Survey of Current Business, Special Supplement.* Washington, D.C.: Government Printing Office.

U.S. Department of Labor, Bureau of Labor Statistics (BLS). 1950. *Handbook of Labor Statistics, 1950.* Washington, D.C.: Government Printing Office.

————. 1975–85. *Current Wage Developments.* Washington, D.C.: Government Printing Office.

————. 1977. *Directory of National Unions and Employee Associations, 1975.* Bulletin 1937. Washington, D.C.: Government Printing Office.

————. 1978. *International Comparisons of Unemployment.* Bulletin 1979. Washington, D.C.: Government Printing Office.

————. 1979a. *Directory of National Unions and Employee Associations, 1977.* Bulletin 2044. Washington, D.C.: Government Printing Office.

————. 1979b. *Employment and Earnings, United States, 1909–78.* Bulletin 1312-11. Washington, D.C.: Government Printing Office.

————. 1979c. *Employment and Earnings, States and Areas, 1939–78.* Bulletin 1370-13. Washington, D.C.: Government Printing Office.

————. 1979d. *Handbook of Labor Statistics, 1978.* Bulletin 2000. Washington, D.C.: Government Printing Office.

————. 1979e. *Earnings and Other Characteristics of Organized Workers, May 1977.* Report 556. Washington, D.C.: Government Printing Office.

————. 1980a. *Directory of National Unions and Employee Associations, 1979.* Bulletin 2079. Washington, D.C.: Government Printing Office.

————. 1980b. *Handbook of Labor Statistics.* Bulletin 2070. Washington, D.C.: Government Printing Office.

————. 1981a. *Characteristics of Major Collective Bargaining Agreements, January 1, 1980.* Bulletin 2095. Washington, D.C.: Government Printing Office.

————. 1981b. *Supplement to Employment and Earnings, Revised Establishment Data.* Washington, D.C.: Government Printing Office.

————. 1981c. *Productivity and the Economy: A Chartbook.* Bulletin 2084. Washington, D.C.: Government Printing Office.

———. 1981d. *Supplement to Employment and Earnings, States and Areas, Data for 1977–80.* Bulletin 1370-15. Washington, D.C.: Government Printing Office.

———. 1981e. *Earnings and Other Characteristics of Organized Workers, May 1980.* Bulletin 2105. Washington, D.C.: Government Printing Office.

———. 1982a. *Employment and Earnings* (Feb.). Washington, D.C.: Government Printing Office.

———. 1982b. *Employment and Earnings* (March). Washington, D.C.: Government Printing Office.

———. 1982c. *Employment and Earnings* (May). Washington, D.C.: Government Printing Office.

———. 1982d. *Employment and Earnings* (Sept.). Washington, D.C.: Government Printing Office.

———. 1982e. *Supplement to Employment and Earnings, Revised Establishment Data.* Washington, D.C.: Government Printing Office.

———. 1982f. *Analysis of Work Stoppages, 1980.* Bulletin 2120. Washington, D.C.: Government Printing Office.

———. 1985a. *Employment and Earnings* (Jan.). Washington, D.C.: Government Printing Office.

———. 1985b. *Employment in Manufacturing: Special Report.* Washington, D.C.: Government Printing Office.

U.S. Office of Personnel Management. 1981. *Union Recognition in the Federal Government: Statistical Summary.* Washington, D.C.: Government Printing Office.

U.S. Union Buster. 1980. *Nation,* 19 April, pp. 452–53.

Veneziale, J. 1978. *Repeal the Taft-Hartley Slave Labor Act.* Chicago: Workers Press.

Voos, P. 1982. Labor Union Organizing Programs, 1954–1977. Ph.D. dissertation, Harvard University.

———. 1983. Union Organizing: Costs and Benefits. *Industrial and Labor Relations Review* 36:576–91.

———. 1984. Trends in Union Organizing Expenditures, 1953–1977. *Industrial and Labor Relations Review* 38:52–63.

Wallerstein, M. 1984. The Micro-foundations of Corporatism: Formal Theory and Comparative Analysis. Paper delivered at the annual meeting of the American Political Science Association, Washington, D.C., September 1984.

———. 1985. *Working-Class Solidarity and Rational Behavior.* Ph.D. dissertation, University of Chicago.

Warren, J. 1980. How the Union Conquered Stevens. *Chicago Sun-Times,* 26 Oct.

———. 1981a. Teamsters Drive Hard to Add White-collar Members. *Chicago Sun-Times,* 7 June.

———. 1981b. Budget Cuts Stymie NLRB: Unions Worried. *Chicago Sun-Times,* 12 Oct.

———. 1982. Labor Department Changes Worth Notice. *Chicago Sun-Times*, 6 July.

Webb, S., and Webb, B. 1894. *The History of Trade Unionism*. London: Longman, Green.

———. 1920. *Industrial Democracy*. London: Seaham Divisional Labour Party.

Weiler, P. 1983. Promises to Keep: Securing Workers' Rights to Self-Organization under the NLRA. *Harvard Law Review* 96:1769–1827.

———. 1984. Striking a New Balance: Freedom of Contract and the Prospects for Union Representation. *Harvard Law Review* 98:351–420.

Weir, M. 1986. The Politics of Unemployment Policy: The Frustration of Policy Innovation, 1960–1980. Ph.D. dissertation, University of Chicago.

Welch, S. W. 1980. Union-Nonunion Construction Wage Differentials. *Industrial Relations* 19:152–62.

Wessels, W. J. 1981. Economic Effects of Right-to-Work Laws. *Journal of Labor Research* 2:55–75.

Wever, K. R. 1983. *Concession Bargaining, 1979–1983: Not Just the Same Old Thing*. Working Paper 1478-83-A. Alfred P. Sloan School of Management, M.I.T.

Widick, B. J. 1975a. Labor's New Brood: The Public Service Unions. *Nation*, 28 June, pp. 782–84.

———. 1975b. Labor 1974: The Triumph of Business Unionism. *Nation*, 6 Sept., pp. 169–73.

Wilensky, H. 1975. *The Welfare State and Equality*. Berkeley: University of California Press.

Wilensky, H.; Luebbert, G. M.; Hahn, S. R.; and Jamieson, A. M. 1983. Comparative Social Policy: Theories, Methods, Findings. Paper delivered at the Science Center Berlin Forum.

Wiles, P. 1974. *Distribution of Income East and West*. New York: Elsevier.

Wilson, J. Q. 1982. *American Government*. Lexington, Mass.: Heath.

Windmuller, J. P. 1981. Concentration Trends in Union Structure: An International Comparison. *Industrial and Labor Relations Review* 35:43–57.

Wolman, Leo. 1916. The Boycott in American Trade Unions. Ph.D. dissertation, Johns Hopkins.

———. 1924. *The Growth of American Trade Unions, 1880–1923*. New York: National Bureau of Economic Research.

———. 1936. *Ebb and Flow in Trade Unionism*. New York: National Bureau of Economic Research.

Wright, D. M., ed. 1951. *The Impact of the Union*. New York: Harcourt.

Zuk, G., and Thompson, W. R. 1982. The Post-Coup Military Spending Question: A Pooled Cross-Sectional Time-Series Analysis. *American Political Science Review* 76:60–74.

Index